THERE WAS NOTHING THERE

There Was Nothing There

Williamsburg, The Gentrification of a Brooklyn Neighborhood

Sara Martucci

NEW YORK UNIVERSITY PRESS
New York

NEW YORK UNIVERSITY PRESS
New York
www.nyupress.org

© 2024 by New York University
All rights reserved

Library of Congress Cataloging-in-Publication Data
Names: Martucci, Sara, author.
Title: There was nothing there : Williamsburg, the gentrification of a Brooklyn neighborhood / Sara Martucci.
Description: New York : New York University Press, [2024] |
Includes bibliographical references and index.
Identifiers: LCCN 2023028401 (print) | LCCN 2023028402 (ebook) |
ISBN 9781479815562 (hardback ; alk. paper) | ISBN 9781479815579 (paperback; alk. paper) | ISBN 9781479815593 (ebook) | ISBN 9781479815609 (ebook other)
Subjects: LCSH: Gentrification—New York (State)—New York. | Sociology, Urban—New York (State)—New York. | Williamsburg (New York, N.Y.)
Classification: LCC HT177.W55 M37 2024 (print) | LCC HT177.W55 (ebook) |
DDC 307.7609747/23—dc23/eng/20231117
LC record available at https://lccn.loc.gov/2023028401
LC ebook record available at https://lccn.loc.gov/2023028402

This book is printed on acid-free paper, and its binding materials are chosen for strength and durability. We strive to use environmentally responsible suppliers and materials to the greatest extent possible in publishing our books.

Manufactured in the United States of America

10 9 8 7 6 5 4 3 2 1

Also available as an ebook

*This book is dedicated to my students,
who always inspire and challenge.
Teaching you and learning alongside you
are my greatest privileges.*

CONTENTS

Introduction: Welcome to Williamsburg   1

1. The Neighborhood: From Industry to Instagram   21
2. Claiming Space: Activism and Ownership over Time   48
3. Dangerous Enough: Crime, Safety, and Identity   74
4. Selling Williamsburg: From Gritty to Luxury   92
5. Views of Change: Convenience and Erasure   118
6. The Myths of Gentrification: What Attachment Style Can Tell Us   145

Conclusion: Williamsburg's Global Reach: Lessons Learned?   161

Epilogue: An "L-pocalypse," a Pandemic, and a New Mayor   175

Acknowledgments   183

Methodological Appendix   187

Notes   197

Bibliography   211

Index   227

About the Author   232

Figure I.1. A summer afternoon at the Northside Bakery, August 2013. Author's photo.

Introduction

Welcome to Williamsburg

October 2008. The Northside Bakery stands out on North Eighth Street in Williamsburg, and not just because of the smell of freshly baked bread emanating from the storefront. The aqua-colored paint job is quite a departure from the rest of the surrounding buildings, mostly two-to-three-story red-brick and beige-sided buildings. Posters taped to the bakery's window advertise the goods sold inside, like rye bread and *makowiec* (poppy seed cake), but there are also flyers, usually in Polish, advertising concerts, religious festivals, and candidates running in local elections. Inside, the display cases and wire racks are stacked with treats: rectangular cakes layered with custard and topped with fluorescent-colored gelatin, wafer cookies with a grainy hazelnut cream, and *paczek*, puffy donuts filled with jelly or Nutella. Squeezed into another corner of the store is a refrigerated shelf holding quarts of homemade soup and enormous jars of pickles. The aesthetic is a hybrid of old-school Brooklyn and post-communist Warsaw: paper coffee cups are stacked on an ever-burning coffee urn, and the highest shelves are lined with tchotchkes from the old country. The bench out front and the handful of stools in the narrow storefront are often occupied by older folks in small huddles or families with young children, most often speaking in Polish.

I'm in line at the bakery waiting to buy a loaf of bread for dinner. Behind me an older man is eating a donut while thumbing through a Polish-language newspaper, another one of the bakery's ethnic offerings. As I'm waiting, some neighbors come in after me and greet the teenage girls behind the counter with "dzień dobry" (good day). Inevitably these customers get served before me. They chatter back and forth a bit with the teenager behind the counter as she fills a take-out container with sausage, sauerkraut, and pierogi from metal pans.

I understand the solidarity of serving compatriots before a random American woman with black-framed glasses and a hipster haircut, but the thing that strikes me is that even when I go to the bakery with my friend Lukasz, a Polish expat, the dynamic doesn't really change. No amount of Polish language quite makes up for his punk rock t-shirts or his expensive bike that he leans up against the storefront when he pops in. At this point, we're both likely viewed as extremely late-to-the-party bohemians, the kind of people who were early gentrifiers in the neighborhood. We're certainly not sleek enough to pass as one of the new, wealthier gentrifiers, who have only just started moving into the neighborhood's first few condominiums.[1]

On my walk home from the bakery that evening, I reflect on the power dynamics at play. The neighborhood is obviously changing around me, with construction going on nonstop. The apartments being built are not for me or seemingly any of my neighbors, who range from unsheltered to middle-class. The concerts, impromptu public art, and loft parties are not spaces where everyone feels welcome; neither are the religious or ethnic social clubs. Both are starting to disappear. I begin to interpret the actions at the bakery not as kinship around a shared language or ethnicity, but rather a conscious effort to prioritize existing residents in one of the few spaces where they were still in control of the social norms.

Everyday experiences of gentrification are at the core of this book. *There Was Nothing There* considers how residents form an attachment to a neighborhood, and how these attachments inform experiences of neighborhood life, perceptions of change, and conflicts over owner-ship in a gentrifying locale. The residents of Williamsburg, filtering in at varying times and for individual reasons, all experience the same neigh-borhood differently. As these varying groups inhabit and make sense of the same physical spaces, tensions play out in daily life: at community events, in local shops, and even in perceptions of crime and safety. This book is about conflicts that arise over feelings of ownership and belong-ing as subsequent "others" come to inhabit and lay claim to a gentrifying neighborhood.

Why Williamsburg?

Brooklyn has been an international city in terms of global migration flows since the mid-nineteenth century. It is represented in literature and movies, and was home to some of the most profitable American industries in the nineteenth and early twentieth centuries, but now the *idea* of Brooklyn carries enough cachet to be used to market businesses thousands of miles away. As one of the borough's most recognizable neighborhoods, Williamsburg was increasingly used as shorthand in the 2010s to refer to the cool districts of cities around the globe. A 2016 phone app called Where Is Williamsburg? perhaps represents the peak of the neighborhood's popularity. The program was created to direct users to "Williamsburg-like" neighborhoods in cities around the globe. The now-defunct app identified hip locales from New Delhi to Detroit, defined by a concentration of Williamsburg-esque businesses—bars, restaurants, cafés, music venues, and boutiques. Malasaña, the "Williamsburg" of Madrid, is even home to a thrift store named Williamsburg.

In the 2000s the neighborhood became synonymous with foodie culture, alternative music venues, hipsters, and gentrification—a contested topic that is on the lips of residents, reporters, politicians, and real estate developers. Over the past two decades, Williamsburg has morphed into a luxury playground. Wealthy residents inhabit the amenity-filled high-rises, influencers watch the sunset from rooftop bars, and tourists book reservations for local restaurants months in advance. Yet beyond the veneer of glittering waterfront condos, Instagrammable street art, and Michelin-starred meals, there is a more complex Williamsburg composed of neighbors with very different needs, desires, and realities, all occupying the same subway stop, park, and even rent-controlled buildings. When "Williamsburgs" are replicated around the world, the tensions, exclusions, and displacements that are characteristic of this level of gentrification are also at risk of being reproduced.

This risk, and the pervasiveness of conversations and concerns about gentrification, reinforced the necessity of an in-depth, qualitative study about how people really experience the process, with Williamsburg serving as a high-profile case study. Aside from its global notoriety, many aspects of the neighborhood's trajectory make it an important subject. First, Williamsburg's high concentration of public housing (over six thousand units, and many more that are rent-controlled or rent-stabilized) means that thousands of residents do not pay market rent and thus can avoid physical displacement. Because of this, *cultural* displacement abounds, an important aspect of understanding residents' experiences of gentrification. Second, Williamsburg witnessed an artist-driven phase of gentrification similar to Los Angeles's Venice Beach, Chicago's Wicker Park, the Alberta Arts District in Portland, Oregon, and many other infamous examples, making it useful as a comparative case.[2] Third, Williamsburg itself has already been the subject of multiple sociological studies.[3] With such rich history and context to draw upon, this study is able to focus on the more micro-level, lived effects of gentrification, while being informed by and updating the findings of existing research. Finally, this is not only a story about gentrification. Williamsburg is a neighborhood that has experienced a large-scale intervention: a rezoning for high-rise housing that precipitated vast changes in the neighborhood's economic, demographic, retail, and physical landscapes. Like the construction of a stadium, a public housing complex, or a convention center, the rezoning can be seen as a catalyst that accelerated the normal pace of neighborhood change. Within just a few years, the results reshaped the neighborhood. This lens allows us to interrogate the effects of state-led interventions on existing communities.

Much of the data collection for this book was focused between 2008 and 2018, a time when Williamsburg's international popularity peaked, and when many of the high-rise condominium buildings were being built and beginning to fill. There are additional scenes from the neighborhood after 2018 via ethnographic visits and news coverage, as late as the spring of 2023. However, major events post-2018, like the impact of the pandemic and commentary on the city's newest mayor, are left to the epilogue.

The G-Word

Once primarily an academic concern, gentrification is now the topic of countless articles from popular media outlets; it has been decried everywhere from *Al Jazeera* to local church bulletins.[4] The process is speculated on by private investors and argued over in community meetings around the world. It's also been the backdrop of novels like *The*

Sellout, There, There, and *The City We Became* and TV shows and movies like *Girls* and *The Last Black Man in San Francisco,* and the target of satire with *The Onion* and *Saturday Night Live* regularly poking fun at the concept, oftentimes with Brooklyn or even Williamsburg as the setting.

While the concept of gentrification has increasingly crept into popular culture in the past two decades, academics have been charting its course for the better part of a century. The discourse surrounding the process has filled anthologies, including Japonica Brown-Saracino's aptly named volume *The Gentrification Debates*.[5] These arguments do not need a full rehashing here, but it is important to locate Williamsburg's trajectory within the scope of existing theories.

When Ruth Glass first coined the term "gentrification," referring to processes in 1960s London, American urbanists were more concerned with disinvestment, suburbanization, white flight, and urban renewal. At that time, Williamsburg was predominantly populated by working-class, (im)migrant families from Puerto Rico, the Dominican Republic, Italy, and Poland, referred to here as the *Old Timers*.[6] Many of these residents worked in the nearby factories, patronized local businesses that were geared toward daily necessities, and participated in the ethnic and religious institutions that dotted the neighborhood. Like much of New York, the area was experiencing urban disinvestment as corporations moved their factories to cheaper regions. At the same time, the city abandoned outer borough neighborhoods to pool its resources into select Manhattan attractions, and the area's tax base decreased as some (usually white) residents moved to suburbs on Long Island or New Jersey. As the 1970s wore on, Williamsburg was stigmatized for high crime rates and the polluted waterfront left behind by the shrinking manufacturing base.

When these patterns of disinvestment were more common, pockets of reinvestment didn't seem to be a problem. Preservationists like Jane Jacobs praised neighborhoods made up of small blocks that were both residential and commercial, lined with houses only a few stories tall and with neighbors and business owners keeping their "eyes on the street."[7] Looking out her window in Greenwich Village, she did not think that the entrance of wealthy individuals posed a threat to the urban villages she celebrated. In contrast to Jacobs, Glass was concerned that middle-class occupants were "invading" and taking over working-class neighborhoods, ultimately displacing inhabitants and altering the "social character of the district."[8] The pattern that Ruth Glass noticed would continue in fits and starts in cities around the world for decades to come, not least of all in Williamsburg.

At its core, gentrification is characterized by a shift of investment into declining city neighborhoods, though the development and extent differ depending on the social, political, economic, demographic, and cultural conditions of a given location. Scholars understand gentrification as either a demand-side process based on individual decisions, or a supply-side progression driven by larger forces. Williamsburg has experienced both versions.

On the demand side, gentrification is viewed as the result of individual economic and lifestyle choices: an aesthetic preference for brownstone houses; an artist's wish for large studios with good lighting; a population's collective desire for good coffee and cool bars. From this position the actors include "urban pioneers" in search of cheap rent near desired amenities.[9] This piecemeal gentrification was characteristic of Williamsburg in the 1980s and 1990s. When apartments in Soho and Greenwich Village, the traditional stomping grounds of New York's avant-gardes, became unaffordable to students, artists, and other creatives, many of these folks slowly migrated out of Manhattan and into North Brooklyn.

The efforts of individual gentrifiers in this piecemeal stage can still have an aggregate effect on a neighborhood's identity. This scenario has played out in multiple New York locales, including the creation of Brooklyn's elite "Boerum Hill" neighborhood, which gentrifiers successfully distanced from the more disparaged Gowanus.[10] In Williamsburg the efforts of early gentrifiers, or *Bohemians*, reoriented the neighborhood's reputation toward art and hipster culture. While seemingly benign, this piecemeal process can help set the stage for supply-side and even state-led gentrification.

All forms of gentrification threaten existing residents with displacement, but state-led gentrification is especially criticized because elected and appointed political figures chronically fail to advocate or provide solutions for vulnerable constituents.[11] In 2005, following the early waves of gentrification and a sharp drop in crime citywide, mayor Michael Bloomberg drastically altered Williamsburg's future with a state-led in-

Figure I.2. The condofication of Williamsburg, September 2017. Author's photo.

tervention in the form of rezoning much of the neighborhood. While most of the housing stock prior to 2005 consisted of three-story apartment buildings and larger public housing units, the rezoning allowed for the building of high-rise condos with tax abatements and kickbacks for developers. Jane Jacobs, then a resident of Toronto, would lament the gentrification she didn't anticipate, penning a letter to Bloomberg and the City Council demanding that they reconsider the rezoning of Williamsburg.[12] Jacobs's words were not heeded, and within a few years large numbers of wealthy professionals, or *Condo Dwellers*, began moving to Williamsburg to purchase apartments that were comparatively cheaper than Manhattan and to partake in what was becoming a luxury neighborhood.

Emerging from similar government policies in Toronto, the term *condofication* refers to a style of gentrification whereby government officials and real estate developers unite to quite literally lay the foundation for high-rise developments, irrevocably altering a neighborhood's demographics and character. This process has been critiqued by sociologists and urban planners as contributing to class-based and racial segregation in cities and creating extreme concentrations of wealth and investment.[13] As a result of the condofication and ensuing corporate investments in the 2010s, Williamsburg became a destination, famous for its restaurants, nightlife, waterfront parks, and boutique shopping.[14]

As gentrification progresses, these changes to the built environment are easy to notice, but the actual rate of residential displacement, or turnover due to increased rents, has proven harder to track.[15] While many residents have already been physically displaced from Williamsburg, the bulk of the Old Timers featured in this book have avoided displacement by living in public housing or rent-controlled units, others by homeownership.[16] Yet even if no physical displacement had ever occurred, the construction of the waterfront condos would have shifted the population and culture of the neighborhood. The number of housing units was set to increase so substantially that zip code boundaries had to be redrawn in 2011. Most census tracts in the hyper-gentrified part of the neighborhood added at least 1,000 residents between 2010 and 2019, with the most developed tract increasing in population from 1,959 to 8,688 in those nine years. For existing residents who dodged physical displacement, this state-led gentrification changed their experiences of neighborhood life and intensified conflict over the use and ownership of public space.

Cultural Displacement

City neighborhoods are not stagnant entities; people move in and out, businesses open and close, and neighborhood reputations are in flux. In the past 150 years Williamsburg's reputation shifted from a collection of bucolic, wealthy estates, to a bustling working-class and (im) migrant enclave, next a locally oriented neighborhood facing urban disinvestment, then an emerging center of cool, and now a more corporate, luxury branded destination. As neighborhoods change, the norms, preferences, and priorities of an in-moving group can come to dominate the locale. As a result, existing residents may experience *cultural displacement*, feeling out of place or that they no longer belong in the neighborhood. These shifts and conflicts are not unique to gentrification, but the class, power, and often racial dynamics characteristic of the process yield particular outcomes. In recent years, understanding these changes has become a central concern for scholars of cities.[17]

As Williamsburg transformed around them, Old Timers who managed to stay put reported experiences of cultural displacement. As nightclubs and hotels replaced grocery stores and ethnic social clubs, the Old Timers' daily navigations through the neighborhood were altered. The elimination of institutions of necessity, less signage in Polish, Italian, and Spanish, and increased surveillance have all contributed to an environment that can feel foreign or even unwelcoming. The Bohemians also feel culturally displaced by increasingly wealthy Condo Dwellers and the entry of upscale retail into the neighborhood. The early gentrifiers who moved to Williamsburg in the 1980s and 1990s opened art galleries and small music venues, created an underground party scene, and jammed with their bands in local bars. Today those spaces and experiences are replaced by the more predictable encounters characteristic of upscale restaurants and chain stores. The remnants of Bohemian Williamsburg have been co-opted by corporate interests. If one needed a sign that the local music scene has all but dissipated, Red Bull's eventual sponsorship of a local music festival serves as a guidepost.

The concept of cultural and social displacement was first noted in urban scholarship in the 1960s. Early research in this field focused on the psychological impact of *physical* displacement. Labeled as a slum in the 1950s, Boston's West End was cleared to make room for high-rise housing for wealthier residents, physically uprooting a working-class Italian American community in the process. Urban sociologist Herbert Gans had critiqued the renewal program in Boston for not considering the *social* cost of displacement for this population. Psychologist Marc Fried's work picked up where Gans left off. He identified effects of relocation among former West End residents who lost not only the physical spaces of their neighborhood, but also their social worlds. Fried found that the loss of networks and spatial identity stimulated a psychological grieving process in displaced individuals.[18]

Two decades later, Peter Marcuse identified *pressures of displacement*, and later added *indirect displacement*, referring to changes to a neighborhood's social and built environment that signaled an important shift: "A family sees the neighborhood around it changing dramatically, when their friends are leaving, . . . when the stores they patronize are liquidating and new stores for other clientele are taking their places."[19] These signals matter because they can herald the *direct displacement* to come, but also because they diminish a sense of belonging in a neighborhood. Such pressures of displacement played out in Greenpoint, a neighborhood just north of Williamsburg, in the 2010s. Anthropologist and organizer Filip Stabrowski observed that long-term tenants in the neighborhood experienced housing insecurity due to increased rents and landlord harassment, while new luxury housing and commercial institutions made them feel out of place in the neighborhood's public spaces.[20] These stressors compounded to create a pervasive *everyday displacement*.

While various terms have been used to describe the process, a common theme in cultural displacement is that the norms and preferences of incoming groups come to dominate over those of existing residents, decreasing their feelings of ownership or belonging in a neighborhood. This includes developments or conditions that alienate or even erase existing residents from a neighborhood's public spaces, or a fluctuation in neighborhood institutions from necessity to luxury.[21] In Harlem, Monique Taylor found that *lifestyle differences* based on class and race led to tensions between existing residents and newcomers, which manifested in public and private spaces.[22] Existing residents knew that the changes were not "for them." Urban sociologist Steven Tuttle conceptualized *alienation from space* to describe how changes to businesses and norms in gentrifying Chicago neighborhoods challenged long-term residents' perceptions of ownership over their neighborhoods.[23]

At the crux of cultural displacement are various groups of local actors—residents, business owners, developers, and others—who have conflicting ideas about what the neighborhood is, or what it should be. These competing frames mean that changes to a neighborhood's environment or demographics are experienced differently. In Williamsburg, waves of cultural displacement have overlapped as gentrification has progressed. Bohemian artists or students did not necessarily have more income than the Old Timers, but they did have different tastes.[24] As large numbers of these avant-gardes moved into the neighborhood, they brought with them a certain set of preferences; soon a local scene of art galleries, underground parties, and quirky bars had emerged. Over the next two decades, the cultures and norms of Old Timers slowly became less visible in the neighborhood. They experienced cultural displacement as the retail, public spaces, and reputation of Williamsburg were increasingly oriented toward the early gentrifiers.[25]

As neighborhoods like Williamsburg gain a reputation for art and cultural consumption, the avant-garde types are often followed by real estate and corporate entities that seek to consume or capitalize on the culture that has been created, catalyzing a second wave of cultural displacement. As urbanist Richard Lloyd documented in Chicago, "artists in Wicker Park help[ed] 'make the scene.' . . . With gentrification these artist groups had to move out."[26] Richard Ocejo noted that in New York's Lower East Side, early gentrifiers saw themselves as "pioneers" because they moved into a neighborhood that was otherwise "forgotten" or undesirable for middle-class whites. As gentrification progressed, these early gentrifiers lamented the loss of cultural character, something they felt lent authenticity to their experiences in the neighborhood.[27]

When certain groups experience cultural displacement, they may also feel a reduced sense of control or ownership over their neighborhoods. As different groups come to dominate the culture of a place, the expectations and norms around public behavior can change. This shift plays out in public spaces like parks, which may see increased investment due to gentrification, but also exclusionary practices that arise with shifting ownership. Sylvie Tissot observed this in Boston's South End, where neighborhood associations led by white professionals exerted control over local parks and community gardens, creating and enforcing strict rules about how plots must be maintained or what activities were allowed in the spaces.[28] The rules and norms instated by these new residents helped them claim ownership over neighborhood spaces with the threat of surveillance or policing.

To be clear, Old Timers, Bohemians, and Condo Dwellers have all tried to claim space, engaged in activities that have excluded others, and felt discomfort in one institution or another. I argue that the claims to ownership and perceptions of neighborhood change are not just dependent on the typical categories we think of when it comes to gentrification. Certainly, race and class are primary determinants for experiences of everyday urban life; much of the literature on neighborhood change confirms its significance in gentrification as well.[29] The focus on attachment style in the present book does not question the impacts of race, class, immigration status, gender, sexuality, physical ability, or other aspects of identity that have very real consequences for everyday experiences of gentrification. Length of tenure in the neighborhood is another common grouping; this categorization can be useful, but it can also obscure nuances and it fails to challenge stereotypes about perceptions of gentrification. The addition of attachment style allows us to include another possible lens through which various residents come to view a neighborhood and to consider why this might matter for their daily experiences of urban life in a gentrifying neighborhood.

Neighborhood Attachment Style

Place attachment has been a popular topic in the social sciences since the 1970s, but the applications of the concept have varied so widely that there has never been a consensus in terms of how to define it.[30] Foundational texts on the subject often claim that time spent in a place is an essential component of attachment.[31] In the 1970s, urban sociologists John Kasarda and Morris Janowitz analyzed an existing survey of over two thousand residents in England to test models of community attachment, identifying length of residence as a "central and crucial factor."[32] Two decades later, anthropologist Setha Low and social psychologist Irwin Altman published *Place Attachment*, an edited volume of twelve essays. The contributors to the book represented a range of fields from landscape architecture and marketing to folklore, and while the authors gave varying definitions for the concept of place attachment, length of tenure was often used as a starting point.[33]

The concept's varied and interdisciplinary use has led to difficulty measuring attachment in different contexts. Some scholars argue that attachment to place is best understood in terms of an individual's behavior, like collective action around a shared goal. Others theorize that feelings and attitudes—for example, the cognitive and emotional processes involved in creating meaning or nostalgia—undergird attachment.[34] There is additional debate over whether attachment is determined more by our own personal identities and experiences or by attributes of the physical spaces we get attached to. Noting a proliferation of studies without an overarching conceptualization, psychologists Leila Scannell and Robert Gifford integrated existing findings into a framework for place attachment using a three-pronged theory that accounts for how people make connections to place as individuals or as members of groups, the social and physical aspects of places that people become attached to, and the emotional and cognitive processes through which people assign meaning to places.[35]

Studies of attachment in urban neighborhoods have predominantly focused on assessing *levels* of sentiment that residents feel toward their locale.[36] Level of sentiment can be impacted by the extensiveness of social networks, physical aspects of the area, the individual's evaluation of their own home and mobility, and whether they own or rent housing.[37] Life stage can also affect attachment. For example, parents of small children may interact with local institutions like schools as well as other families, generating greater feelings of attachment to their community. By contrast, single people may feel less attached since their social lives might play out in other locales.[38]

Existing research on neighborhood attachment has concluded, or taken for granted, three things: first, longer-term residents exhibit higher levels of attachment than newcomers; second, increased attachment leads to more involvement with local organizations; and third, these attachments yield benefits for both the individual and the neighborhood.[39] I argue that the *level* of attachment or neighborhood sentiment alone is too simplistic for understanding how our attachment to a place can impact our perceptions, experiences, and actions. I propose a model of neighborhood attachment *style*, building on urban sociologist Albert Hunter's theory of how neighborhood conditions can impact residents' interactions and attempts at building community.[40] In his essay in the *Handbook of Contemporary Urban Life*, Hunter argues that communities develop along sequential stages dependent on neighborhood characteristics and the context of mass society and that these factors would influence the type of attachment residents would have to their local community. According to Hunter, residents of *residual communities* have little shared attachment and community is based solely on proximity, while *emergent communities* come about through conflict, or banding together to combat a perceived threat. *Conscious communities* are chosen and arise around an "articulated set of central values," and in the final stage, *vicarious* or *symbolic communities*, individuals choose to be part of the community, even if they do not necessarily participate or even share in central values.

My theory departs from these community categories to develop styles of attachment that more directly relate to gentrifying neighborhoods, a phenomenon that was likely of little concern to Hunter in the 1970s. Building on his categorizations of how communities develop, and incorporating Scannell and Gifford's framework that takes account of how individuals form attachment, I propose a theory of neighborhood attachment style. Attachment style refers to an individual's motivation for moving to the neighborhood and the conditions of the area at that time. The cultural, social, and physical aspects of the neighborhood interact with an individual's personal biography, influencing their perceptions and experiences. I have identified three attachment styles among the residents of Williamsburg: necessity, identity, and investment (see table 1.1).

TABLE 1.1. Neighborhood Attachment Styles

Motivation for Moving to Williamsburg	Born into neighborhood or moved there for work, local immigrant community, or economic necessity.	Moved into the neighborhood because of cultural institutions, networks of artists/students, and inexpensive rent compared to other artist enclaves.	Moved into the neighborhood to invest in luxury housing, as a neighborhood to raise children in, and/or opportunities for consumption.
Conditions of Williamsburg Upon Entry	Presence of factories/production, limited city services, higher crime rates, businesses catered toward necessity.	Declining presence of factories/production, increasing city services, high to moderate/decreasing crime rates, businesses catering toward necessity as well as artist/musician/student culture.	Improved/better-funded city services, low crime rates, businesses catering to necessity, arts, upper-class necessity, and luxury.
Attachment Style	Necessity-based	Identity-based	Investment-based

A *necessity attachment* can emerge when a resident chooses a neighborhood because of basic needs that the locale can meet. Old Timers in this study (or their parents) were drawn to Williamsburg for the following reasons: access to work, affordable housing, (im)migrant networks, and institutions like ethnic grocery stores or places of worship. Generations of Old Timers moved to the neighborhood during its industrial period and through its transition into an avant-garde cultural hub. They chose the neighborhood because it provided essential goods, services, and networks, even in its early days of gentrification.

Individuals may also choose a neighborhood for more symbolic reasons, like what the neighborhood represents—in this case residents have an *identity attachment*. What is important is not necessarily the goods or services one can get in a neighborhood, but how the neighborhood conditions or reputation relate to aspects of an individual's identity. Perhaps there is a concentration of art galleries or renowned restaurants, or maybe the neighborhood has a reputation for being popular among families or young professionals. The networks here are based on interests or lifestyle rather than a more constraining variable like economic conditions or immigrant status. Individuals with an identity attachment often have some choice of where to move to, though it may be influenced by housing prices. In this style, the decision is at least partially made with consideration of the identity-affirming activities, networks, or institutions present in the neighborhood. In 1980s and 1990s Williamsburg, the neighborhood's material conditions (emptying warehouses and proximity to the East Village) created fertile ground for a burgeoning art and music scene. Eventually, artists and young people were attracted to the neighborhood because of specific arts institutions, material conditions, and an emerging subcultural scene.

A third reason why an individual might choose a neighborhood is the existence of, or potential for, future benefits: an *investment attachment*. The housing may be comparatively inexpensive but likely to increase in value, or perhaps the area has a good school district. For these individuals, their choice of neighborhood goes beyond meeting necessities or providing some kind of lifestyle or identity affirmation. In fact, an investment attachment to a neighborhood may mean that an individual moves there even if they feel that it does *not* fit their immediate needs or identity—with the expectation that it eventually will or that these concerns are less important than the investment being made. This was the case for the Condo Dwellers, who moved into the neighborhood after the construction of luxury housing post-2005.

These are the broad categories that reflect most of the participants in this book, but certainly not all of the residents of Williamsburg. While people can still move into the neighborhood for any of the above motivations, the social, cultural, and physical neighborhood prevents certain attachments from forming. A resident who wins a housing lottery will be motivated to move to the neighborhood out of economic necessity—that is, affordable rent—but the current conditions of Williamsburg preclude a full necessity attachment, as many other daily needs are unlikely to be met in the neighborhood. Similarly, an artist would not be able to move into the neighborhood and have a robust identity attachment for long after the rezoning. For example, Annie, an actress who rented in the neighborhood from 2008 to 2014, enjoyed the local restaurants and bars, but the performance spaces, artist networks, and avant-garde culture that would have facilitated an identity attachment were already waning. The constant construction in the neighborhood prevented the feelings of discovery that Bohemians fondly recalled. By the early 2020s, newcomers to Williamsburg were less likely to be motivated by a sense of economic investment; three-bedroom apartments were selling for over $3 million. New residents to Williamsburg may now be moving into the neighborhood for identity-focused reasons, this time to participate in a luxury neighborhood instead of an artistic one. Because of the time frame of data collection, those people are not included in this account, though a comparison of identity-attached residents at different times would be worthwhile.

In this case study, attachment style was important in the analysis of experiences of gentrification and neighborhood life. The emphasis on attachment style allows us to go beyond typical gentrification categories like ethnic background, class, or length of tenure in the neighborhood, revealing distinctions that otherwise might not be captured. Henryk and Gosia were both immigrants from Poland and in their mid-twenties in 1990. That year, when Henryk followed other family members to New York, he moved to Williamsburg even though his family put down roots in Queens. For Henryk, the move to Williamsburg was an identity-related choice to be around other young people and artists like himself. Gosia had immigrated to Williamsburg with her mother in the 1970s out of necessity, because her father already owned a house there. With different attachment styles, identity-attached Henryk remembered the 1990s undeveloped waterfront as "beautiful," in stark contrast to Gosia, who described the waterfront as "decrepit and dangerous." For Henryk, disused piers and decaying factories provided an exciting backdrop, while for Gosia they signaled decay.

Penny, a white American woman, moved to Williamsburg in the late 1990s because her artist husband wanted to live in the area. She was not interested in participating in that aspect of Williamsburg's culture, and she detested her Old Timer neighbors. With a very early investment-minded lens, Penny bought a building on the Southside, describing the neighborhood at the time as empty and unfriendly: "There were practically tumbleweeds blowing by." Unlike identity-attached artists, she found no redeeming qualities for that part of Williamsburg's history. When the Northside condos began to open, she sold her building and moved to a waterfront tower, finally enjoying life in Williamsburg. She moved into the neighborhood around the same time that Henryk did. In another framing of gentrification, Penny and Henryk might be grouped into the same cohort because of tenure in the neighborhood, but their attachments to the neighborhood and their perceptions of change are quite different.

Consider also Arnold, a Dominican man who was a Former Resident from the Southside. He is around the same age as Henryk and Penny, but was born in the neighborhood and has a necessity attachment to Williamsburg. This is reflected in his dismissal of the nightlife obsession in Williamsburg, which he feels has overtaken the local culture. Josie, a Latina woman, is newer to the neighborhood. Even though she wanted to move to a place with a lot of diversity, she described Williamsburg from her first visit in 2007 as dirty and empty. As an investment-attached Condo Dweller, she sticks to the Northside for her shopping and socializing rather than the predominantly Dominican and Puerto Rican Southside. In these examples, a resident's age, tenure in the neighborhood, and socioeconomic or ethnic status were not reliable variables for understanding their experiences of Williamsburg.

Attachment styles are reflective of differences in lifestyles, priorities, and perceptions for residents. The differences can lead to conflicts over space and over the issue of who has the power to shape that space in any urban neighborhood. During gentrification, existing and new residents may have incompatible ideas about what types of behavior are considered deviant, which businesses are needed or desired, or how public spaces like parks should be used. As residents with varying attachment styles struggle for ownership over a neighborhood, their efforts often lead other groups to experience cultural displacement.

These conflicts are more complicated than differences solely along demographic lines. Since residents move to the neighborhood for various reasons, their personal histories get layered onto existing patterns of (im)migration and flight, austerity and reinvestment, segregation and rezoning, and so on. This book reveals how neighborhood attachment styles create competing frames that affect how residents experience the neighborhood, claim control over space and the neighborhood's trajectory, and perceive daily life in a gentrifying neighborhood.

There Was Nothing There

The idea that there was "nothing" in a neighborhood before gentrification is a common trope. Gentrifiers measure "nothingness" in terms of (un)available goods and services, aesthetics, and perceived social disorder. At times, it's even simpler: gentrifiers don't see themselves, their tastes, and their lifestyles reflected in the neighborhood. Bohemians and Condo Dwellers have both perceived Williamsburg in this way, though at different times. The rhetoric of "nothing" frames gentrification in a positive light. If the place was empty, gritty, or even dangerous before, then the neighborhood's upscaling is only a boon. Narratives of Williamsburg as a void are important to gentrifiers' accounts, and these are reflected in media reports of the neighborhood and the city's treatment of Williamsburg through cycles of disinvestment and reinvestment. This framing works to erase the cultures and histories of existing residents. Today, it is the Old Timers who are starting to feel that there is nothing in the neighborhood. While they welcome some of the changes of reinvestment, they face a lack of relevant goods and services and are increasingly excluded from public spaces in both overt and subtle ways. *There Was Nothing There* explores how residents' attachment styles impact their daily experience of gentrification, and why these dynamics matter far beyond the borders of Brooklyn.

Before delving into the specifics of gentrification in Williamsburg, the reader must be immersed in the neighborhood's physical and cultural environment. Chapter 1 begins with an ethnographic tour of the neighborhood. This section is followed by a history of Williamsburg covering the key policies and socioeconomic trends that shaped the neighborhood. The macro picture of Williamsburg situates it in the context of other locales that have experienced an advanced level of gentrification, while an overview of demographic trends of the neighborhood center us back in North Brooklyn. Finally, the chapter concludes with an introduction to the resident groups that comprise the perspectives in this book.

Chapter 2 explores how residential cohorts utilized various forms of community organizing to assert power and claim ownership over the neighborhood. Old Timers were active in a neighborhood that suffered from city disinvestment and deindustrialization. They took actions to make their neighborhoods safer and to advocate for services that the city failed to provide. Bohemians rallied around environmentalism, and later protested the rezoning as it threatened their artist enclave. Condo Dwellers have organized for the addition—and regulation—of parks and public spaces in the neighborhood, changes that will support a continued return on their financial investments. A case study of Williamsburg Walks, a street-closure event, provides an in-depth look at how the planning of a community event worked to further investment-related goals, claiming space for some residents while excluding others.

The relationship between gentrification and crime is complex, to say the least. Chapter 3 begins with a survey of academic literature on this muddled relationship before turning to perceptions and experiences of crime among Williamsburg residents. Crime peaked in Williamsburg and New York in the early 1990s, then steadily decreased through the 2010s. Old Timers and Bohemians both lived in Williamsburg during its highest crime rates, but members of each group had different interpretations of crime and indicators of social disorder. All Old Timers acknowledged that there was a period of high crime in the neighborhood, even if they did not feel personally threatened by it. Bohemians perceived the crime and aesthetic disorder of Williamsburg as more alarming, but also "exciting" and "real." The third chapter ends with a discussion of the significance of crime for Bohemians and their identities as "pioneers" in Williamsburg.

Chapter 4 considers the changes in Williamsburg's most public sphere—the neighborhood's main commercial street. This chapter investigates the role of local shops in the trajectory of gentrification, pairing ethnographic description with quantitative data about retail change and the accounts of residents and store owners. The evolution of Williamsburg's Bedford Avenue is traced as the neighborhood shifts from local to global and necessity to luxury. This chapter examines how the decisions of local business owners act to welcome or exclude various residents' groups, and the implications these decisions have in a rapidly gentrifying neighborhood.

After understanding how attachment style impacts community organizing, perceptions of crime, and experiences of neighborhood retail, we turn to an analysis of how residents view gentrification overall. Chapter 5 focuses on three themes that emerge from these accounts: the perception of Williamsburg as a family neighborhood; the transition from narratives of void or nothingness to convenience; and the shift from a local neighborhood to a global destination as well as Condo Dwellers' attempts to reclaim a more local vibe. The chapter closes with the contemplation of a mural that was emblematic of many of the themes and tensions discussed.

Chapter 6 examines pro-gentrification rhetoric that continues to be promoted in the popular press, by politicians, and even in some academic literature. According to these sources, gentrification makes neighborhoods safer, improves local retail and access to amenities, and helps to socially integrate neighborhoods. These myths of gentrification are challenged, drawing on examples from Williamsburg's case study, and reiterating the impacts of state-led gentrification on existing communities.

The concluding chapter presents two additional examples of state-supported gentrification. In these descriptions, we hear echoes of the tensions and narratives present in Williamsburg, showing that this case study extends beyond the time and place it was conducted. Ideas for future research inspired by this project are shared, as well as thoughts on how residents and organizers can resist state-led change.

Finally, an epilogue considers the impacts of two events that happened after data collection ended: the threat of a long-term transit shutdown and the COVID-19 pandemic lockdown in the spring and summer of 2020. The first exemplifies the power amassed by new residents and business owners, and the second shows the limits of that power. We briefly hear the experiences and perceptions of a Bohemian resident who stayed in the city and two Condo Dwellers who left Williamsburg temporarily, posing more questions for the future of urban research. The epilogue closes with a contemplation of how Eric Adams, New York's current mayor, might deal with problems of gentrification and housing. A methodological appendix follows, documenting information about the sample and recruitment in this study, as well as further details of the mixed methods utilized in this book.

1

The Neighborhood

From Industry to Instagram

September 2016. The waves ripple out underneath a ferry departing from Williamsburg's Northside, heading toward Manhattan. It will return with commuters in professional attire who work in Midtown and live in the condos on this shore's waterfront. It's a weekday afternoon in early fall and the East River State Park[1] is well manicured—sanitized, even, as evidenced by a list of prohibited items, including dogs and alcohol. It is markedly different from its past incarnations.

This park was once the site of bustling factories and warehouses. Later, the abandoned structures provided housing for a small population of unsheltered people. In the 1980s and 1990s, this stretch of the waterfront was occupied by skateboarders, musicians holding band practice, fire spinners, performance artists, and old men fishing off the piers into the murky waters of the East River.[2] The park officially opened in 2007, around the same time as the first Condo Dwellers were moving into the new developments. On weekends, part of the park is now taken over by Smorgas*burg*, an expensive food market that has opened other branches throughout New York, as well as Jersey City and Los Angeles. Occasionally, the entire park is closed for ticketed music concerts. On a pleasant weekday afternoon like this one, the East River State Park is populated with tourists photographing the perfect view of the Manhattan skyline, a few Hasidic Jewish mothers with their small children, and Black Caribbean nannies pushing expensive strollers. The adjacent space to the north, Bushwick Inlet Park, is even newer, with pristine soccer fields, a dog run, and a small playground.

To the south, the autumn sunlight catches on one of a dozen buildings that range from six to thirty stories. The Edge Towers, the Northside Piers, and the Austin Nichols House are all luxury housing opened in or after 2008. Prior to the flood of real estate development, the highest

Figure 1.1. Street-level view of waterfront condos, January 2023. Author's photo.

building on the waterfront was the old Domino Sugar factory, which is currently under construction and will be another upscale housing development, reportedly with some affordable units and another waterfront park. In the years preceding the rezoning, this waterfront was completely different—no high-rises, no ferry service, no landscaped new parks. These are all evidence of the private investment that has flowed into Williamsburg in recent years, with the support of public subsidies and infrastructure.

To the east, at the park's entrance, even more high-rises jut up into the sky, rising above the three- and four-story homes that are more typical in this area. Pedestrians look both ways before exiting the park and walking onto Kent Avenue, not for cars, but for bikes. Kent, once an important delivery route for the factories along the waterfront, also had a nighttime economy of drug sales and sex work. After Williamsburg's

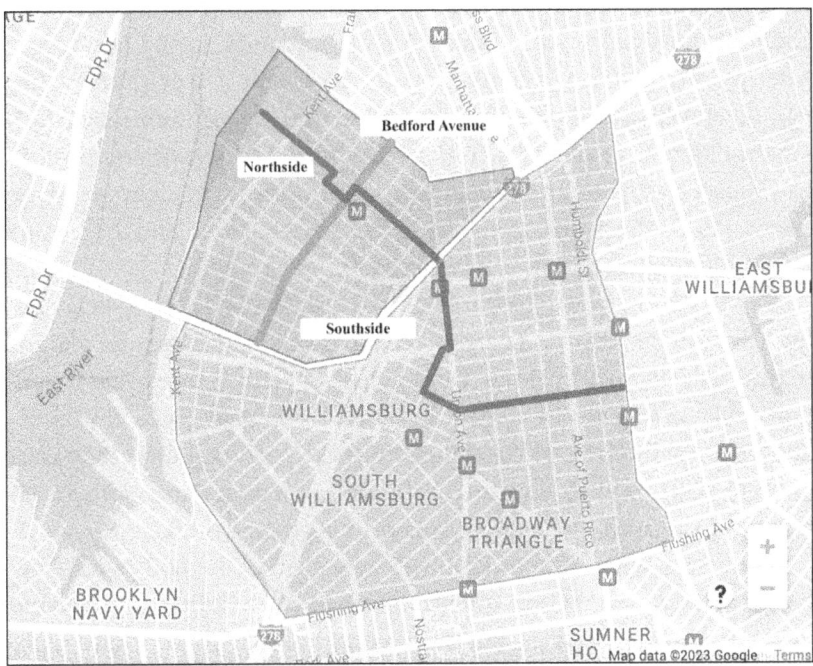

Figure 1.2. Map of Williamsburg. The dark line marks the route described in this chapter; the lighter line is Bedford Avenue. The neighborhood is segmented to single out the most gentrified section, the northwestern corner. Map courtesy of Google Maps, 2023.

rezoning, the street was altered to have just one lane of car traffic and a two-lane, protected bike path. The green-painted path, part of the derisively nicknamed Great Hipster Silk Route, covers approximately ten miles in North Brooklyn, connecting a few gentrifying neighborhoods. Further down Kent Avenue are many more waterfront condos, most anchored on the ground level by retail ranging from upscale grocery stores and chain pharmacies to gourmet ice cream shops, boutique gyms, and indoor play spaces for children. Past the Williamsburg Bridge, the neighborhood transitions dramatically into a Hasidic Jewish community. Many of the businesses in that area have served the Hasidic residents for decades. The area even has its own local school bus company, run by Central Satmar Transportation, as well as Hatzalah, their volunteer emergency medical services.

If we walk southeast out of the park and onto North Eighth Street, the first street we encounter inland is Wythe Avenue. In the late 2000s Wythe was a quiet street. It had several vacant buildings as well as three- and four-story houses and remaining light manufacturing businesses. After years of constant construction, there are now two extravagant hotels, several cafés, bars, nightclubs, and multiple music venues, including Brooklyn Bowl, a hybrid concert hall/bowling alley with outposts in Las Vegas, Nashville, and Philadelphia. Cabs line up at all hours of the evening to shuttle people to and from these destinations, and the pulsing music and excited crowds can be heard for blocks.

As we continue down North Eighth, the smell of fried food emanates from Teddy's Bar & Grill, a neighborhood institution for decades that has transferred hands many times. On warm days, patrons sit outside at sidewalk tables over plates of burgers and fries. By the mid-2010s, the lunchtime crowd at those tables has shifted from older adults and working-class locals to Williamsburg mom groups (founded on virtual spaces but meeting in person) with a battery of strollers lining the sidewalk.

Aside from a few condos on this block, most of the houses have between three and eight apartments. Some of the buildings are covered in vinyl siding or shingles, but more savvy building owners have renovated their houses and stripped down to the original brick that the new in-movers seem to prefer. It's afternoon and a parade of parents and children are exiting the Montessori preschool as Marcin, an elderly Polish immigrant, watches the street from his normal perch, a lawn chair

Figure 1.3. A typical street view on the Northside: Wythe Avenue and North Eighth Street, January 2023. Author's photo.

set atop his stoop. Bedford Avenue is just ahead, ground zero for retail gentrification in the early 2000s and the main transportation hub on the Northside. There are dozens of boutiques, specialty coffee shops, restaurants, and bars on Bedford, and the side streets have attracted commercial activity as well. Several of the newer businesses include large corporations like Apple and Whole Foods as well as branches of international banks.

One block south on Bedford, there is a seemingly endless flow of people trudging up and down the subway stairs. Black and Hispanic teenagers tease each other as they hover around the station after a long school day; a Polish mother gets help carrying her baby stroller up the stairs; young Japanese women huddle around a phone trying to figure out which direction to walk in as a few white men in suits hustle by on their way home to the waterfront. Tourists and locals merge without interacting and in the span of a few minutes, English, French, Japanese, German, Polish, and Spanish can all be heard.

Snaking around the crowd on the sidewalk, we see that the neighborhood begins to open up into a section that feels more quietly residential. The condos and retail peter out for a few blocks that are dotted with older institutions like Our Lady of Mount Carmel, an Italian Catholic church with a diminished congregation. North of here is McCarren Park, the barrier between Williamsburg and Greenpoint, an adjacent neighborhood that is also in the throes of gentrification.[3] The thirty-five-acre park has lots of open space, a track, dog runs, and baseball fields. A farmers' market sets up in one corner on Saturdays and, no matter the season, older Polish men can be found in the park, socializing and hiding their beer cans in brown paper bags. But the park's main attraction is its Olympic-size swimming pool, completed in 1936 by the Works Progress Administration. At first it was a neighborhood treasure, but disinvestment and racial tensions in the 1970s and 1980s culminated in white residents petitioning the city to close the pool; it would not be reopened for nearly thirty years.

Ahead of us, and in contrast to the green space to the north, is Robert Moses's imposing Brooklyn-Queens Expressway (BQE). Completed in 1964, the elevated stretch of highway casts a shadow where hundreds of homes used to stand. The structure cuts through a large swath of Williamsburg, and during its construction in the 1940s and 1950s several blocks were demolished to make room for it. The BQE runs north to south, bifurcating the neighborhood into eastern and western sections, which is why the Italian church is disconnected from much of today's Italian American community on the opposite side of the highway. Passing under the structure with the whir of cars speeding overhead gives the feeling of entering a different neighborhood. The eastern portion of Williamsburg has restaurants, bars, and condos too, but it isn't as homogeneously gentrified as the Northside.

Union Avenue heads southeast from the expressway and divides the historically Italian neighborhood to the north from the predominantly Puerto Rican and Dominican neighborhood to the south. In the Italian neighborhood, the housing stock is much the same as the Northside, three- and four-story homes on tree-lined streets with the occasional high-rise climbing up above the rest. The Italian population has dwindled, but a few longtime Italian businesses are still around—a butcher, a fish market, a pastry shop, and a bread bakery—some of which are patronized by long-termers and newcomers alike.

The intersection of Union and Grand heralds the beginning of a more concentrated Latinx community. Grand Street itself is in transition. Longtime dollar stores and Mexican taco shops sit next to punk rock dive bars and newer restaurants that look more like the ones on Bedford Avenue. This area has been slower to gentrify, at least partially because of the high percentage of public housing and rent-stabilized units in the neighborhood, which have assisted lower-income families staying in place even as market rents spike. The southern portion of Williamsburg also suffered the most from disinvestment, including racist redlining practices compounded by limited city services. Turning down Hooper Street, we still see some vacant lots, a reminder of the arson fires and landlord neglect of the 1970s and 1980s.

It's only a mile's distance, but this area feels worlds away from the amenity-filled high-rises of the western portion of the neighborhood. There are more shuttered businesses and less corporate advertising, the sidewalks are cracked, and there are fewer trees—but there's also a lot more public, neighborhood life. Residents regularly congregate at the church for worship and to pick up supplies from the food pantry. This afternoon, neighbors are grilling on the sidewalk and playing music while children shriek and chase each other; a few older kids on bikes are stopped at a corner debating their next move. This informal, unstructured play is rarely seen on the Northside.

There are signs of gentrification here too, from Big Irv's, a longtime gallery and artists' residence, to the more obvious Rough Draft, a sleek co-working space. Rough Draft opened in response to the growing population of creatives who frequently work from home but sometimes prefer the atmosphere of a communal workspace. Individuals can pay twenty-eight dollars to work there for the day, or three hundred dollars to work there full-time each month. Down the street, City CoPilot has just opened in a space formerly occupied by a small grocery store. This new business is a concierge service for the economy that has developed around the hundreds of Airbnb rentals available in Williamsburg. Owners pay to leave keys for their visitors and can also arrange to have someone clean the apartment for the next Airbnb guests; visitors can leave luggage at the storefront and coordinate airport transportation. The idea that there would be enough visitors on the Southside to warrant this sort of business was unthinkable even a few years ago.[4]

Figure 1.4. Street-level view of Southside Williamsburg: Hooper Street and South First Street, April 2018. Author's photo.

Turning left and heading up Scholes Street, we end at the Williamsburg Houses, the oldest public housing in the borough and the largest in Williamsburg, with 1,620 units. These are a stark contrast to where this walk began on the Northside waterfront. Just like the new condos, the twenty towers that make up the complex are the sites of dense urban living, but there are no rooftop patios or heated pools here. The anchor institutions on the first floor of the Northside condos include both necessities and luxuries, but at the Williamsburg Houses the first-floor retail is empty, aside from a few convenience stores and a daycare. One thing that is present here, but lacking in most of Williamsburg, are police—a sign of control and securitization over the neighborhood's non-white population. This is not the Williamsburg that has international renown, and while they might find affordable Airbnbs in the area, most tourists do not spend much time in this section. The Southside, especially the public housing units, are home to Old Timers and residents who aren't facing immediate physical displacement. Still, their local environments have shifted significantly over the past two decades. In the following chapters, we will explore how residents experience these changes as their neighborhood continues to gentrify.

A Brief History of Williamsburg

Standing in the canyon of luxury towers along the heavily curated waterfront parks, we may find it hard to imagine previous versions of Williamsburg. Through the seventeenth century, this area was part of the Lenapehoking region, occupied by the Canarsee. These Natives fished and farmed tobacco and corn in much of modern Brooklyn and Queens.[5] Long before the word "gentrification" was coined, the Canarsee were displaced from this area by European colonization. The Dutch West India Company claimed ownership over the land as early as 1638, but the first European settlement wasn't chartered until 1661, when the town of Bosjwick, now Bushwick, was established. At that time, the interior part of Bosjwick was used for farming, and Het Strandt, the area that is now the Williamsburg waterfront, was a launching point for ferries to move crops and other goods to Manhattan, foreshadowing the neighborhood's future importance as a hub of trade.

In 1802 Richard Woodhull hired John Williams to survey a thirteen-acre patch of waterfront land that he had purchased with the intention of creating a ferry route. By 1827 Williamsburgh, named for the surveyor, became its own incorporated village within Bushwick. Dropping the *h* by the 1850s, the city of Williamsburg was an industrial center, attracting manufacturing because of its location on the East River and also welcoming wealthy New Yorkers as a desirable, less crowded suburb of Manhattan. Williamsburg became part of Brooklyn in 1855, and into the twentieth century the area continued to attract industry, including the Domino Sugar factory, Pfizer Pharmaceuticals, oil processing, and breweries.[6] Wealthy New York families had built estates in Williamsburg, but in 1898 Brooklyn was incorporated into New York City and in 1903 the Williamsburg Bridge opened. These two factors encouraged a migration of poor and working-class people from Manhattan, particularly the Lower East Side, who were attracted to the manufacturing jobs.

For the next several decades, Williamsburg's demographics shifted from wealthy New York entrepreneurs to working-class migrants and immigrants, accompanied by the construction of tenement housing stock and later public housing. Williamsburg's population grew through chain migration as individuals and families from Europe and the Caribbean followed networks of relatives and acquaintances to Brooklyn.[7] In 1938 the Williamsburg Houses were completed on the far eastern end of the neighborhood, as part of the Public Works Administration. The Houses were the first New York City Housing Authority (NYCHA) buildings in Brooklyn, and they were followed by eight more in Williamsburg, totaling seventy-four buildings and approximately six thousand apartments.

Polish immigrants have populated Williamsburg and its northern neighbor, Greenpoint, since the late nineteenth century. Subsequent generations immigrated after both World Wars, and again in the 1980s and early 1990s after the end of communism in Poland. Immigration from southern Italy followed a similar pattern, with peaks in the late nineteenth century and in the decades after World War II. Jewish families migrated from the Lower East Side after the completion of the Williamsburg Bridge in 1903 and the opening of the L subway line in 1924. Jewish people of Satmar-Hasidic origin began moving into Williamsburg before World War II, but the community grew with Holocaust survivors in the late 1940s and early 1950s. The advent of commercial air travel increased the migration of Puerto Ricans to New York, especially to Williamsburg. Dominicans began settling in Williamsburg in larger numbers after the Immigration Act of 1965 repealed quotas favoring Europeans. Compared to other Brooklyn neighborhoods, Williamsburg has never had a large population of African American residents.[8]

Many of these people were drawn to Williamsburg because of the availability of factory jobs and cheap housing in the neighborhood, in addition to established (im)migrant communities. However, by the 1960s New York's tenure as a manufacturing center was coming to an end. In *Branding New York*, Miriam Greenberg carefully traces the political and economic conditions that led to disinvestment in New York.[9] Changes in technology and deregulation meant that factories could employ fewer workers, and companies began moving out of New York and later the United States in search of cheaper, non-unionized labor.[10] Deindustrialization, racism, and suburbanization funneled white middle-class populations out of many American cities, as the economy went through a fiscal crisis as well as a global oil crisis. At the same time, cities were hotbeds for social justice movements around race, gender, and sexuality, as well as protests against the Vietnam War. In response, conservative politicians at the federal level began cutting urban funding under presidents Richard Nixon and Gerald Ford, culminating with the famous 1975 *Daily News* headline "Ford to City: Drop Dead," after he offered New York bankruptcy instead of a bailout.[11]

With the combined, related issues of deindustrialization, suburbanization, and a reduction in federal funds, New York City had a budget problem. In places like Williamsburg, poverty and criminal activity increased as jobs and resources became scarcer. In an attempt to increase revenue via tourism, politicians considered a policy of planned shrinkage. While many decried the concept put forth by Roger Starr, then the housing and development administrator, the outer boroughs experienced significant cuts in services, with funds being redirected toward central Manhattan tourist attractions, including Broadway.[12] As a result, Williamsburg and similar neighborhoods experienced a lack of funding for education, hospitals, and police departments. Subway and bus service was limited, firehouses faced closure, and sanitation trucks visited with varying regularity. At the same time, housing values plummeted and landlords refused to repair buildings, leaving some tenants without heat or water; other landlords participated in a trend of arson fires, hoping they could recoup some of their house's value through insurance claims. At the same time, redlining and other banking practices made it all but impossible for minorities to get loans to buy or improve apartments, while white ethnic Old Timers exerted control in the Northside by refusing to rent to people who were not white.[13]

Despite these challenges, Old Timers in the neighborhood insist not only that they could get groceries, clothing, and other necessities in the area, but also that they had rich religious and ethnic-based social lives and generally felt insulated from crime. Most of them actively resisted the term "slum" and showed pride in their neighborhood by creating many successful community-based organizations and neighborhood groups that advocated for or provided services that the city neglected.[14] This period of disinvestment persisted, but it didn't keep away another flow of migration from Lower Manhattan. This time it was artists and students moving to Williamsburg for the cheap rents, studio spaces, and easy access to the city. As demonstrated in recent studies by sociologists Stacey Sutton and Zawadi Rucks-Ahidiana, the racial segregation kept in place by Old Timers likely helped prime Williamsburg for gentrification.[15]

By the early 1980s, Williamsburg's demographics began to shift with this migration of young, middle-class students and artists, most of whom were white Americans, along with some European and Asian avant-gardes. These Bohemians came to Williamsburg seeking inexpensive rent but also to be part of a growing artist network. The newcomers described Williamsburg at the time as both desolate and magical, and their creativity flourished in the vacated factories and overgrown waterfront of Williamsburg's industrial landscape. Violent crime rates dopped throughout New York City in the 1990s, and Williamsburg was no exception. Repairs to the L train line made transit to the East Village even easier—a place where many of the early gentrifiers worked, showed their art, and may have even lived before coming to Williamsburg. Eventually, entrepreneurs opened new restaurants and bars in the area and the neighborhood became a draw for nightlife. Soon the L train did not just transport people into Manhattan for work and play, but also shuttled Manhattanites across the river to check out the burgeoning art, music, and party scenes.[16] The cultural changes spurred on by Bohemians were certainly not inconsequential for the neighborhood's trajectory; still, much of the power wielded in Williamsburg is beyond the reach of Old Timers, Bohemians, or Condo Dwellers.

Even before Michael Bloomberg's development-focused mayoral tenure, Jason Hackworth and Neil Smith noted an increase in state-led gentrification in New York City.[17] This shift transformed the face of gentrification in New York and beyond, moving it from a smaller-scale, piecemeal process into larger projects, more similar to the urban renewal of the 1950s and 1960s. In her 2009 reflection on power and gentrification, Sharon Zukin reminds us that a potent blend of international capital and local politics is often behind this type of development, creating a homogeneous urbanism that is replicated around the world. This is certainly the case in Williamsburg, as a series of decisions by city government in the 1990s and early 2000s led to a virtually unrecognizable neighborhood two decades later. While mechanisms exist to give residents a say in these processes, the final decisions are often made by local politicians whose decisions more often align with global capital flows and the interests of real estate developers than with their local constituents.

Although gentrification was underway in Williamsburg, city officials viewed the area as degraded after decades of their own policies of disinvestment and planned shrinkage. In 1994 the city proposed a waste transfer station for the neighborhood, but a coalition of residents successfully protested it. In 2001 the neighborhood was again threatened with the proposal of a power plant on the nearby Greenpoint waterfront. Local organizations predicted that if the power plant was defeated, the area might instead be rezoned for denser residential use. Anticipating development of the waterfront, neighborhood organizations and the Community Board devised a 197-a plan, a community-based advisory document that detailed the requests of neighborhood residents in light of the potential rezoning.[18] In the plan, residents demanded public access to the waterfront, open space, and affordable housing, while raising environmental concerns. In 2002, after much conflict between the city and Northside residents, the City Planning Commission and the City Council eventually approved a modified version of the advisory 197-a plan that would include affordable housing, light industry, and waterfront access. However, the city soon came up with its own rezoning agenda that disregarded much of the 197-a plan. In 2005, despite opposition from residents and community-based organizations, the New York City Council approved Mayor Bloomberg's plan that rezoned almost two hundred blocks of Greenpoint and Williamsburg, including the entire waterfront. At the time, the 421-a Inclusionary Housing Program provided generous tax abatements to developers and let them build higher as long as 20 percent of the total units would be affordable housing.[19] This program has now been adopted in other parts of New York, as nearly 40 percent of the city was rezoned during Bloomberg's twelve-year tenure, part of his effort to create a luxury city. Predictably, the affordable housing stock has been slow to emerge, and what has been built has been criticized as not being affordable for longer-term residents.[20]

Bloomberg's enticement of real estate kicked off a decade of development, escalating gentrification in the neighborhood, which only stalled briefly in the wake of the 2008 financial crisis. To drum up business during the downturn, real estate developers passed the tax abatements and other bonuses on to potential buyers. The owners of one condo building, Rialto (named for a Venetian bridge), became so desperate during this period that in April 2009 they offered a free trip to Venice to anyone who would purchase a unit.[21] Williamsburg had a surplus of luxury housing—even as the existing housing stock was becoming too expensive for many residents—so these units became lucrative investments for people who were already looking to buy real estate in New York.

While the sleek new buildings have drawn comparisons to Miami Beach, much of modern Williamsburg's branding has relied on the "rustic" historical charm of the neighborhood's industrial past. Exposed brick in dozens of upscale restaurants and apartments in restored factory buildings offer a highly romanticized version of Williamsburg's working-class history. In reality, past industry means that the area is still reckoning with centuries of pollution, and some of the long-term issues have yet to be resolved. The Northside's Starbucks currently sits on the site of a former electroplating and metal finishing firm that left behind seven thousand gallons of hazardous materials, since cleaned up by the EPA.[22] Beginning in the 1950s, an oil company now owned by Exxon Mobil spilled between seventeen and thirty million gallons of oil into Newtown Creek, which lines the northern shore of East Williamsburg and Greenpoint. One of the largest spills in American history, it was first noticed in 1978, but it wasn't until the area became an upper-class destination that the state successfully took action against the corporation. In 2007 the construction of luxury housing near McCarren Park was stalled because oil was seeping up from the ground, assumed to originate from the Newtown contamination.[23] In 2010 New York's then attorney general Andrew Cuomo settled with Exxon Mobil to clean the spill. The company was ordered to pay $25 million in penalties and environmental support and to remove the oil.[24] The plan for the cleanup isn't expected until 2028.[25]

Still, the oil discovery did not prevent Warehouse 11 from opening on the site in 2009. Promotional materials from the high-end building promise residents a chance to "unwind in style in your modern gallery lounge, exercise to perfection in your state-of-the-art fitness center, be spiritually awakened in your yoga garden."[26] After opening in 2009, studios in the building sold for $399,000, and in 2020 went for as much as $639,000; the floor plan showed a built-in Murphy bed in the combination living/dining/bedroom.

Throughout the neighborhood, luxury housing has attracted wealthy newcomers, the Condo Dwellers, who would have previously been more likely to settle in Manhattan or the earlier gentrified neighborhoods of Brooklyn like Park Slope or Brooklyn Heights. The rezoning and development in the western portion of Williamsburg have created even starker contrasts between the neighborhood's condofied Northside and the public housing in the southern and eastern sections, which were victim to decades of disinvestment and municipal neglect. Millionaires and former factory workers now share the same subway stop and neighborhood park, and more upscale shops and restaurants have replaced many of Williamsburg's older establishments. The residential towers and the corporations that comprise condofication have sanitized the public spaces of the avant-garde culture and contributed to drastic rent increases. Units once occupied by poor and working-class families have "filtered up" to wealthier people.[27] As a result, the Old Timer communities of Dominicans, Puerto Ricans, Polish, and Italians, though still very much present, have been successively diluted by swells of newcomers.

Defining the Neighborhood

The geographic boundaries of Williamsburg have shifted over time, and the current popularity of the neighborhood has encouraged real estate agents to stretch the name further and further east along the local subway line. Literature on neighborhood effects, the indicators of (re)investment, show that they are generally "clustered geographically," and this is certainly true for Williamsburg, with the improved subway station, medical services, increased retail, and new park space all concentrated on the Northside.[28] The purpose of this study is to understand how people experience gentrified neighborhoods, and thus, many aspects of this research are focused on the Northside section of Williamsburg, which has witnessed the most intense gentrification.[29] Still, participants in the study lived in a variety of areas throughout the neighborhood.

At the time of research, the area that experienced advanced gentrification, based on income levels, housing value, and changes to retail and public spaces, has a natural boundary of the East River to the west, McCarren Park to the north, the Brooklyn-Queens Expressway to the east, and the Williamsburg Bridge to the south. This part of Williamsburg is also bisected by Grand Street, the dividing line between numbered streets designated North or South. Before gentrification, the Northside was more traditionally Polish and Italian, and has seen the most dramatic rates of gentrification. The Southside was primarily Puerto Rican and Dominican; this area has also changed significantly, if less rapidly.[30] Using US Census Bureau data from the decennial census and the American Community Survey, we can track demographic changes in Williamsburg over time.[31] The following data focus on ten census tracts in Williamsburg, six on the Northside and four on the Southside, all in the more heavily gentrified western portion.

The residential population of Williamsburg changed as the area shifted from a working-class factory town to an internationally known cultural hub, and then to a site for upscale consumption. In figures 1.5 and 1.6, Williamsburg is compared to itself over time and also to the borough of Brooklyn for a broader context. In figure 1.5, we see that from 1970 to 1990, Williamsburg lagged behind Brooklyn averages when it came to proportion of residents who attended college. In 2000, leading up to the rezoning, Williamsburg's rates approached the overall borough levels, and by 2010, the percentages of Williamsburg residents with at least some college education shot past the rest of Brooklyn and continued to increase through the 2010s. If we consider only the condofied Northside, the numbers are even more stark: in 2019 nearly 87 percent of Northsiders had at least some college education, compared with just under 80 percent of all residents of Williamsburg and 56 percent for Brooklyn overall. Similar trends are noted for the proportion of residents in professional jobs.

Yet poverty rates remain high in Williamsburg, relative to Brooklyn as a whole. In the borough, the percentage of adults living below the poverty level has hovered in the low 20 percent range from 1980 on (see figure 1.6). Williamsburg had been an outlier with a high poverty rate, which spiked again in 2010, before decreasing closer to the Brooklyn average by 2020. The high rate in 2010 was concentrated among older adults who were living in the Southside tracts, in contrast to previous years, when Williamsburg's poverty was more widespread throughout the neighborhood. This indicates that while the entire neighborhood has gentrified, the increase of wealth has been especially marked on the Northside and in the waterfront condos.

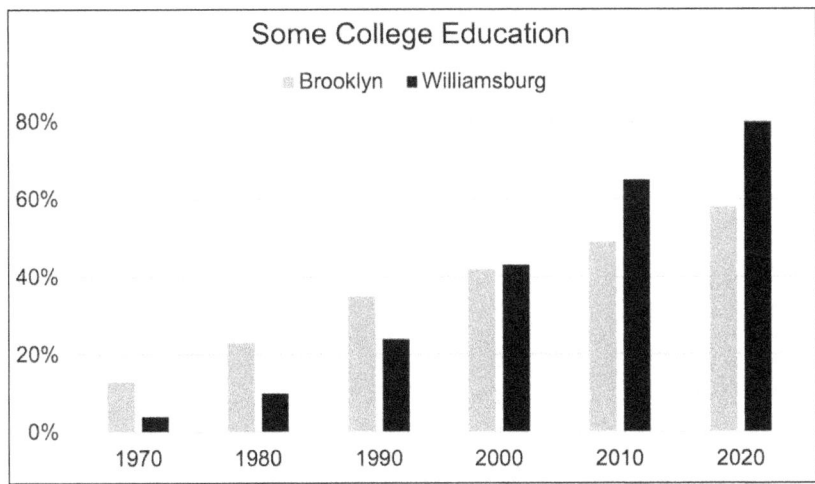

Figure 1.5. Percentage of Williamsburg adults with some college, compared with Brooklyn rates, 1970–2020. Data from the US census (1970–2000) and American Community Survey (2010–2020), via Social Explorer. Chart created by author.

The presence of a younger population is another way Williamsburg's gentrification has played out demographically. By 2010, a third of all Williamsburg residents were between twenty-five and thirty-four years old, compared with 17 percent for the borough. The newest residents are more likely to be educated and in professional careers, and also more likely to be coupled, married, and/or parenting compared to earlier gentrifiers, who were often fresh out of undergrad.[32] These in-moving Condo Dwellers are very different from the Bohemians who made Williamsburg's youth culture during the first wave of gentrification in the 1990s. The current generation of artists and students cannot afford the neighborhood today; they are moving to relatively cheaper neighborhoods like Bushwick, Ridgewood, and Bedford-Stuyvesant and, in the absence of rent regulations and other protections, spurring gentrification there.

In the mid-2000s Williamsburg broke away from the slower changes of the 1980s and 1990s and moved into a more rapid and dramatic shift. The greatest factor in this was the rezoning of the neighborhood for higher-density housing. The number of housing units increased by over 50 percent in a mere four years, between 2010 and 2014; the overall in-

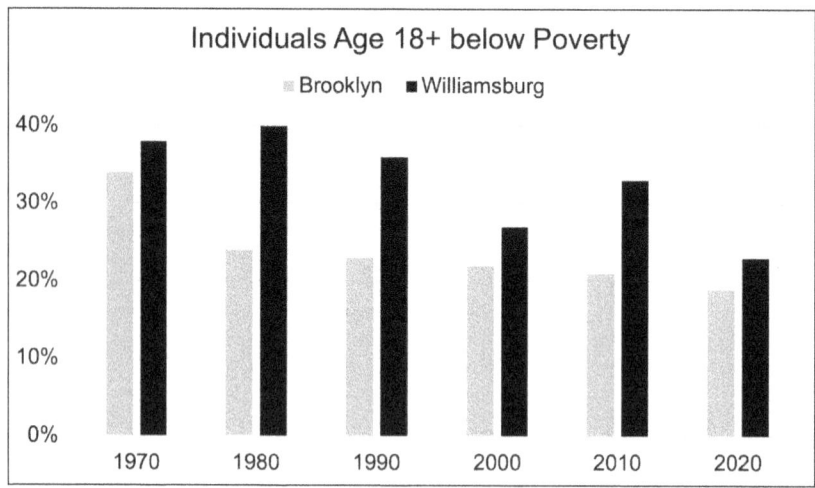

Figure 1.6. Percentage of Williamsburg adults living below the poverty level, compared with Brooklyn rates, 1970–2020. Data from US census (1970–2000) and American Community Survey (2010–2020), via Social Explorer. In 1970 data were collected for people ages fourteen and over; in all subsequent years, the data incorporated adults only. Chart created by author.

crease in Brooklyn over that time was 2.6 percent. With the increase in housing came a population boom: eight thousand additional residents in those same four years. Williamsburg was beginning to lose the "small village" feel that many Bohemians and even Condo Dwellers have praised.

Despite these changes, there is still a significant presence of Polish, Dominican, and Puerto Rican residents who have remained in the neighborhood, even as it transformed around them. The neighborhood's (im)migrant populations peaked in the 1970s. In 1980, 59.5 percent of Williamsburg residents were of "Spanish" origin, as it was presented on that census; and 9.6 percent were Polish. Forty years later, a decade into the neighborhood's condofication, 26.8 percent of residents were Hispanic and 5.4 percent were Polish.[33] The decrease reflects movement out of the neighborhood, whether by choice or because of rent increases, but it also reflects the overall growth in population. The actual count of people of Polish ancestry increased from 2,143 to 2,242 and the total count of Hispanic residents decreased from 13,193 to 11,160. There have been extreme demographic changes in Williamsburg over time, but these numbers also tell us that a significant portion of the existing community may have remained in the neighborhood as advanced gentrification was occurring. What were their experiences of staying put in a gentrifying neighborhood?

Meet the Neighbors

The changes to Williamsburg's physical environment, demographics, and reputation are beyond the individual choices of existing residents and in-movers. The patterns of disinvestment and state-led gentrification were precipitated by larger political and economic trends that Williamsburg, New York City, and other global cities have experienced. Still, local actors like residents and business owners do have an impact on how gentrification plays out in their neighborhood, especially in the social and symbolic spheres. As sociologist Janet Abu-Lughod urged, we must conduct neighborhood case studies to fully understand the "interactive effects of micro and macro forces."[34] With this understanding of the underlying currents connected to Williamsburg's gentrification, we turn to the residents to get a clearer picture of how these macro changes played out at the individual level.[35]

Old Timers: Necessity-Attached

The Old Timers are residents with a necessity attachment to the neighborhood. Most of the Old Timers in this book were living in Williamsburg by the 1970s, although a few younger participants were growing up in the neighborhood through the 1990s. Many Old Timers came to Williamsburg (either themselves or through their parents) because of the presence of well-paying factory work or because other people from their hometown had moved there; frequently participants said it was both reasons. They raised families, opened ethnic businesses and social clubs, participated in religious institutions, and formed community organizations to insulate their neighborhood from the city's disinvestment.

Paul was born in Williamsburg in the late 1980s, a few years after his parents moved to Brooklyn: "A lot of people from my dad's town [in Puerto Rico] came to Williamsburg. So a lot of the neighborhood was neighbors [from Puerto Rico]." The same was true for Omar, whose mother moved to the neighborhood from Puerto Rico in the 1960s: "My mother . . . had older generations beforehand helping her." And George's family from the Dominican Republic also had a network of people when they immigrated in the 1970s: "It's been very helpful to have a lot of my family here. My parents were able to make this their home." Former Old Timer Arnold recalls coming from the Dominican Republic as a child and settling in Williamsburg: "My uncle was kind of like the point man for immigration. He had set up there, so that's how we went there."

Back then, the Northside of the neighborhood was mainly home to European immigrants and white ethnics. The Italian American community was diminishing due to white flight, but at the same time Polish immigrants were moving into the neighborhood. Marcin arrived in Williamsburg in 1965: "I came because I have family here." Gosia's father moved to New York in the early 1970s and moved his family over in 1976: "Basically [he] got off at JFK and at that time a family friend who he knew from the village back in Poland was here and he ended up [in Williamsburg]."

Sections of Williamsburg continued to develop around ethnic, racial, and religious communities that were fairly homogeneous, at least for a few blocks. Neighbors were often extended family members, or from the same regions, creating insular villages within the neighborhood. Old Timers who were (im)migrants or second-generation benefited from social networks and the cultural businesses that thrived in these ethnic enclaves. These various ethnic groups coexisted, sometimes less than peacefully, within less than one square mile of each other.

Bohemians: Identity-Attached

When Old Timers discussed how Williamsburg had changed over the years, several of them mentioned "the Village people." They were referencing Manhattan's Greenwich and East Villages to categorize the artists, students, and other young people who were indeed coming to Williamsburg partially due to gentrification and increasing rent in those Manhattan neighborhoods.

Bohemians took over abandoned manufacturing spaces with varying degrees of legality. They threw parties, opened businesses, played music, and showed their art in local galleries. They came to be part of a growing community of artists and musicians, and the neighborhood became a symbol of an avant-garde movement. In an artistic version of chain migration, Rob, a musician, remembers several members of his band moving into the neighborhood: "I was the first one in [the band] to move here and the rest of the band followed, and for a while we were all living in the same neighborhood and one of us owned a bar and the other one was a bartender at the bar. Magical time." James and his girlfriend, both artists, came in the mid-1980s: "She got invited to go and live in Williamsburg. We were just a big crowd of twenty-somethings from five or six different countries. . . . Everybody was an artist or an architect or a writer."

Later-arriving Bohemians came to the neighborhood because it was already known for its concentration of artists and was compared to former iterations of SoHo and the East Village. By 1992 there were estimated to be over two thousand artists in Williamsburg, at a time when the Northside had a total population of only about nine thousand.[36] Patrick, a musician, visited in the late 1990s and moved in soon after because of how he related to the creative atmosphere: "My impression was that it was a place where artists could live for not a lot of money and feel like they were in their element, because there was an artistic community and the environment was conducive to art-making."

Williamsburg was becoming a cultural touchstone in the way that Greenwich Village had been decades earlier. Many of the Bohemians moved to New York from suburban American towns. For them, the environment of Williamsburg was integral to their identities as artists and avant-gardes. Williamsburg's industrial environment and relatively high crime rate in the 1980s lent authenticity to their urban experiences. In addition to the growing scene of art, music, and nightlife that Williamsburg was becoming known for, these other factors helped Bohemians establish themselves, honing an identity that was closely associated with the neighborhood itself.

The concentration of artists and their institutions, including galleries and event spaces, began to influence the culture and reputation of Williamsburg. Later identity-attached in-movers were attracted to the neighborhood because it provided opportunities for cultural consumption, without actually participating in the creation of art. Courtney informs us about her decision to move to Williamsburg in 2003: "I came the day of the marathon and it had a really nice feeling. . . . People were out at the cafés and it just felt like a neighborhood, and I liked the idea of loft living." As Williamsburg garnered outside attention, Bohemians fought to stay in the increasingly expensive neighborhood because their identity was tied to the creative community that had thrived there.

At the turn of the twenty-first century, the city began to restore services that had been cut for more than three decades. Residents noted an increasing police presence at that time, and transportation was overhauled to keep up with the growing population. All the while, Williamsburg was beginning to attract a broader range of visitors from around the city and the world.

Condo Dwellers: Investment-Attached

In the mid-2000s a new group of Manhattanites began visiting Williamsburg for the parties, galleries, and bar scene that the area had become famous for. These were not the artists or students who made up Williamsburg's youth culture, but instead slightly older individuals with professional jobs and incomes to match. Many of the newest residents in this study reported that they came to Williamsburg once or twice in the mid-2000s but didn't imagine themselves coming back to purchase an apartment a few years later. To them it was dirty—okay for a party but not a place they'd want to live in. They evaluate its recent past as sketchy, unsafe, or "less classy" than other gentrified neighborhoods like Park Slope or Brooklyn Heights.

Many of the Condo Dwellers in this sample moved to Williamsburg because luxury apartments were selling for discounted prices. Caithlin and her husband purchased an apartment in 2009, at the height of the real estate panic: "We wanted to invest some money. He got a bonus that year which was pretty nice, so we wanted to invest it. . . . We were in the recession, and we got a huge deal on the apartment." Ella echoed the real estate-as-investment strategy. She and her husband had been living in a loft in Chelsea since the 1970s, but decided to sell their larger space and invest that money in Williamsburg: "Well, we were looking in the recession. It was just 2011 and this part of the neighborhood, with all of these buildings, they were still looking for people to live in them. . . . And I thought this would be a good move because I figured it would appreciate, because real estate is sort of an investment." While condos were slower to sell during the recession, sales picked up by 2010, and the Northside's population doubled over the next ten years from 11,309 to 22,507 residents.

Some Condo Dwellers reluctantly moved to Williamsburg after finding more traditional "Brownstone Brooklyn" neighborhoods unaffordable. Sarinda, a British woman of South Asian descent, was living in Fort Greene when she and her husband began looking to buy an apartment around 2010. They realized that they could get more space for their money in Williamsburg, and while Sarinda found it to be "less classy" than Fort Greene, she felt that the schools in Williamsburg were better. Josie and her husband were planning on buying a home in Park Slope for about a year before they decided to check out Williamsburg in 2010. She had visited the neighborhood in her early twenties and remembered that "it felt unsafe and dirty to me before, back in, like, 2006." Although Williamsburg was not their first choice of neighborhood, "we found the condo and it was exactly what we wanted, so we bought it." These newcomers had heard of Williamsburg because of its avant-garde scene, but that was something they were more likely to tolerate than gravitate toward, and certainly not participate in. Convenience and a return on investment were most often the priorities.

Caithlin, Ella, Sarinda, and Josie unanimously felt that the neighborhood had improved during the 2010s, with the addition of upscale restaurants and boutiques along with the minimization of graffiti tags and underdeveloped space—signs for them of social disorder. The new residents have attracted and celebrated the arrival of corporate stores, which has further shaken the Bohemians' identity attachment. Residents in this group express that they gambled on Williamsburg, since it was not previously known for luxury and convenience, but that their risk has paid off. Because these Condo Dwellers invested in property in Williamsburg, they are also invested in the aesthetics and the amenities the neighborhood has to offer. They have organized for increased park space as well as the exclusion of certain activities—and therefore people—from public spaces, helping to establish their neighborhood as a wealthy enclave.

Former Residents

This book includes ten Former Residents, who nearly always share the same perceptions about the neighborhood as their original attachment cohort—that is, the group they would have been a part of if they hadn't moved out of Williamsburg. There are four main reasons why residents leave Williamsburg: (1) Some residents were physically displaced because of rent. They often tried to stay in the neighborhood, looking for other apartments in Williamsburg before expanding their search to neighboring spaces in Brooklyn and Queens. This was common no matter how long the individual had lived there. (2) Other residents moved because they felt that they no longer fit into the neighborhood. This was not often a motivation for Old Timers, but as the culture of the neighborhood shifted from artsy to corporate, some Bohemians decided to leave because they already felt culturally displaced. This was also sometimes a result of aging out, as some of the Bohemians hit their mid-thirties and the neighborhood didn't hold the same appeal. (3) People might leave Williamsburg when they "cashed out"—that is, they left the neighborhood because they owned property that they then sold. No one in the study fell into this category, but some people reported that friends, family members, or former landlords had done this, moving to nearby suburbs, Florida, or even home to Poland or Puerto Rico. (4) Two of the Former Old Timers left the neighborhood because they perceived that they or their children would have better opportunities elsewhere.

All Former Residents, regardless of race, class, or original attachment cohort, felt that Williamsburg has become too much of an attraction. They noted that the neighborhood no longer serves its residents and compared it to Manhattan to emphasize how the tourist crowds, population increase, and upscale retail had changed their experience of the neighborhood either before leaving or on visits back. Regardless of the reason they left, nearly all Former Residents of Williamsburg experienced cultural displacement before moving. For the most part, Former Residents had less in common with each other than they did with their original attachment cohorts. In the coming chapters, these residents are usually incorporated with their original group, though noted as being Former Residents. Including this category lends insight into perceptions of neighborhoods and gentrification after a resident is displaced, a point of view that much of the literature on gentrification fails to account for.

Conclusion

The luxury buildings that have come to dominate Williamsburg are among the most visible markers of the neighborhood's transformation. With the months or even years of construction, out-of-context architecture, expensive amenities, and the demographic changes they bring, the condos are an obvious and frequently mentioned target when people are asked about how Williamsburg has changed. These new additions to the landscape exemplify how the same neighborhood spaces hold different meanings for Old Timers, Bohemians, and Condo Dwellers.

Perhaps one of the most conspicuous examples of the cultural displacement resulting from condofication is the Spire Lofts, a former church and school on Williamsburg's Northside. The building, constructed in 1869, now boasts a gym, roof deck, bike room, and co-working space along with forty rental units, including a two-bedroom that rented for $7,300 a month in 2018. Redevelopments like the lofts are lauded for their unique, historical touches: vaulted ceilings, wooden beams, and exposed brick. But the preservation of historic buildings stripped of their meaning falls flat for existing residents who see their neighborhood changing around them, their cultural touchstones and institutions increasingly pushed out. In an interview with the *Brooklyn Paper* after the Spire Lofts were announced, one long-term resident complained, "All you see now is big buildings—they need to keep a little bit of old Brooklyn here."

The church hadn't been operational for a decade before the lofts opened; it was sold to developers by the Brooklyn Diocese after it was closed in 2005. Yet the conversion into lofts represented a symbolic loss well after the church ceased operation. This comment about the "old Brooklyn" is revealing. Old Timers often react favorably to some of the neighborhood changes, but long to also keep a few of their own institutions in place. Over lunch at a community center one day, Antoinette, a retired beautician and lifelong resident in her seventies, observed that the condos had turned the Northside into an "elite section" of the neighborhood and worried that "in the future [this] will only be for the rich." Agata nodded in agreement and added that while the "skyscrapers" had welcomed new people, there were also disadvantages. The women mentioned aspects of change that they liked, such as being able to take their grandchildren out for ice cream at a new shop or accessing a clinic within a few blocks from home. They were realistic in their outlook—they didn't expect Williamsburg to stay the same, but they wanted the neighborhood to at least retain some of its old character. They were displeased with what they referred to as "Little Manhattan."

Old Timers are not the only ones who feel out of place in today's Williamsburg. While the neighborhood still has some of the cafés, bars, and art institutions that originally put it on the "hip" map, many have been replaced with upscale or big-box establishments. According to the Where Is Williamsburg? app, by 2016 the Williamsburg of New York was actually the nearby neighborhood of Bushwick, signaling that the next generation of Bohemians and the establishments that cater to them had moved on due to unsustainable rents. Former Residents in this study who were part of the Bohemian period discuss their own cultural displacement. Alex lived in Williamsburg from 2001 to 2007, but a few years later he felt that the condos, corporate stores, and crowds made the neighborhood unrecognizable to him. He noted that what made Williamsburg interesting—art, subculture, a sense of spontaneity—was gone. "The scene in Williamsburg," he said, "is over." Jessica, a hospital administrator who lived in the neighborhood from 2002 to 2008, felt similarly; she eventually moved because she felt "like I didn't really fit. . . . It had gotten so popular that it was annoying." She recalls going to the waterfront to drink and pass the time with friends. Once the construction of the condos began, Jessica remembered, she felt melancholy because what she loved about the neighborhood was starting to disappear: "I remember when all this stuff was being built and we were like, 'Oh, this place is done.'" Carol, a Bohemian resident who still lives in the Williamsburg, commented that the changes had been so drastic that she sometimes felt disoriented after more than thirty years in the neighborhood. In the past decade, old landmarks have disappeared and entire new blocks' worth of housing have been built: "I can walk down the street and not know what street I'm on. There's so many new buildings that I can't remember where I am."

For the Condo Dwellers, the high-rise housing signals that Williamsburg has been sufficiently upgraded. Most of the investment-attached residents in this book would not have come if the luxury housing had not been built. Condo Dwellers decided that moving to Williamsburg made financial sense, though they found the neighborhood to be too grungy. Caithlin explained that she really didn't want to move to Williamsburg, but their broker had pushed them in that direction. She summarized the decision as "the best bang for our buck," an investment that would continue to grow: "We kind of predicted it would be worth a little more a couple years later. We had no idea it was going to get like this!"

The identity-attached Bohemians see the new buildings and businesses as stripping Williamsburg of its creative scene, and necessity-oriented Old Timers view the condos as symbolic of an increasingly elite and unaffordable neighborhood. In contrast, the Condo Dwellers, with their focus on investment, see convenience, cleanliness, and most tellingly, "a full-on neighborhood" where they felt one hadn't existed before. They view the process of condofication as greatly improving the neighborhood and their own financial portfolios.

Despite the Old Timers' plea to keep some of the "old Brooklyn" in Williamsburg, the high-rise construction that is emblematic of the "new Brooklyn" or "Little Manhattan" has increasingly bled out into surrounding areas. The process that contributes to feelings of cultural displacement for Old Timers and Bohemians has been replicated throughout New York, partially built on Williamsburg's model. When local politicians and real estate developers unite to rezone urban spaces, the needs of existing residents are chronically ignored, resulting in a diminished sense of ownership over neighborhood spaces. The attachment styles of Old Timers, Bohemians, and Condo Dwellers inform how they interpret and experience Williamsburg's ever changing physical, social, and cultural landscapes. These perspectives also matter for how residents define and solve neighborhood problems and how they attempt to claim space in Williamsburg.

2

Claiming Space

Activism and Ownership over Time

September 2011. Red police lights bounce off a luxury building under construction. Down the street, Widespread Panic, a self-described neo-psychedelic jam band, has just wrapped a concert at the waterfront park. The concert may be over, but the party is not—dozens of people, mainly white men in their twenties and thirties, mill about on a residential street on the Northside, holding on to brightly colored balloons. Every few seconds someone takes a sip out of a balloon filled with nitrous oxide, or laughing gas. I have a confession to make: this is a digital ethnography; I wasn't in Williamsburg that night. This description comes from a video shot by a woman named Susan. Throughout the video you can hear her yelling at the revelers, "Hey, no, you can't hang out here!" She uploaded the video under the handle StopOSAConcerts, OSA being short for Open Space Alliance, a local organization that puts on concerts in the nearby park. A few days later the local *Brooklyn Paper* interviewed Susan for a sensationally titled article: "Post Concert Open Air Drug Market in Williamsburg!"[1]

The videos (there are five) go on for twenty minutes, as people continue to purchase balloons and obstruct traffic despite the presence of police and fire engines. The incident speaks to a broader conflict shaping neighborhood tensions in Williamsburg. In a changing neighborhood, various groups compete for ownership of public space. In later communication with Susan, I found out that she was an artist and writer who had moved to the neighborhood in 1992. As a Bohemian resident, Susan may well have participated in concerts and public space events during Williamsburg's avant-garde heyday. Now, as more investment-focused individuals and companies come to dominate Williamsburg, Susan observes the neighborhood norms changing, to her frustration.

Tensions over Space

The Open Space Alliance (OSA), now the North Brooklyn Parks Alliance (NBPA), is a nonprofit that was founded in Williamsburg in 2003 by Steve Hindy, owner of the internationally famous Brooklyn Brewery. Hindy's business interests give him a long-standing investment attachment to Williamsburg. Strictly adhering to tenure, we might categorize the OSA as a Bohemian community organization, but the alliance began around investment-related goals of raising the neighborhood's profile and dictating public space. The group raises money that board members then use to upgrade public space in the neighborhood. Where the money goes and what constitutes "upgrading" are entirely at their discretion. In 2021 the alliance's website listed twenty-five board members, who are required to make annual contributions to the organization to secure their position. The price tag for the annual fee is not disclosed on the website, but the board members include lawyers, doctors, directors of real estate agencies, and stockbrokers—careers that are atypical for the average Old Timer or Bohemian resident.[2]

The alliance utilizes profits made from the concerts and other events to shape public spaces around board members' preferences. This is not unlike other exclusionary practices throughout the city where non-elected elites, like commercial and residential property owners, have the power to make decisions for and about neighborhoods. The same process goes on in Manhattan's Union Square, just a ten-minute subway ride from Williamsburg. There, the Union Square Partnership, a non-profit, exercises power over a public park by adding security and commercial programming—strategies of control that affect who uses the park and how. In changing neighborhoods, tensions arise as new groups come to dominate local norms and exert control in public spaces.

The OSA did not initiate large, outdoor concerts in Williamsburg. Public space concerts, as opposed to those occurring in music venues, began in 2005, when Clear Channel donated a quarter of a million dollars toward the restoration of the disused McCarren Park pool. This marked one of the first major corporate investments into modern Williamsburg and an early co-optation of the Bohemian culture. The next year, Live Nation, Clear Channel's outdoor venue branch, began holding ticketed concerts at the still-empty pool while a small, Williamsburg-based marketing company organized free shows, nicknamed Pool Parties, in the same space. In 2008 OSA took over programming in the park after winning a bid with the Parks Department. When renovations began on the pool, OSA moved both concert series to the new East River State Park, a few blocks away on the waterfront. The OSA/Live Nation ticketed concert series continued on the waterfront while the free Pool Parties departed for alternate Brooklyn locations after financial disputes with OSA.

Within three years of gaining control of concert scheduling, the alliance had driven out a free concert series that reflected the DIY/artistic culture of many Bohemians, while maintaining a corporate concert series that charged up to fifty dollars per ticket. Ironically, the ticketed concerts meant closing a heavily used public park for up to twenty nonconsecutive days during the hot summer months. During these events, tarps boasting "Open Space Alliance" hung from the park's gates, completely closing off residents' views of the waterfront and sending a message that this space was *not* open to them.

Actions by the alliance reflect the neighborhood's transition from the DIY hipster culture that fostered the original Pool Parties to a wealthy, corporate, and securitized location where public spaces are closed for expensive, ticketed events. Events like these raise funds for the alliance to then upgrade public space to its desires, although the Widespread Panic debacle may have temporarily done more harm than good for Williamsburg's luxury image. Tension over the waterfront concerts is an example of an investment-attached organization trying to raise the neighborhood profile as existing identity-attached residents grapple with the shifting neighborhood character and the corporate co-optation of the neighborhood. This is the latest outcome in a gradual departure from the necessity-based activism of Old Timers or identity-focused advocacy of the Bohemians. In gentrifying neighborhoods, community organizations and local events are an important mechanism by which groups claim space and how one competing narrative succeeds above others.

Whether working to improve some perceived problem or attempting to control how public spaces are used, struggles for ownership and tensions between residents have played out over decades in parks, pools, and streets in Williamsburg. This chapter details some of these struggles, while also looking at how attachment style has influenced residents' goals for the neighborhood. Examining community organizations over time allows us to see how residents shaped their neighborhood through collective action.

The Significance of Community Organizations: Ownership and Displacement

Some gentrification literature suggests that there is an uptick in political activity as wealthier, more educated residents flow into a locale, though Derek Hyra has noted decreased political engagement among existing residents in gentrifying Washington, DC.[3] In the case of Williamsburg, civic groups flourished even at a time when American culture was characterized by a shift away from local engagement.[4] Each attachment cohort in Williamsburg has engaged in its own form of activism, but the conflicting realities, needs, and desires of these groups have yielded different actions.

Residents' attachment styles and the changing nature of Williamsburg meant that successive groups identified and defined neighborhood issues differently and responded accordingly, affecting the trajectory of Williamsburg in their own ways, even as more politically and economically powerful forces continued to shape the neighborhood around them. In the 1970s and 1980s necessity-attached Old Timers responded to the city's policy of planned shrinkage by creating both temporary and enduring community-based organizations (CBOs) as methods of survival in a neglected environment. In doing so, they exerted their agency and claimed ownership over a neighborhood that the city was leaving behind. In the 1990s and early 2000s Bohemians came together to organize against the intrusions of pollution and city-sponsored gentrification in the form of a large-scale rezoning—usually allied with the neighborhood's Community Board, an appointed, advisory arm of city government. Their struggles against gentrification, globalization, and environmental degradation were, at least in part, driven by their identity attachment to an artistic, bohemian neighborhood. They knew that if those projects advanced, the identity of Williamsburg would be threatened, and *their* ownership over the neighborhood would be jeopardized.

Condo Dwellers have also organized in Williamsburg, including a battle with the city to fund a new waterfront park. The efforts of newer residents differ from previous groups because their activism is focused on improving neighborhood aesthetics, attracting additional investment, and increasing the value of their property.

This evolution of community organizing in Williamsburg can be viewed as representative of competing narratives and changing ownership. The practice of *symbolic ownership* was identified in Los Angeles's Venice Beach, as the neighborhood's reputation shifted from a nineteenth-century seaside resort town to a neglected urban neighborhood and finally to a gentrified enclave.[5] Sociologist Andrew Deener examined how local actors, like wealthy new residents and entrepreneurs, exerted their ownership of Venice, utilizing high-profile events and fostering an upscale retail cluster to signal who the neighborhood belonged to. Through these actions, certain groups achieve an ownership or heightened presence in a neighborhood's public space.[6] In Venice, these attempts at ownership created an image of the neighborhood that focused on its new attributes and attractions as a site of consumption, effectively erasing claims to space by the neighborhood's Black, Latinx, and homeless populations.

As this process of claiming space continues, "the tastes of new residents . . . dominate the landscape" and cultural displacement of existing residents occurs.[7] Through aesthetics, events, retail options, and real or invented histories, neighborhoods become defined around one or more of these competing narratives. Although North Brooklyn still has working-class, poor, and (im)migrant populations, it has come to be symbolically owned by young, upper-middle-class singles and families with more disposable income and different social and cultural capital.[8] In Williamsburg, ownership has been claimed through events that promote the neighborhood as a destination for tourists, or at least foodies or music connoisseurs from around the city.

Studying New York's Hudson Valley, Richard Ocejo explored how competing narratives played out in political and other organized actions of gentrifiers and existing residents.[9] Ocejo focused on the moral framing of gentrification by in-movers to Newburgh, New York, a city of twenty-nine thousand residents. He argues that gentrifiers' sense of community affects their interpretation of, and actions around, development. Similar to the Bohemians in Williamsburg, the gentrifiers whom Ocejo interviewed chose to move to Newburgh despite having other options for housing. They created a community buttressed by a local creative economy, which many of them took part in. As a result, these in-movers viewed their decisions that led to gentrification as good and moral, interpreting many of their actions as helping to promote the city. The Newburgh gentrifiers also didn't want the city to gentrify further, at least not if it was outside their control. This led them to interpret larger-scale developments as having a negative impact on the city, even if their own actions primed Newburgh for further investments. These gentrifiers found themselves in conflict with both longer-term residents and developers as they sought to maintain their ownership over the city. The actions of Williamsburg's Bohemians are not dissimilar, as they worked to curb the city-led gentrification that was at least partially in response to the cultural hub they had created.

Claiming symbolic ownership over space reflects the power that a group holds. Urbanists Jean-Paul Addie and James C. Fraser detailed how gentrifiers, specifically "pro-development actors," shaped the Over-the-Rhine neighborhood of Cincinnati. Framing gentrification as settler colonialism, they exposed the process that displaced individuals and cultures from both public and private spaces in the changing neighborhood.[10] In Over-the-Rhine this was often carried out through policing and other tactics of intimidation. The long-term, predominantly Black community as well as in-moving gentrifiers both interpreted spaces created by the other group as not for them. In this scenario, one group has more financial and political power to assist it in claiming, maintaining, and increasing what is considered "their" space. In Williamsburg, there is less often direct conflict in terms of policing, but groups in positions of relative power have tried to control access to and norms in the neighborhood's public spaces, sometimes along racialized lines.

The Evolution of Community Activism in Williamsburg

Old Timers: Fighting for Necessities

As Williamsburg was depleted by deindustrialization and disinvestment, residents saw a reduction of municipal services. Budget cuts forced the closure of some schools and hospitals, police presence was minimal, and the city threatened to close firehouses in the neighborhood. All of this was occurring as working-class jobs disappeared from Williamsburg, fostering a drug economy that local gangs and mafias participated in. Most Old Timers did not mention feeling personally threatened by criminal activities, but they did feel that their neighborhood was being left behind and neglected by the city. In response, they created formal and informal CBOs to protect themselves from negligent landlords or to provide their communities with the necessities that the city failed to. Similar to the residents of Mario Small's Villa Victoria neighborhood in Boston, long-term residents exercised agency and social capital to organize for improved housing and services, rejecting the notion that their neighborhood was a slum.[11]

As with many neighborhoods suffering disinvestment, residents in Williamsburg demanded policy changes through community organizing efforts. Coalitions of these groups were somewhat successful at wielding political power. Residents and organizations on the Southside also bargained through the area's political machine, led by Assemblyman Vito Lopez and his Ridgewood Bushwick Senior Citizens Council. In exchange for political loyalty, constituents and local organizations received services, employment, and funds toward affordable housing development.[12]

The Northside

On March 3, 1977, Northside residents had something to celebrate. After sixteen months of resident occupation, the city finally reversed its decision to close a local firehouse. In November 1975, when the city first ordered the closure, Northside residents began a resistance movement called the People's Firehouse to keep the needed service in the area. Families, elderly residents, and even Boy Scout troops took turns occupying the building twenty-four hours a day. Residents slept on mattresses inside the firehouse, organized fundraisers, and even held Christmas celebrations in Engine Company 212.[13] For nearly a year and a half, they struggled to maintain a basic city service in their neighborhood, building a community movement to fight back against city policies of disinvestment and planned shrinkage. Decades later, the People's Firehouse Inc. still exists, now focused on tenants' rights, affordable housing, and economic development in the neighborhood.

Just up the street from the firehouse, the Norman Street Block Association was initiated in the 1970s. The organization started as part of the Federal Block Associations, which created "self-help programs aimed at reducing maintenance costs for the city."[14] The Norman Street chapter was created with police assistance, but the residents drove discussions toward their own needs. They organized a summer lunch program, arranged for play streets or street closures during summer vacation, and attempted to turn a vacant lot into a park—although the city sold the land to a developer after promising it to the association. Additionally, the Northside Neighborhood Community (NNC) and the National Congress of Neighborhood Women (NCNW) were also grassroots organizations that advocated for needs like housing rights and transportation, and resisted budget cuts to daycare and senior citizen centers.

Another Northside organization was formed in 1974 after a fire destroyed buildings on the eastern side of the BQE. Parishioners of St. Nicholas Roman Catholic Church worked together to help neighbors who lost their homes. The volunteers formed the St. Nicholas Neighborhood Preservation Corporation, later the St. Nick's Alliance. They went on to establish housing for seniors, advocate for factory work, and rehabilitate buildings, while providing jobs for local community members. Still operating today, the alliance has worked together with Southside organizations around necessity-oriented goals like an after-school program, senior citizen center, and the borough's first charter high school. Through these organizations, Northsiders exerted control over the narrative of Williamsburg, promoting it as a functioning, working-class neighborhood despite the city's neglect.

The Northside's CBOs often succeeded in restoring or maintaining city services and advocating for tenants. Occasionally people who were typically divided along ethnic or racial lines worked together toward goals like maintaining a local bus line or tenants' rights.[15] However, racism among the mostly white Northside residents also influenced local organizing. In the mid-1980s, racial tensions mounted around public space—the neighborhood's McCarren Park pool. Crime rates had risen in the city, and the pool was not immune, with

Figure 2.1. An intergenerational and multiethnic coalition of necessity-attached residents protesting the threatened eviction of the Swinging Sixties Senior Center, March 2015. Author's photo.

robberies and fights being reported. As a result of disinvestment, the pool had fallen into disrepair, with a multimillion-dollar renovation project scheduled after the 1983 season. A group of Northside residents lobbied the city to permanently close it instead of renovating it, even chaining themselves to the fence during construction efforts. In their own attempts to dictate ownership of public space, nearby white residents didn't want "outsiders" coming to their neighborhood (from less than a mile away). They advocated to keep the neighborhood pool closed rather than share it with their non-white neighbors.[16]

The Southside

While Northside residents struggled against planned shrinkage and the constraints of class, many Southside residents had the additional obstacle of systemic racism—both formally in terms of city policy and informally by the actions of local whites. Their organizations reflected this, not only by providing services and advocating for residents, but also by giving them a platform to celebrate their cultures with festivals and parades.

Los Sures was founded in 1972 as the Southside United Housing Development Fund Corporation. It began as a housing rehabilitation cooperative in response to abandoned buildings and illegal evictions by landlords. Los Sures continues to advocate for housing management and ownership to be controlled by community members, while also managing city-owned properties. In addition, the organization provides social services on the Southside, including a food pantry and a senior center. In the face of gentrification, Los Sures and other CBOs face a new challenge: maintaining and adding to the neighborhood's affordable housing stock. As local demographics change, Los Sures has a stated goal to "preserve the history of the neighborhood's residents."[17] It achieves this by hosting Dominican and Puerto Rican cultural events, block parties, and El Museo de Los Sures, which holds exhibits on the history of Williamsburg and showcases local artists. While Los Sures was focused on the necessity of housing, Nuestros Niños began filling another gap in the neighborhood: daycare for local preschoolers. The organization continues to thrive with three sites in South Williamsburg, serving hundreds of local families.

In the early 1980s, when crime was at its peak in Williamsburg, yet another necessity-based community organization was founded, this time to combat gang violence. The founders of El Puente "called together church leaders, artists, educators, health providers, and other community activists" to quell violence in the neighborhood.[18] The organization continues to focus on empowering the community through health, social justice, arts, and environmental initiatives, including a high school, the El Puente Academy for Peace and Justice. Similar to Los Sures, the organization has shifted its goals and activism over time from neighborhood revitalization to preservation of the long-term community as it is threatened by gentrification. By providing necessities like childcare and housing assistance, and by hosting cultural events in public space, Southside Old Timers achieved ownership over their neighborhood. Like the Northsiders, CBOs allowed Southsiders to resist negative evaluations of Williamsburg. Today, these events and institutions assist them in maintaining visibility and agency as their neighborhood gentrifies.

These community-based organizations were prevalent in Williamsburg's North and Southsides partially because of the Comprehensive Employment and Training Act (CETA), a 1973 federal law that provided local organizations with funds to hire part- and full-time employees.[19] CETA was a job-training program aimed at employing neighborhood residents in jobs like "highway maintenance, sanitation, clerical work and other areas to be determined by local officials."[20] The People's Firehouse, National Congress of Neighborhood Women, St. Nick's Alliance, and Los Sures all received CETA funding, giving at least some aid to organizations that were fighting for basic services in their neighborhoods. In the end, the activism that helped insulate the community from the ravages of disinvestment contributed to readying the area for gentrification starting in the early 1980s.

Bohemians: Identity and Protecting the Artist Enclave

Early gentrifiers who came to Williamsburg in the 1980s and 1990s were moving into a neighborhood that was still being affected by the city government's disinvestment, but the existing activism had already improved the neighborhood's trajectory. As a result, issues like restricted city services and dilapidated housing conditions were being dealt with, but these were also of less concern to in-movers, who were often young and single and who thought of Williamsburg as a stopover between college and family life. At first, Williamsburg was a bedroom community to the artists and students who worked, showed art, and went to school in Manhattan. Later, Williamsburg became its own cultural nucleus, sometimes referred to as the New East Village or New York's latest "bohemia."

This reputation as a bohemia developed because of early gentrifiers' attempts to claim space in the neighborhood through events, businesses, and public art. For Bohemians, there was "nothing" in Williamsburg when they moved there; they added the culture, art, music, and buzz. But similar to the gentrifiers in Ocejo's account of Newburgh, Bohemians viewed these changes as positive until they were no longer within their control. As artist James laments, "By the end of the '80s it turned into a subculture.... I wouldn't have jazzed it up nearly as much as I did had I known . . . how much that would exacerbate the social relations and spur on gentrification. I now believe that art is a serious stimulus for gentrification." Most Bohemians did not participate in community organizing until the area's reputation as an artist colony became threatened.

In 1993, when the city first expressed interest in the rezoning and development of the waterfront, the new artist and student residents attempted to change the course of the proposed plan. Coming together as Williamsburg/Greenpoint Organized for an Open Process (WOOP), the coalition began working on a plan that claimed to represent the various groups in the community. WOOP and other organizations held meetings where community members could voice their hopes for the waterfront rezoning, contributing to the 197-a plan that called for mixed-use zoning, affordable housing, waterfront access, and environmental protection, among other demands. Bohemians were more likely to resist the area's political machine that Old Timers sometimes relied on; instead, they lobbied for the support of Community Board members. WOOP is credited in the final 197-a plan, submitted by the Community Board, but eventually the goals, strategies, and actors of WOOP were absorbed into other CBOs.

Additional Bohemian organizations developed around environmental concerns in the 1990s and 2000s. Neighbors Against Garbage, or NAG, was founded in 1994 in opposition to a proposed expansion of a waste transfer station on the Northside's waterfront. The acronym was changed in the early 2000s to Neighbors Allied for Good Growth. This modification alone suggests how the organization adapted to the shifting landscape and demographics of Williamsburg. Later, NAG members were involved in the planning of the rezoning, pushing for waterfront parks as part of the 197-a.

In 2000 Greenpoint/Williamsburg Against Power Plants, or GWAPP, was founded to protest the construction of a power plant on the Greenpoint waterfront. The group successfully defeated two proposed power plants with the help of NAG, but then the neighborhood got hit with the rezoning instead. GWAPP also changed its name to the Greenpoint Waterfront Association for Parks and Planning as its focus shifted. NAG and GWAPP recently merged into North Brooklyn Neighbors, focused on issues of public space and environmental concerns and typically organizing alongside investment-attached groups.

Naturally some of these groups counted Old Timers among their members, and they sometimes partnered with existing CBOs on specific issues. In the aftermath of the rezoning, groups like NAG, as well as Los Sures and the People's Firehouse, joined with Brooklyn Legal Services Corporation to form the Greenpoint-Williamsburg Collaborative Against Tenant Displacement. Yet overall, Bohemian organizations focused on environmentalism and urban planning that would protect or advance the neighborhood's avant-garde reputation. Early gentrifiers didn't have the same concerns as Old Timers in part because the basic necessities of the neighborhood were already in place, thanks to the work of earlier activists, but also because many of them did not plan on living in Williamsburg long-term. The successes of their organizing against power plants and waste transfer primed the neighborhood for the rezoning plan that would further gentrify the neighborhood, now with investment-minded professionals instead of identity-attached artists.

Condo Dwellers: Investment in Aesthetics and Reputation

Today, wealthy newcomers to Williamsburg are moving into a neighborhood that was curated with them in mind, the result of an influx of private capital following decades of disinvestment, resistance, and community organizing. They are welcomed by luxury real estate, upscale restaurants, new amenities, big-box corporations, and several new parks and outdoor spaces, a materially different neighborhood than Old Timers or Bohemians moved to. However, the earliest Condo Dwellers bought apartments in a neighborhood that had not yet transformed into the destination that it is today. As a result, much of their organizing has been focused on improving neighborhood aesthetics and sometimes attempting to exert control over the use of public spaces in an effort to enhance their financial investments in the neighborhood.

Participation in traditional community organizations is lower among Condo Dwellers than it was for Old Timers and Bohemians in this study.

When asked about participation in community organizations, many of the Condo Dwellers referenced the Brooklyn Baby HUI, a website for Brooklyn parents (almost entirely mothers). Users share advice on chat forums, sell or donate outgrown baby clothes and furniture, and plan events for each other and their children, like social events for mothers and holiday parades for kids. The Condo Dwellers also discussed joining their child's school or daycare parents' associations, and some mentioned participation in neighborhood activities like park cleanups or consumption-based fundraisers, but these were mostly onetime events rather than actions toward a long-term goal. The only organization that new residents occasionally mentioned being part of was Friends of Bushwick Inlet Park.

As part of the 2005 rezoning, Williamsburg and Greenpoint residents were promised an extensive swath of parkland along the borough's northwestern edge. Some of it would be state park, some of it city, and other parcels would be semi-public spaces maintained by condos. However, an eleven-acre plot of riverfront property (adjacent to the existing portion of Bushwick Inlet Park) was privately owned by Norman Brodsky, who operated CitiStorage, a massive archive storage building on the site. For years Brodsky and the city could not come to an agreement on how much the land was worth. The issue was debated between the city, the Community Board, organizations like NAG, and the property owner for over a decade. In 2008 Friends of Bushwick Inlet Park was founded to organize Williamsburg residents in a fight for the park. Activity picked up in 2015 after a fire tore through CitiStorage, and Brodsky threatened to sell the land to private developers.[21] Under the rallying cry "Where's Our Park?," some Bohemians and many Condo Dwellers held fundraisers, staged protests and marches, petitioned the City Council, and even camped out one night at the would-be park. New residents especially rallied behind this cause, utilizing their considerable social and political capital to raise funds, and bringing their children along to the marches in designer strollers. By December 2016, the city struck a deal, agreeing to pay $160 million to Brodsky. Millions more in city funding were needed for the cleanup and design of the park. Critics argued that the time and money spent on this parcel of land (in an area that already has several waterfront and inland parks) should have gone to Brooklyn neighborhoods with less green space, like Bed-Stuy or East New York.

The actions of Friends of Bushwick Inlet Park have positive implications for Williamsburg broadly. The waterfront parks are always bustling, a place where residents and visitors alike gather to play, picnic, and watch the sunset. Yet the democracy and diversity of these parks can be limited by investment-oriented attempts to control public space. The rhetoric and community action around other public spaces in Williamsburg make it clear that not everyone is necessarily welcome, so if the Friends of Bushwick Inlet Park feels a particular ownership over the park, it may pose a challenge to others' use of it.

In the summer of 2012 the McCarren Park pool was reopened after twenty-eight years, and less than a mile away barbecue pits were proposed for Cooper Park. Both sparked community outcry from Condo Dwellers. While they did not organize against the pool's reopening, they were vocal about the event online. According to a *New York Times* article published at the time of the pool's reopening, "Some of the blog posts and comments in recent days have echoed the racially tinged dialogue of the 1980s, with neighbors of the pool blaming teenagers from outside the community" for fights and other behavior that led to arrests.[22] Local news and media outlets interviewed individuals at the pool's grand reopening and published stories about the long lines and excited crowds. A common theme in these reports was residents' concern that the pool would bring people from outside Williamsburg, specifically teenagers of color. This sentiment was repeated by one of the Condo Dwellers, who was in disbelief that non-white families live in the neighborhood:

> MILO: I remember the first summer when it opened, I was like, "Oh, that person's obviously not from around here but they're going to McCarren Park, to the pool."
> SM: How did you know the person wasn't from around here?
> MILO: Black and Latino teenagers? They can't afford apartments here.

These comments reveal Milo's opinions not only about who should use the pool, but who is even expected to be a resident of Williamsburg.

Conflicts about who belonged in public space also arose at East Williamsburg's Cooper Park when the city announced a plan to install barbecue pits as part of the park's renovation. New residents, many who lived in condo towers around the park, lamented that the proposed barbecue pits would lead to a loss of green space. In anticipation of the installation, Condo Dwellers complained that they would potentially smell the smoke in their houses and that trash would be left behind: "Now my children will be dodging rotten chicken bones along with the garbage that is already there."[23] Others worried that additional renovations would compromise their pets' experience of the park: "The intent of our park should be to provide a safe haven for our dogs to run freely with their canine friends." Condo Dwellers spoke at Community Board meetings and signed an online petition to prevent the pits being dug in the park, but Old Timers from nearby public housing were in support of the new grilling area. Karen Leader, a NYCHA resident and Community Board member, advocated for long-term residents: "We're not allowed to barbecue on NYCHA's property and this would give us a place to barbecue and enjoy the taste of grilled food during summer."[24] In response to protests launched by the Condo Dwellers, another NYCHA resident was quoted as saying, "It makes me annoyed to deny us this space. . . . This is something we've wanted in Cooper for a while, just a little area for us to cook."

Eventually the barbecue pits were installed, but the controversy around them reflects the ongoing tensions of a gentrifying community where resident groups have different expectations and desires for the use of public space. Condo Dwellers attempt to claim their ownership over the space by couching it in terms of their children's safety, and even privileging the experiences of their dogs over those of established residents. In trying to elevate the aesthetics and reputation of Williamsburg, and by default the value of their real estate investments, new residents have organized to increase, but also control the use of, public space in Williamsburg.

Gentrified Community Events: A Case Study of Williamsburg Walks

Recent community organizing and events in Williamsburg have centered on public space. These spaces afford city residents the opportunity to interact, socialize, consume, and relax beyond the private realm of their apartments. In most urban neighborhoods there are three types of public space: the shops and institutions that are visited daily (grocery stores, churches, subway stations, schools); places to spend leisure time (parks, cafés, restaurants, pedestrian malls); and special-event public spaces like block parties and festivals. As outlined in *Public Space*, a volume of case studies written by architects, environmental psychologists, and urban designers, public spaces—whether daily, leisure, or special-event—should be responsive, democratic, and meaningful.[25] The authors of the case studies argue that public spaces should serve the needs of users, be open to all people, and allow individuals to interact and make connections between their private lives and the larger neighborhood context. The situation becomes problematic when residents do not feel comfortable in their neighborhood's public spaces, as a result of retail changes, special events, or other interventions.

Events like movie, music, and culinary festivals held in parks and on side streets have helped to brand Williamsburg as a destination of leisure and culture, but they also impact Old Timers' use of neighborhood public spaces. This dynamic is especially visible at Williamsburg Walks, a street closure event on Bedford Avenue.[26] This section details the inception and development of the first three years of Walks, utilizing ethnographic observations at planning meetings and at the event, a review of internal documents created by the planning committee, and brief encounters with residents during the street closure. An in-depth analysis of this event illustrates how uses of public space reflect the tensions of ownership and cultural displacement. Because Williamsburg Walks is part of a broader "Summer Streets" initiative proposed by the Department of Transportation (DOT) and the city of New York, it is important to understand how these events are planned and how they affect residents of gentrifying neighborhoods.

Evolution of Williamsburg Walks, 2008–2010: Planning and Execution

Williamsburg Walks was initially proposed to be "a celebration of the Williamsburg community, centered around a pedestrian-only Bedford Avenue." The event took place each summer from 2008 to 2016, and by 2017 had merged with an event called the Northside Festival, which ceased in 2018. The duration of the Walks event varied each year; some years it was just one weekend, and at other times it spanned six weekends throughout the summer. When the event was on, a few blocks of Bedford Avenue were transformed from a heavily car-trafficked street into a venue meant for picnics, art, and neighborly interaction.

While the event changed significantly over the first three years, the slogan "Rethink your public space" remained constant. With this mantra the organizers insisted that the event should be about community—neighbors getting to know one another and using the newfound public space for just about anything noncommercial. Flyers in 2008 reminded residents and visitors that the event was not a street fair: "There will be no funnel cake and no cheap tube socks," a derogatory reference to existing ethnic and religious street festivals in the neighborhood. "We simply want the community (YOU) to come out and enjoy the public space."[27] The purpose of Williamsburg Walks, at least how it was marketed, was as a social experiment—a new way of building community.

The opening event took place on July 19, 2008. Volunteers set up barricades to prevent car traffic while some businesses extended their storefronts by putting racks of clothing or tables with free samples onto the sidewalk. For the most part, people simply walked down the street as if it were the sidewalk, but some made use of tables and chairs that had been set up by organizers, and others sat down with a book or even suntanned. The event wasn't well publicized in the neighborhood and many residents were confused about why the street was closed. Organizers later acknowledged that promotion was done mainly on NAG's blog and by word of mouth. From my observations at the event, as well as photographs that were later posted on the Williamsburg Walks website, the event was overwhelmingly homogeneous. Most people in attendance were young white Americans; older adults and Polish, Italian, Puerto Rican, and Dominican residents were almost completely absent.

After the first few Saturdays in 2008, individuals began to vend on the street. A few people were selling food or having yard sales. Something that the planners did not anticipate was that for many people, amateur entrepreneurialism was how they would use their public space. Local business owners complained that the commercial activities taking place on the street were detracting from their own stores, so for 2009 only street vendors who already had licenses to operate on Bedford were allowed to sell during Williamsburg Walks.

After the inaugural year, planning for Williamsburg Walks was taken over by NAG, which hosted a planning meeting for the second year in April 2009 at a community center. Representatives from the nonprofit Transportation Alternatives discussed findings from a survey of the 2008 Walks, reinforcing that most residents did not understand the purpose of the street closure. Respondents also mentioned that they would like some activities to be provided. While commerce was a concern, the focus of the 2009 planning meeting was how to bring more programming to the street and to better promote Williamsburg Walks. The meeting attendees decided to have components that catered to "art, music, community organization, local food [and] family activities."

The 2009 Walks was better attended, a result of more programming and activities for visitors. Many of the restaurants and cafés had once again extended their services onto the sidewalks, a few of the boutiques placed merchandise outside their stores, the usual street vendors set up their wares, and the event was a bit more active than the previous year. Children colored on a giant roll of paper unfurled on one of the streets, there were intermittent performances—some planned, some spontaneous—and several local community groups had information tables on the street. According to the planners, only vendors with preexisting permits would be allowed to sell, but some people had still set up makeshift food carts—one family cooked plantains under a tent; another woman poured horchata from large jugs on a stoop.

While the 2009 events were more successful in getting people to use public space, organizers were still concerned about street vending. An internal summary document that the planners wrote after the 2009 event stated, "Several people at the wrap up session complained that too many activities were taking place reinforcing the feeling of Bedford Ave as a 'permanent Mardi Gras' and diverting people from shopping."[28] This indicates that the purpose of Williamsburg Walks had shifted from being a "social experiment" to an event focused on local commerce, specifically businesses with storefronts on Bedford.

Illustrative of this shift, the 2010 Williamsburg Walks Community Brainstorming Session was held at a neighborhood restaurant as opposed to a community center, as it had been in 2009. That year, the Project for Public Spaces (PPS) was involved, in addition to NAG. Representatives from PPS, a New York-based "place making" nonprofit, gave a presentation on the mission of the year's event: celebrate the neighborhood, relax, shop at local stores, and rethink public space. Illegal vending was a major theme at the meeting; the organizers stated that over the past two years they had realized the importance of enforcing a "no vending" rule. As a result of pressure from local businesses, the organizers decided that having a police presence at the event would be necessary to dissuade vending. They maintained that vendors who were normally permitted to sell on the street would be allowed to continue, but additional vendors would be prosecuted. When one resident asked why it was such a problem, organizers replied that the extra vendors made it too crowded, and they were trying to promote the established businesses. While promoting local businesses was viewed as one of the many benefits of Williamsburg Walks, it was evident from this meeting that it had become a primary goal. As the brainstorming continued, people shared ideas about how to get Walks visitors to patronize stores, including a scavenger hunt or a booth where you could sew your own bag to use while shopping. After meeting with local business owners, one organizer said he wanted any ideas "that connect the programming with the merchants."

The 2010 Walks was heavily programmed and well attended, at least by some residents. The children's block had an outdoor gymnasium, an art competition was staged throughout the avenue, and the local community-supported agriculture (CSA) group set up a picnic area. Williamsburg businesses that did not have a presence on Bedford Avenue were allowed to use some space in the street. A boutique had a table where employees handed out flyers for their shop. Jungle, a garden supply store, set up a green oasis at one end of the event. Brooklyn Brainery, a collective offering DIY classes, and Green Mountain Energy, a renewable energy company, each had booths set up in the street, although they are not local to Williamsburg. Despite not being neighborhood institutions, these businesses fit in with the ideals of the organizations that planned the event, so their presence was permitted.

Someone who did not fit in with this image was Aaron, who was selling costume jewelry at the corner of a side street. His location away from the main event was surprising since he was clearly a permitted New York City vendor. Aaron showed me a letter he received from Williamsburg Walks planners stating that there would be no street vending allowed and police action would be taken if he set up his booth on Bedford Avenue. Aaron claimed that he was a usual fixture on Bedford, and had been for a few years—longer than some of the newer boutiques and bars. He said he appreciated what Williamsburg Walks did for the community, but he found it unfair that he was suddenly not allowed to sell on the main strip. Companies like Brooklyn Brainery and Green Mountain, although not local, were encouraged to take up space on Bedford Avenue because these organizations reflect the concerns and hobbies of Williamsburg's new, wealthier residents. Aaron's "street boutique" does not fit with these tastes, so he was explicitly excluded.

Although the 2010 event was more successful in attracting families, it was still not representative of the entire community. Flyers advertising the event were deliberately vague, with their message "Are You Suffering from Don't Talk to Your Neighbor-itis?" The materials were never translated into other languages, despite translation being discussed at planning meetings. The lack of outreach to the Polish, Italian, Puerto Rican, and Dominican communities in the neighborhood inhibited their participation.

Lillian and Stan, a Polish and Ukrainian couple, were sitting on chairs on the sidewalk at the periphery of the event. I asked whether they had participated in any way. "There's nothing here for us," Lillian replied, and she gestured at the street where earlier in the day young people had hosted a "garden party" art exhibit, complete with Astroturf lawn and lemonade. Gladys, a Puerto Rican woman, was studying the activities map with her husband and daughter around 5:00 p.m. on a Saturday when the event was packing up for the day. Gladys explained to me that they had just wandered over to the event because they were wondering why the street was closed. She wished that she had known about Williamsburg Walks in advance so that her family could have attended.

The lack of outreach to Old Timers coupled with the increasing focus on consumption reflects broader tensions over ownership in Williamsburg. Williamsburg Walks is a special event that takes place in an "everyday" public space—a commercial street. While the event is taking place, the space becomes a medium to highlight Williamsburg as a leisure destination, focusing on the neighborhood's status as a site for consumption, while minimizing the presence of existing residents. Old Timers are further excluded from the event by the organizers' level of

Figure 2.2. The "garden party" art exhibit at Williamsburg Walks, June 2010. Author's photo.

control over the activities, coupled with an ideology that rejects a "carnival" atmosphere. These actions are dismissive of events like block parties, Dominican Day and Puerto Rican Day celebrations, and the Italian neighborhood's Giglio Feast—a century-old festival that takes place for two weeks each summer. Different aesthetics and rules apply at these long-standing neighborhood events; thus Walks contrasts with Old Timers' expectations and scripts for public space events, making their participation and presence at Walks even less likely.

Williamsburg Walks as a Mechanism for Ownership and Displacement

Community events send signals about the locale. During events like Williamsburg Walks, select actors organize activities and make the rules. At public space events, the neighborhood is symbolically owned by the groups and businesses that have a presence on the street, in this case communicating the aesthetics of luxury and consumption that

Williamsburg has become famous for. Williamsburg Walks could have provided many benefits to the neighborhood. A car-free street could ideally give everyone an opportunity to enjoy more public space. Residents and visitors could use the street to relax outside, share food, play games, make crafts, and indeed, talk to their neighbors—undoubtedly leading to a stronger, if temporary, sense of community among participants. However, the event quickly became a strategy to reinforce the norms and values of investment-attached residents, leading to the privileged inclusion of some and adding to the exclusion and cultural displacement of others. Old Timers were rarely present at the event, despite the fact that they often socialize in other public spaces. The problem is that there is nothing at Williamsburg Walks to attract these groups *by design*, and thus they are left on the periphery if present at all.[29] Although the initial concept of the event seems benign, a critical exploration of the planning exposes it as a microcosm of gentrification and the fight for ownership in the neighborhood.

In addition to Walks, other outdoor festivals and events occupied Williamsburg's public spaces in the late 2000s and early 2010s as Condo Dwellers came to symbolically own the neighborhood. Programming like Taste Williamsburg (a display of local "food and beverage purveyors") and Willifest (a film festival), along with more regular events, like the Smorgasburg food market, utilize public park space to advertise the neighborhood as an upscale cultural destination. Writing about New York's transformation into a tourist destination, Miriam Greenberg notes how poor, ethnic, or otherwise diverse neighborhoods are branded for tourists. The histories and less mainstream aspects of the neighborhood are ignored while opportunities for consumption are emphasized: "None of these branded visions made reference to . . . [the] famously polyglot, racially diverse, proudly working class culture, except to extol the shopping and entertainment opportunities such culture at times provided."[30] These events celebrate the diversity of a neighborhood in only the most superficial way—as a means of consumption for people who can afford it. A few local, ethnic restaurants were featured at Taste Williamsburg and Smorgasburg; Willifest occasionally includes Polish- or Spanish-language films, but participating in these events is expensive and they usually do not have multilingual advertising campaigns.

The original purpose of Walks was to create temporary public space, but at the 2010 event nearly everything one could do on the street served as advertising for local businesses.[31] Returning to the idea that public space should be responsive, democratic, and meaningful, we can see where events like Williamsburg Walks fall short. Since the event was focused on consumption, less wealthy residents were not engaged in the activities; the event was not responsive to their needs and desires of public space. The event is not democratic in outreach or programming. At Williamsburg Walks, residents like Lillian, Stan, and Gladys do not feel a meaningful connection to their local public spaces. Events like Walks have the capacity to bring diverse neighbors into contact with one another, but they also have the potential to exacerbate existing tensions when they serve as a strategy for new residents and organizations to claim ownership over Williamsburg's public spaces.

A Blank Canvas

The increasing investment focus of Williamsburg Walks is reminiscent of Bohemian attempts to claim symbolic ownership in the 1980s by co-opting an existing public space event, the Grand Street Waterfront Festival. The festival was an end-of-summer carnival organized by Southside Latinx residents, but one Bohemian recalled her peers' attempts to utilize the event for identity-attached goals. Morgan refers to herself as "not really an artist" who nevertheless participated in Williamsburg's avant-garde culture. A lifelong New Yorker, she moved to Williamsburg in the 1980s after finishing a bachelor's degree at an art school just outside the city. Morgan arrived in Williamsburg at the beginning of the Bohemian art scene and continues to live in the neighborhood, giving her a long view of how art and gentrification have interacted there. She remembers one specific turning point when the original purpose of the Grand Street Waterfront Festival was threatened.

Morgan's memory of the event in the late 1980s was of a harmonious block party where newcomer artists created programming for children who attended: "Their parents would be eating and drinking and dancing . . . and the kids would just be tearing through all the stuff we made. We just did simple things like having kids paint, and make little rides for them and games. . . . And the parents would just gush appreciation at us and bring us food and buy us beer and [it was] just a beautiful event." However, Morgan became discouraged at a planning meeting for the next event. She recalled potential contributors asking about the media strategy, thinking of the festival as more about exposure for themselves than connecting with the Old Timer community: "They just couldn't imagine participating in something where their career wasn't the issue."

By 1990, artist involvement in the event had increased. An article published on a local artist's digital archive describes how the event shifted with the Bohemians' influence: "The Waterfront Festival existed happily for many years as a traditional three-day Labor Day Weekend bash . . . where Grand Street meets the East River . . . and then come these Weird Things, these 'publicly relevant phenomena . . . wherein the public was invited to wander freely.'"[32] Local writer Mark Rose went on to describe some of the public art at that year's event, including installations called *This Is Your Office* or *The Weird Thing Zone*. In the article, artist Ebon Fisher, who created *The Weird Thing Zone*, refers to his art as a "media organism which protrudes into public space and exchanges unmentionable nutrients." The creation of public art that "protrudes into public space" helped Bohemians claim symbolic ownership. Years later, Bohemians are not appreciative of the investment of corporations and real estate developers that also "protrude into public space," like Susan's upset earlier in this chapter at the investment-minded concert series.

Although she was entrenched in Williamsburg's avant-garde moment, Morgan was critical of it: "People had all these ideas of what they wanted to do here. I feel like Williamsburg has this kind of curse where people come here and just project their own fantasy on it and they just assume that's what Williamsburg needs to be." While she felt that initial Bohemian involvement in the street festival was integrative, it became a more contested relationship as artist participation became more about exposure and claiming space. Morgan insinuates here that Bohemians viewed the neighborhood as a blank canvas where they could afford to live and make art with a community of like-minded newcomers, alternately ignoring or co-opting the neighborhood's existing cultural touchstones. Just as Williamsburg Walks helped to mark the neighborhood as one oriented toward consumption and symbolically owned by gentrifiers, the introduction of performance art into the Grand Street Festival was a way for Bohemians to claim ownership and reorient neighborhood spaces and events toward their own interests.

The perception of gentrifying neighborhoods as blank canvases is a convenient narrative for waves of newcomers who can make their mark artistically or invest in property, viewing their contributions to the neighborhood as undeniable improvements over what was, or wasn't, there before. Yet the conditions of Williamsburg, its problems and its draws, have been interpreted differently by cohorts of local residents. Where an Old Timer sees a neighborhood block party and barbecue, a Bohemian sees a mundane gathering and an opportunity to elevate their artistic portfolio; where a Condo Dweller sees a street closure that highlights exciting opportunities for consumption, an Old Timer sees a confusing event that feels irrelevant. Residents living in Williamsburg simultaneously have disparate experiences of the neighborhood, in part due to their attachment style. In the next chapter we turn to perceptions of safety, danger, and social disorder, aspects of urban life that have held different meaning for Old Timers, Bohemians, and Condo Dwellers.

3

Dangerous Enough

Crime, Safety, and Identity

I first met Omar on a drizzly day in September 2014. We walked around the neighborhood before settling in a park to people-watch and speculate about gentrification. A lifelong Williamsburg resident, scholar, and artist, he was putting together a podcast about the neighborhood when he came across some of my work and reached out. Of my informants, Omar is the most outspoken against gentrification, as well as the most poetic about it. He grew up on Williamsburg's Southside in the 1970s, experiencing firsthand the troubles and joys of that period of local history. He considers himself an infiltrator, a Puerto Rican lifelong resident and an artist who played in neighborhood punk bands before attending a liberal arts college north of the city. Omar pairs his Old Timer credentials with a savviness of Bohemian networks and aesthetics.

In the winter of 2021, amidst reports of increasing crime in New York, he shared the following on Facebook:

> I lived on South Third and Bedford Avenue for the past 4 or so years. Shortly after I moved in, I lost the key to my room from the hall . . . Gentrification is no secret here, but my block, and especially the front stoop of my building, is one of those few spots on the Southside where the Afro-Puerto Ricans endure in groups. Constantly harassed by the police, snitched on by neighbors, even at times looked down upon by their own Peoples, my building drew crowds in the summer, and there were cheers, roars, fights, and loud music into the night and early in the morning, especially in the warmest weather. Tough kids among them. Passionate women. Fighting boys. Maligned Peoples celebrating their commiserations and commiserating their celebrations. And I never replaced that lost key. In the time I lived there I never locked my door.

Omar is describing a neighborhood scene that is familiar to him, even comforting, as evidenced by not feeling the need to lock his door. At the same time, he acknowledges that this scene is viewed as problematic by his newer neighbors who "snitch." Where one resident sees neighborhood life unfolding, another sees disorder. These conflicting views of safety and danger point to the complicated relationship between attachment, gentrification, and crime.

Crime, Gentrification, and Perceptions of Disorder

Early studies on gentrification and crime rates found conflicting results. One report analyzed data between 1970 and 1984 and noted a decrease in personal (but not property) crime in gentrifying neighborhoods of Boston, New York, San Francisco, and other cities.[1] By contrast, a study of gentrifying parts of Baltimore found that in the 1970s robberies increased in gentrifying areas.[2] The authors also found that larceny rates decreased less in changing neighborhoods, compared to ones that were already well-off and where housing values were continuing to appreciate. A third study focused on Seattle neighborhoods in the 1980s and 1990s and found a curvilinear relationship, showing that some types of crime, like theft and larceny, saw an increase with the onset of gentrification and then a decrease as gentrification progressed.[3]

These variations in findings can be partially accounted for by differing neighborhood conditions and demographics prior to gentrification and the category of crime being measured. Sociologists studying Chicago have even found evidence that the style and trajectory of gentrification might impact the frequency of certain crimes. Chris M. Smith analyzed gang homicide rates in Chicago from the mid-1990s to the mid-2000s and found that certain styles of gentrification were associated with a decrease in gang-related murders, while state-led gentrification that destabilized public housing led to an increase in homicides.[4] Another study of Chicago during the same period used a unique measure of gentrification—number of coffee shops—and found an association between coffee houses and increases in robberies in predominantly Black neighborhoods but decreases in white or Latinx locales, and with decreasing murder rates in all contexts.[5] In a study of crime rates in New York, Michael Barton found a negative association between gentrification and violent crimes citywide.[6] However, in most of these analyses, the associations are just that—evidence that a relationship exists, but not a causal statement. Violent crime rates dropped swiftly in the second half of the 1990s in New York and many other American cities, and some researchers suggest that decreasing crime rates have more likely been a prerequisite for gentrification, rather than an outcome of the process.[7]

Regardless of the direction of this relationship, it does not impact residents equally. Individuals who are particularly vulnerable to gentrification, like unhoused, lower-income, immigrant, and non-white residents, are more likely to be the targets of harassment or are physically displaced from a neighborhood and therefore unable to enjoy the benefits of a safer locale.[8] Part of this harassment includes increased policing in gentrifying communities. In her study of 1990s Chicago, Mary Pattillo identified conflicts around policing and safety that arose as a low-income Black neighborhood was gentrified by Black professionals. Tensions between the groups culminated in a request by gentrifiers to expand the nearby University of Chicago police rounds into the area, a potentially dangerous claim to space by newcomers.[9]

The relationship between policing and gentrification proves to be a delicate balance. Sociologist Brenden Beck analyzed New York City data during a period of rapid gentrification from 2009 to 2015 to assess whether increasing property values as well as in-mover demographics (including income, profession, education, and poverty rates) affected arrests, crimes, stops, and non-emergency 311 complaints. He found that policing increases during earlier stages of gentrification—what he terms "development-directed policing"—but that additional growth does not cause increased policing in already gentrified or wealthy areas. These findings are supported by an additional study of policing in New York during the same period, showing a higher police presence and rate of stops in areas surrounding gentrified locales, but not in already gentrified places.[10]

In recent years, data from non-emergency call systems like 311 have been utilized in gentrification research because the complaints can often reflect a discordance between social norms and expectations for public space between gentrifiers and existing residents. Referred to as "citizens' hotlines," these services can be used to request sanitation pickups and report negligent landlords, but from 2010 through 2022, noise complaints were by far the most common use of New York's 311 service, with over 5.5 million calls in regard to residential, street, vehicle, and commercial noise.[11] These types of complaints, known as "quality of life" issues, can also include reports of graffiti, the state of buildings, the presence of homeless individuals, and uses of public space. A 2019 report for the Community Service Society of New York identified important trends between gentrification and quality of life complaints. Economist Harold Stolper analyzed 311 calls around New York City that were referred to the police department and determined that while the frequency of referred calls increased citywide in the mid-2010s, the increase was significantly higher in low-income and majority non-white areas that had large influxes of white residents during that period.[12] While arrests from these calls are infrequent, they are three times as likely in these neighborhoods. Tellingly, the largest increases in police-referred 311 calls were in census tracts with new market-rate housing developments, but even more so when affordable public housing was also present.

Similar to how community events assist in claiming symbolic ownership of a place, quality of life complaints exhibit residents' attempts at shaping and dictating local norms. While non-emergency services for quality of life issues have been around for about twenty years, the practice of policing perceived social disorder is a few decades older. In 1982 criminologist George L. Kelling and political scientist James Q. Wilson published their influential article "Broken Windows: The Police and Neighborhood Safety," not in an academic journal but rather a more public forum, the *Atlantic* magazine. In the article they proposed that visible signs of a neighborhood's disorder—like graffiti, public drinking, and buildings in disrepair—would indicate that an area lacked social order or surveillance, leading to an increase in crime.[13] Kelling and Wilson recommended the policing of these smaller infractions to prevent more serious crime by way of signaling that the neighborhood was cared for. Their ideas influenced an era of controversial policing tactics in New York and other US cities.

Violent crime did decrease in New York at the same time that broken windows policing and CompStat—a method of tracking crimes by location—were implemented. Yet scholars have called into question how much of the drop-off in crime was due to these policing tactics. Some research suggests that the waning of the crack cocaine public health crisis, improved economic conditions, and demographic shifts that led to a smaller population of eighteen-to-twenty-four-year-olds also influenced the decrease in crime.[14] Many of the policing strategies inspired by broken windows or quality of life policing were racist and classist, targeting people of color and poor and homeless populations.[15]

The causality between visible signs of disorder and actual occurrence of crime has been debated and critiqued by criminologists, sociologists, and law professors.[16] Still, urban scholars have explored the idea that these signs of disorder can influence *perceptions* of crime and safety, and residents also differ on what they view as social disorder. In an early study of gentrification in Boston, incoming residents identified signs of disorder that included trash accumulation, noise, what they perceived as dirty streets, and complaints that the neighborhood had too many dogs (a quality that is now viewed as a marker of gentrification).[17] A study using American Housing Survey data from the 1980s and 1990s reported that white people perceived more crime and disorder than non-white residents and that women and longer-term residents also perceived more disorder. Conducting surveys in three gentrifying neighborhoods in Portland in the 2000s, researchers again found that white residents perceived more disorder, and that homeowners perceived more than renters.[18] Feelings of agency and integration in a neighborhood might also influence perceptions of crime. Robert J. Sampson has written about crime and neighborhood effects throughout his career. He has asserted that collective efficacy—trust, cohesion, and social integration—is negatively associated with violent crime.[19] Other sociologists have since debated whether collective efficacy has an effect on actual crime rates, but a quantitative study found that collective efficacy helped to alleviate fear.[20]

These findings around perceptions of disorder and safety along with the 311 data indicate that in-moving gentrifiers may not only perceive more disorder or crime in their new neighborhood, but also may be more likely to report behavior or conditions that they feel interfere with their quality of life. In Williamsburg, where Omar sees neighborhood life and feels no need to lock his door, he believes newer residents see disorder and summon the police. There is an inconsistency between how different residents evaluate the presence or threat of crime. While race, the physical environment, and level of collective efficacy can all play a role, I argue that neighborhood attachment style can also predict how individuals interpret signs of disorder and crime.

Crime in Williamsburg

Crime dropped off significantly in Williamsburg, and throughout New York, from its peak in 1991.[21] The precinct that patrols the Northside reported a 70.2 percent drop in crime from 1990 to 2015, and a 69.4 percent decrease on the Southside. Yet certain crimes, or at least the frequency with which they're reported, have increased over time. Throughout Williamsburg, grand larceny (defined as $1,000 or more but discounting cars, which have their own category) increased 72.6 percent from 2001 to 2015 (642 cases in 2015); in the Northside precinct alone, it increased 182.1 percent (488 cases in 2015) in that time.[22]

For many Old Timers and Bohemians, Williamsburg was a place where dangerous things sometimes happened. Gang fights, muggings, and/or drug use were the most frequently mentioned disturbances, at least by residents who lived in the neighborhood in the 1970s, 1980s and early 1990s. Yet with all of this activity, most Old Timers did not report feeling unsafe. In the anecdotes that follow, Old Timers sometimes note that personal safety was protected within ethnic territorial divisions. As newcomers, Bohemians do not make as much of a geographical distinction between the North and Southside, and were less likely to follow the tacit rule of staying in the territory of one's ethnic or racial group. When it came to questions about crime and safety, Condo Dwellers admitted that their perception of Williamsburg pre-condos was as a gritty, cool, but dangerous neighborhood that they would not feel comfortable raising a family in. Occasional reports of violent crime are shocking to them, but they do not personally feel at risk. Concerns about property crime were expressed in several interviews with newer residents.

Old Timers

Typical of New York, the demographics and social scene of Williamsburg can change noticeably over the course of a few blocks. The occurrence of crime in Williamsburg varied starkly between sections of the neighborhood, specifically between the North and Southsides. In the 1960s and 1970s, when crime was starting to climb, residents of both sections reported that the neighborhood felt safe as long as you stuck to the territory where your ethnic group—Italian, Polish, Puerto Rican, or Dominican—dominated.

The Italian mafia on the Northside and gang activity on the Southside introduced some forms of crime into the area, but Old Timers may have also benefited from organized criminal activity in their locales. Using ethnographic and quantitative data to study New York from the 1960s through the 1980s, Mercer Sullivan noted that certain patterns of street crime could bring resources and services into an otherwise poverty-stricken neighborhood. Sullivan reasoned that stolen items became affordable goods, and when protecting their turf from rivals, gang activities had the consequence of providing security for locals. Like the Southside gangs, the Northside's Italian mafia presence afforded some level of protection to residents and businesses, even when citywide crime rates were high.[23]

Southside

Maria is a middle-aged Puerto Rican woman who grew up on the Southside, raised a family there, and is now helping raise grandchildren in addition to working at a community center for aging Southside residents. When asked to describe her neighborhood in the 1970s, she immediately spoke about crime and visual signs of disorder: "There were gangs, there were shootings, there were a lot of abandoned and burned buildings. Chaos." However, she claims that this environment did not necessarily feel dangerous to residents: "Honest to God, I've never felt unsafe. . . . Being raised here, you knew everyone, you knew the street dealers, you knew the thugs. . . . If gang violence was gonna start, they'd warn the people, you know, 'Pick up your kids, something's gonna happen.' . . . I've never been robbed, burglarized, mugged, anything like that." Maria wasn't even aware of how dangerous her neighborhood was perceived to be until she started high school in Manhattan: "Once—you do an introduction, and I said Southside Williamsburg. Everybody looked at me like, 'Oh my god, they kill people over there,' and that's the first time I got the feeling of how bad my neighborhood was perceived."

Arnold is a Dominican man and Former Resident around Maria's age. He was a teenager in the 1980s and has a memory of a rougher version of the neighborhood. Like Maria, he acknowledged that you generally could rely on your neighbors and that people had a choice to take part in the "chaos" that Maria described: "When I was growing up, Williamsburg was basically a slum, . . . gutted, burned buildings. . . . The nice thing about it was it was a Latino neighborhood, so we were, I think by default, forced to be a sort of insular community . . . but I knew where the trouble was and I was getting into trouble and I had to decide—keep going down that path or not." Although he was briefly caught up in what he describes as a troubled scene, his biggest complaint about the neighborhood at the time was how the problems were ignored by the city until wealthier residents moved in. Arnold described Williamsburg at the time as "dangerous poverty, it's not getting the right protections from the people who are supposed to protect you, like the police and the firemen, . . . until someone decides it's a really cool place to live."

Growing up about a decade later, George, a Dominican man in his late thirties, experienced the height of crime in Williamsburg as a teenager. Looking out the window of his rent-stabilized Southside apartment, George recalled what the neighborhood used to look like: "Growing up it was . . . a lot of vacant lots, a lot of blight, a lot of drug paraphernalia around. You still see it now but not as much as before. It was very blatant." But like Maria and Arnold, George was entrenched in the community, with many cousins, aunts, and uncles living nearby: "Even given all of that, it was great that it was a lot of, predominantly Puerto Rican/Dominican at the time." George also felt insulated, even though he was aware that the neighborhood could be dangerous:

> I pretty much always felt safe, but there were times where, if it was late at night and in a strange area, you had to be careful. . . . Nothing really ever happened. . . . If you weren't out there trying to blatantly disrespect somebody, that wasn't going to happen. It was very rare instances. But there were people that I knew that were involved in nefarious things. . . . But if you weren't involved with that, you didn't really have much to worry about.

Paul was the youngest of the Southside residents in this study. He said that when he was growing up in the 1990s, "Everyone basically knew everyone, . . . [but] it did have its rough patches, gangs, individuals just robbing, no cops around, a lot of drugs." Echoing Maria and George, he was aware that the neighborhood had problems, but never felt particularly threatened. Like Arnold, Paul noted the lack of cops in the neighborhood, at least until it started to gentrify:

> I think I was in high school and I noticed a cop car, then another, and I thought, "Whoa, either someone's getting robbed or they're looking for someone," but it was just a regular patrol. That's when I really started to realize . . . things are changing, cops are starting to come by, people are fixing up broken-down buildings. . . . It started growing. Now it's all rich people.

Not everyone was as integrated into the neighborhood's familial and institutional networks. Rosa, a sixty-seven-year-old woman who has lived in Williamsburg for most of her life, is one such person. Although she stated that she was Puerto Rican, she was adamant that she did not identify with her ethnic background: "I'm not a typical Hispanic female." She described growing up and raising her own children in Williamsburg: "There were drugs and there were gangs for quite a few years there." Rosa did not feel as at ease in Williamsburg as other Southsiders did, likely because of her lack of identification with the local community.

Renaldo, a sixty-nine-year-old Mexican American, moved to the neighborhood in his late twenties after returning from a deployment in the Vietnam War. He came to Williamsburg to work in the "sugar house," the Domino Sugar factory. Renaldo came to Brooklyn from the Midwest and although he spoke Spanish, he felt that he was an outsider to the existing Puerto Rican and Dominican communities. He remembered driving upstate when he had weekends off and spending time out of the city. As he told it, this was to keep himself out of trouble:

> There was nothing but drugs here. . . . People around here had fear to go out at night or in the evening because all the drug trafficking and [sex workers], a lot of bars and killings, drug sales on every other block. . . . I didn't hang out in the neighborhood at all. If you did, you were taking your life in your own hands.

Renaldo's experience was closer to Rosa's than those of the other necessity-attached Old Timers. Both of them did not feel protected by the "insular community" that Maria and Arnold described, nor did they have the family attachments that George and Paul mentioned. Rosa and Renaldo were both outsiders, seemingly by choice—because they actively did not identify with the community. They experienced less integration and collective efficacy of the neighborhood because they participated less in its institutional and social life. As a result, they had more fearful perceptions of Williamsburg's crime rates than their more integrated counterparts.

Northside

Peter, Mike, and Anthony were all members of the Swinging Sixties Senior Center, an older adult program that provides meals, activities, and education for older residents. I chatted with the three men over their lunch one afternoon as they reminisced about their neighborhood in the 1960s and 1970s. They acknowledged that there were drugs and gangs in Williamsburg back then but maintained that their neighborhood was safe overall. Peter recalled a story from his youth that, to him, indicated the safety of the neighborhood: "I was drunk, I had change, money in my pocket, fell asleep outside and I woke up, still had all my money." They echoed other Old Timers, mentioning that social norms of Williamsburg at the time were based around racialized territories:

> MIKE: Usually the groups stuck together. The Italians stuck together; the Puerto Ricans stuck together.
> ANTHONY: Like, you gotta stay on your own territory, and then there's no problems.
> PETER: That's why they say there's a Northside, a Southside. The Spanish had the Southside, and we had the Northside.... Once you got out of your area you were at your own risk.... We knew we weren't allowed to go over there, they knew they weren't allowed to come here...
> MIKE: ... the territory, this is my neighborhood, that's yours. You get caught over there, you get a beating, that's all. It was stupid.

Territory was not mentioned as often among Southside residents in this study, but in the 1980s and 1990s, Northside white ethnics were preoccupied with maintaining the racialized boundaries of their neighborhoods. Marcin, who moved to Williamsburg from Poland in the 1950s, talked about when Williamsburg was "bad": he remembered "Puerto Rican people burning houses." While arson rates were higher on the Southside, it is unlikely that Puerto Rican residents were responsible. Several studies on arson in New York and other cities at the time maintain that these fires were most likely to happen in non-owner-occupied buildings in disinvested neighborhoods, often structures with housing code violations or tax arrears where it was more profitable for a landlord to collect insurance money than attempt to rent or sell the building.[24] But attributing these actions to Southside residents justified the racist actions that kept the territories intact.[25]

The effects of deindustrialization and disinvestment were slower to hit the Northside compared with the Southside, where these effects were compounded by racist housing policies and later policing tactics. Crime rates remained relatively lower on the Northside, but by the 1980s some residents did find a noticeable shift in the neighborhood. When describing the neighborhood that she grew up in, Gosia named many signs of disorder but denied ever having experienced danger personally: "There were empty factories, broken glass, a lot of homeless people, [sex workers] on Kent Avenue." She recounted that the area felt dangerous, deserted:

> You just didn't go out after eight o'clock. Once it got dark you didn't go out. . . . There was a firehouse across the street, and I think that was the reason we didn't have break-ins. . . . Other neighbors did have break-ins. The cars got vandalized quite often. . . . It was so desolate and a place you didn't walk down to the water. There were barbed wire fences and tons and tons of garbage, and you just didn't go there, you didn't park your car there and the only time the neighborhood gathered there was during the Fourth of July.

Coming from a small town in Poland could only have enhanced Gosia's lack of security in the neighborhood, but her memory of the bad old days are more about aesthetics than actual crime. While she did not feel safe hanging out in the neighborhood, her two brothers felt free to explore. Additionally, these comments are referencing a time when Williamsburg's popularity as a nightlife destination was growing. The difference is that for Gosia, these aesthetics signaled danger, whereas the postindustrial landscape and vacant buildings were intriguing to Bohemian newcomers.

Bohemians

James, a white artist, lived in the same neighborhood just a few years after Gosia's family moved there. He grew up in a suburban American town and lived short-term in a few European cities, before moving to Williamsburg in 1983, following a small network of friends and fellow artists. James is now an art dealer in another gentrified Brooklyn neighborhood. He gestured theatrically as he told me stories of Williamsburg's bad old days in the 1980s and 1990s, remembering it as "a very degraded, beleaguered place." He relished recounting a story of a time when his storefront apartment was "invaded" and he called the cops, who responded not from the neighborhood, but from Queens. As he tells it, "The cops were like, 'What are you living here for, anyway? This place is a sewer.'" James painted a Wild West portrait of the neighborhood: "And there were gunfights all the time and people would get held up. Getting held up at gunpoint was like paying a tax. And it would be like, 'Yeah, that's my $15 quarterly tax.'" But then he immediately retracted the severity of it upon probing:

> SM: So you had said earlier that Williamsburg was not a violent place . . .
> JAMES: No, no, no, Williamsburg was not a violent place, it was not especially violent. That's a myth. It wasn't this big, urban, you know, South Bronx.
> SM: I feel like people would say that getting held up at gunpoint multiple times . . .
> JAMES: Only on certain . . . that didn't actually happen that often. I was only held up once. Most friends of mine were held up once or twice.

Owen, also a white artist, moved to Williamsburg after art school in 1985 and remembered that "there was a big difference between the

Southside and the Northside. . . . [On the Southside] there were a lot of drugs and there was a lot of violence. You would hear things all the time." According to Owen, as long as you took precautions you weren't at risk, but he also remembered one day when he let his guard down. He was taking photos while doing a series on "derelict buildings" and he ventured to the Southside with his camera: "That wasn't a good idea, taking nice cameras to corners where drug deals were going on, and I got chased by kids, like, 'Don't take our picture.'"

Visible, if exaggerated, signs of disorder were also recounted by Rob, a white musician who moved to the neighborhood in 1994, who claimed that there were "[sex workers] on every street corner." While he didn't recall being physically threatened himself, he shared stories of run-ins that his friends had, some of which served as inspiration for his song lyrics. He remembered one story about a man delivering pizza to his building getting mugged in his vestibule, "probably by the [sex worker] that sometimes slept there."

Kristy first came to Williamsburg in 1985 for a party. She visited a few times before moving there and described the neighborhood in the 1980s as feeling abandoned: "When I first moved here, someone was honking at me at midnight when I was walking by the waterfront [where sex workers would engage clients]. There was a drug dealer and a drug addict that lived across the street from me. So yeah, it was dangerous enough." Dangerous enough to feel edgy, but not so dangerous that she, or most other young newcomers, would leave.

The accounts of Bohemians (including Former Residents who moved there in the 1980s and 1990s) were in line with those of the Old Timers when it came to actual experiences of crime. While both groups acknowledge its presence, they weren't necessarily victimized. Later in their interviews, James and Owen altered their descriptions of Williamsburg. James said, "The violence was gang-related and drug-related and focused on certain streets. So it was concentrated. It wasn't . . . random. Most of the neighborhoods were really tight, nice places you could walk through day or night." Owen qualified his earlier statements as well: "I never heard of anyone getting mugged. . . . I don't think the violence was really that frightening."

Around the late 1990s and early 2000s, the narratives shifted. Women were still concerned with crime, or at least more than men were, because they are far more frequently targeted for sexual assault. But people who moved to Williamsburg toward the later end of the Bohemian cohort were more likely to talk about "grit" than crime, and this narrative comes with its own set of implications.

Alex, who moved out of Williamsburg in 2007, felt out of place when he visited in the early 2010s. His nostalgia for the neighborhood relied on its previous, gritty reputation: "Williamsburg used to be kind of dirty. Williamsburg used to be a place where my family would come or my friends would come and say, 'Why are you living here?' . . . There was a dirtiness to it, and I feel like now with all the condos in there, it's kind of, it's just like the East Village." He noted that the earlier incarnation of Williamsburg was "more interesting. There was more excitement, there was more realness to it."

Anna, a Latin American woman, was among the last of Williamsburg's Bohemian cohort, and some of her perceptions of the neighborhood straddled the identity/investment divide. She moved to the Southside in 2003 to enjoy the neighborhood's dwindling art and party scene. Anna lived in a few apartments before moving into a condo with her husband in 2012. She remembered that in 2003 it "definitely felt more dangerous. . . . I lived across from the projects, so you know, that felt a little dangerous." For Anna, the mere presence of public housing was enough to feel threatened, although she had never been targeted. Anna's condo overlooked the same housing that she lived next to in 2003, but she said she barely noticed them because the neighborhood has gentrified so much: "I don't even really think about that kind of stuff anymore . . . and by now the neighborhood is so safe. I barely notice that there's projects over there." She reports feeling mostly safe in the neighborhood now, but

> it's still a little bit sketch. . . . There are very drunk people walking around. That can be a little bit intimidating. There's a guy with an electric guitar and he hangs out near the Grand stop and he's just ranting and raving. . . . There was a guy with a knife just walking down the street and angrily stabbing our garbage cans and I'm pretty sure I called the police. . . . Yeah, so that's the main thing, just sometimes really drunk people hanging out.

Williamsburg had so many bars that in 2011 the Community Board considered a moratorium on liquor licenses for new businesses. Every night of the week, drunk twenty- and thirty-somethings spill out of bars, onto the street and into the subway stations. Of course, the "sketch" that Anna referred to was not the young professionals at happy hour, but the residents of NYCHA housing being visibly drunk in public space—a population that she can otherwise forget exists. While many Bohemians have a nostalgic, romanticized memory of Williamsburg's grit, Condo Dwellers have a different perception of it. To them it wasn't a backdrop to their artist colony or adventurous youth, but rather something that discouraged them from imagining Williamsburg as a place they would want to live and invest in.

Condo Dwellers

I interviewed Stephanie in her tenth-floor condo, which she shared with her husband and two children. The living room was crowded with toys for her toddler and infant, with large windows that looked out onto New York's East River and the Manhattan skyline. Stephanie, a white woman then in her forties, first started visiting friends in the neighborhood in 2001. "We'd take a car service to get to a bar or something. We wouldn't want to walk around at night. . . . I kind of thought of it as dangerous." She no longer felt that way about the neighborhood: "There were just a lot of crazy things, that don't really exist anymore, I don't think, or not as much out in the open."

In 2010 Jenny and her husband, both white, moved into one of the waterfront buildings after their broker showed them an apartment. They thought that it was a good investment, and Jenny didn't plan on living in the area long-term. She had first visited a friend in the neighborhood in 2005: "I thought it was gritty." When they moved here in 2010, Jenny felt uncomfortable because there were a lot of carjackings: "We've had a few break-ins into our garage, bikes were stolen, stuff like that. I never felt like my safety was ever compromised but I felt like my stuff's safety was compromised." This is consistent with some of the literature that suggests that property crimes increase during gentrification, but the presence of theft did not act as a deterrent in the way that aesthetics had.[26]

Josie, a Mexican American woman who had a psychiatry practice in the neighborhood, first came to visit Williamsburg in 2006. Her friend encouraged her to come check it out, but she viewed the same attributes that the Bohemians romanticized as undesirable: "So we came, and I was like, 'Yeah, it's cool stuff but . . . too much graffiti, and lots of empty factories.'" When she and her husband returned to look at apartments in 2010, she still felt that the waterfront was unsafe, but also felt that the stores and new buildings made Williamsburg feel like more of a neighborhood. They eventually purchased an apartment in a converted former factory.

Today murals have replaced the graffiti that Condo Dwellers saw when they visited; chain businesses and the increase of families like their own have made newer residents feel more comfortable. More often, newcomers' reactions stressed the security they feel living in Williamsburg: "it's safe, convenient" and "generally safe and genuinely a happy place to be," and "people say that it's much safer now." Property crime still exists as well as occasional violent crimes, but luxury housing residents feel separated from the crime by virtue of living in buildings with doormen or private security who control access to the building, an urban gated community.[27] With their dominance in the neighborhood, investment-attached residents get to define problems, focusing instead on quality of life issues like who is using public space and how it is being used.

Urban Pioneering in Williamsburg

Depending on attachment style, Williamsburg's graffiti, abandoned lots, burned buildings, and gang activity were either background noise to be tuned out, authentic grit, or justification for redevelopment. Like Omar, most Old Timers acknowledged that social disorders existed without feeling that their personal safety was compromised. However, residents who lacked social integration were more likely to feel threatened or intimidated; this included both Old Timers and Bohemians who didn't socialize with neighbors or participate as much in local institutions. The important distinction here is that Bohemians incorporated crime-related anecdotes as part of their narratives of life in Williamsburg or their identities as artists. Old Timers' necessity attachment to Williamsburg meant that the crime wasn't romanticized or exaggerated; it simply existed.

Williamsburg's aesthetics made the neighborhood interesting to Bohemians, the bad reputation kept the rent cheap, and the illegal loft parties were mythic. Nearly every one of the Bohemians recalled a specific threatening incident that they or their friends experienced. It's likely that while living in a neighborhood with high crime rates, Old Timers at some point experienced a criminal act either personally or through a close friend or family member, but they didn't recount these stories specifically or in the detailed and personal ways that Bohemians tended to. The fact that James, Rob, Kristy, and Owen had precise stories to call back to, complete with fragments of conversations from thirty years ago, implies that this was not their first telling. In fact, these anecdotes were shared with a bit of nostalgia. The incidents, their brushes with Williamsburg's infamous street life, have been incorporated into their narratives of their time there.

The exaggerated "quarterly tax for mugging," the industrial, "dangerous enough" environment, and the fact that their parents and friends (and in some cases cops) questioned why they lived there contributed to the thrill of participating in an authentic avant-garde lifestyle. This narrative of settling dangerous territory is nowhere more apparent than in *The Last Bohemia: Scenes from the Life of Williamsburg, Brooklyn*, Robert Anasi's memoir about the neighborhood from the late 1980s to 2008.[28] Anasi states that white flight "brought the frontier to Williamsburg," perpetuating the colonist trope that geographer Neil Smith criticized in his analysis of gentrification on the Lower East Side.[29] In her film *Gut Renovation*, documentarian Su Friedrich refers to gentrification as an evolutionary process and makes the claim that artists were pioneers who "were making the streets safer by populating them at night."[30]

The imagery of taming a frontier is frequently evoked by gentrifiers, but it is also not lost on developers.[31] The "urban pioneering" done by middle-class artists and students marked a crucial moment in Williamsburg's trajectory.[32] The presence of Bohemians and their cultural institutions, along with media acknowledgment of both, helped set the stage for further gentrification. Bohemians and Condo Dwellers are not dissimilar from each other in a few key ways. Both populations are predominantly college-educated, white Americans from middle-class or wealthy families. Late Bohemians, moving to Williamsburg at the height of its avant-garde popularity, are even around the same age as the first surge of Condo Dwellers. The presence of people who were demographically similar and the shifting reputation from working-class, industrial enclave to artist community were necessary in instilling the confidence of the investment-attached.

Indeed, the hipster culture that arose out of Williamsburg's bohemianism was heavily relied on in advertising campaigns for the Edge condo towers. In one flyer, a man with a skinny tie and black-framed glasses leaned over a kitchen counter; the Rolling Stones' song title "Gimme Shelter" written above him, but with the first word crossed out. A second ad featured a tattooed woman with a trendy haircut in a penthouse apartment with the copy "Street Smart," again with the first word crossed out. Another set of advertisements contained only words and also referenced two stereotypical aspects of hipster culture: "While you were busy contemplating which flannel to wear . . . I moved on up" and "While you were busy cultivating your mustache . . . I moved on up." The ads exploited Williamsburg's cool factor while suggesting that potential buyers were smarter than people who had simply had a good time in the neighborhood, but did not financially invest in it.

The edginess imparted upon Williamsburg by Bohemian culture, narratives, and, as we will see, retail institutions shifted the neighborhood's reputation from a dangerous, neglected neighborhood to one worthy of real estate and corporate investment. By the late 2000s, companies and business owners were eager to align themselves with the Williamsburg brand. In joining the retail landscape, upscale stores have continued to transform the neighborhood's identity.

4

Selling Williamsburg

From Gritty to Luxury

As late as 2012, a single block of Bedford Avenue featured necessities that included a pharmacy, an independent food store, a pet supply shop, and New York essentials like a bagel shop and a pizzeria. This retail coexisted alongside Whisk, a kitchenware store that was one of the first bastions of the street's commercial upscaling.[1] Just five years later, Whole Foods, Citibank, and Apple had opened, later joined by Sephora and Equinox Gym, all on one city block. Early among the higher-end stores, Whisk could not survive the street's latest transition. The owner closed in 2019, a decision made after the landlords asked for $26,500 a month in rent. Eleven years earlier, when they first opened, their rent had been $8,625. In an interview with *Gothamist*, the owner, Natasha Amott, speculated on the reason for the sharply increasing rents: "So many of these multinational brands want Williamsburg. They think Williamsburg is the place to sell their brand to, so they're willing to treat the high rent as an advertising dollar," thereby inflating the asking price for retail rent throughout the neighborhood.[2]

Amott's observation about the Williamsburg brand is nowhere more apparent than at Alo, an indulgent yoga clothing line and studio, which opened just steps away from the space Whisk used to occupy. In a promotional video of its "Williamsburg Sanctuary," a barista in the store's café peels back the top of a fresh coconut, the company's logo branded into the fruit's flesh. Alo does most of its business online, with two dozen boutique/studios in expensive locales including Beverly Hills, Aspen, SoHo, and La Jolla, San Diego. While its Williamsburg rent is not disclosed, the company made headlines for signing a lease in Manhattan to the tune of $250,000 a month for the next seven years.[3] But with revenue of $200 million per year and expanding, it is worth it to have the brick-and-mortar location, to have the Alo branded coconut aligned with the sleek, urban luxury branded Williamsburg.

Figure 4.1. "Style Comes from Williamsburg" advertising campaign in the subway, September 2014. Author's photo.

Wealthy outsiders viewed Williamsburg as dangerous, gritty, and grungy through the late 2000s. For the neighborhood to become the condofied, corporate destination that it is today, it had to undergo a serious rebranding. How did a working-class neighborhood disinvested by the city transform into the center of hipster culture and then a hypergentrified locale, all within just a few decades? The 2005 rezoning was a major factor in the neighborhood's gentrification, but it may have never happened if the image of the neighborhood did not shift in the 1980s and 1990s.[4]

The Williamsburg Brand

Travel and lifestyle blogs have compared neighborhoods (and even entire cities) to Williamsburg. In the 2010s, drawing a comparison to Williamsburg meant that a neighborhood was cool, cutting-edge, and artsy. This sentiment is on display in articles heralding Berlin, in its entirety, as "the New Williamsburg," Shimokitazawa as the "not as pretentious or annoying" Williamsburg of Tokyo, Tulum as the "Williamsburg of Mexico," and Fitzroy as "Melbourne meets Williamsburg."[5] These bloggers reference Williamsburg as an established, cultural touchstone to promote or characterize places around the world. In these cases, "Williamsburg" was used as shorthand for a neighborhood catering to young people, streets lined with bars, restaurants, yoga studios, vintage clothing stores, and murals.

Some neighborhoods become popular because of grand projects, cultural institutions, or star architects.[6] In New York, dozens of neighborhoods have utilized business improvement districts (BIDs) to promote commercial areas.[7] Such attempts at organizing businesses have seemed superfluous in Williamsburg.[8] The Northside Merchants Association (NMA) was a loose grouping of local business owners in the most gentrified section of the neighborhood. The group occasionally organized services like trash collection or decorations during the holiday season, but it is now generally dormant; its websites and social media accounts have not been updated since 2013. At first, the promotion of Williamsburg did not occur in a top-down way as it has in other places. The artists, musicians, and eventually the Bohemian business owners promoted the neighborhood on their own by engaging local media and eventually attracting an international hipster scene.

Bohemians opened galleries, bars, coffee shops, and music venues, creating an atmosphere that soon garnered attention from around New York City and beyond. Richard Lloyd observed a similar trend in Chicago's Wicker Park, where, he noted, "such local institutions both drive neighborhood identity and reflect it."[9] These businesses are essential in the transformation of once working-class neighborhoods into districts that cater to avant-gardes. Neighborhoods with a critical mass of these businesses eventually become attractions for visitors and tourists.

Local shops contribute to an area's aesthetic, and in turn influence the perceptions and narratives about neighborhoods. Soon the atmosphere created by Bohemian businesses and hyper-local media started to attract broader attention. In 1996 ArtNet, an international website that listed parties and festivals around the world, began including Williamsburg galleries on its site.[10] In 1997 Williamsburg was hailed as one of the "15 hippest neighborhoods in America" by *Utne Reader*, a self-described "digital digest of the new ideas and fresh perspectives percolating in arts, culture, politics, and spirituality."[11]

By the second half of the 1990s, Williamsburg started getting more mainstream attention, with the *New York Times* as a significant promoter of the neighborhood. Although it is an international paper, the *Times* is also an important driver and mirror of gentrification locally. I accessed the *New York Times* online archives to get a better understanding of the interaction between media representation and Williamsburg's reputation. Searching for any mention of Williamsburg every five years from 1980 to 2000, I categorized the articles to track how reporting about the neighborhood changed over time (see figure 4.2). The total number of articles annually devoted to Williamsburg nearly quadrupled over the twenty-year period, but the topics of the articles also changed during the neighborhood's early gentrification (see figure 4.3).

In 1980 there were twenty-two articles about crime, arson, and disorder, the most popular category of Williamsburg articles at that time, accounting for 41 percent of the fifty-three articles mentioning the neighborhood, while only five articles, or 10 percent, were about artists, cultural events, or local restaurants. In 2000 the *Times* published 186 articles about

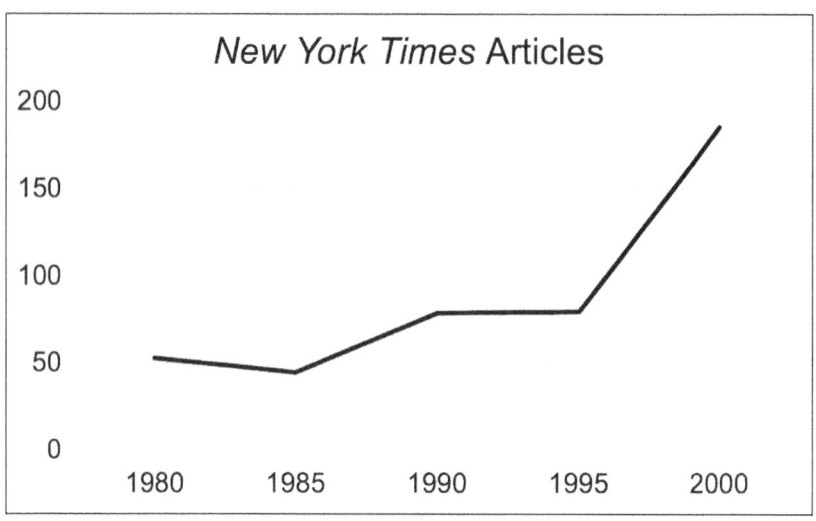

Figure 4.2. Count of *New York Times* articles mentioning Williamsburg, five-year increments from 1980 to 2000. Data collected by author from *New York Times* online archives. Chart created by author.

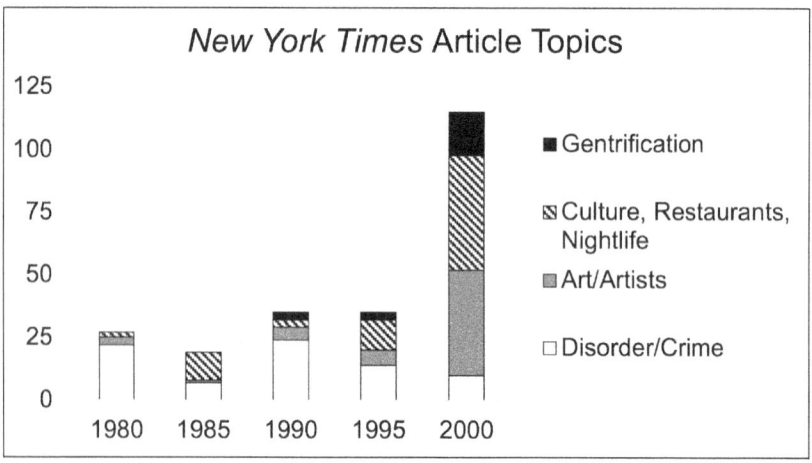

Figure 4.3. Popular categories of *New York Times* articles mentioning Williamsburg, five-year increments from 1980 to 2000. Data collected by author from *New York Times* online archives. Chart created by author.

Williamsburg, with 47 percent of them (88 articles in total) focusing on profiles of artists and gallery openings, cultural events, restaurants, and nightlife. These articles usually directed readers to specific institutions in Williamsburg. The *Times*' reporting on Williamsburg peaked around 2012, a few years into the neighborhood's condofication. In that year there were hundreds of articles mentioning Williamsburg, with eighty pieces in the paper's food section and sixty-four in the style section.

Citywide tourism efforts also began focusing on Williamsburg during this period. In the mid-2000s the now defunct VisitBrooklyn.org, partially funded by the "I ♥ New York" campaign, featured 103 attractions in Brooklyn. Over half of the destinations were art-related, including galleries, film festivals, music spaces, and artist collectives, many in Williamsburg. The site also profiled 227 restaurants. Of the twenty-three Brooklyn neighborhoods listed on VisitBrooklyn.org, Williamsburg had the most destinations.

Williamsburg was becoming an established brand that attracted international attention for its underground parties, curated thrift shops, concerts, restaurants, and other destinations. Writing about the neighborhood in 2010, Sharon Zukin noted how these parties and "places for cool cultural consumption" changed the image of the neighborhood.[12] Institutions that were central to the Bohemians' culture helped pave the way for an upgrading of retail. Retail has played a key role in the neighborhood's identity, as Williamsburg shifted from a focus on production and necessity to artist culture, and now is seen as a global destination for luxury consumption. Of course, not all residents have experienced this shift in the same way. As the Northside's commercial strip has transformed, Old Timers and even Bohemians have been culturally displaced, while Condo Dwellers experience convenience, comfort, and excitement in the area's abundant retail.

Identity and Exclusion through Retail Gentrification

Along with housing stock and public spaces, shops and businesses are part of an urban neighborhood's built environment. As the uses and character of localities shift, retail businesses help create a new, though sometimes contested, neighborhood identity. Storefronts and businesses can communicate an area's aesthetic, function, and even demographics to residents, visitors, and media. They can also signal who does and does not belong in a space.

Prior to advanced gentrification, stores in Williamsburg contributed to a sense of familiarity or belonging for existing residents. Ethnic businesses can be important resources for immigrant populations.[13] The Italian, Polish, Puerto Rican, and Dominican businesses of Williamsburg did more than serve the necessities of locals, they also contributed to residents' sense of ownership over the neighborhood through the presence of ethnic goods, signage in their languages, and the general visibility of their cultures.

Local institutions signaling an artist enclave (and the beginning of gentrification) dotted Williamsburg in the early to mid-1990s. The L Café, opened in 1992, was among the first, serving coffee and small meals in an environment that catered to students, artists, and other newcomers. A local writer recalled that it was not "a place to work, rather to discuss your work, the work you intend to do, or the work you have no intention of taking on but are more than happy to go on about."[14] Galapagos, a bar and performance space, opened in 1995 and "helped put Williamsburg on the art map."[15] Six years later, Supercore, a Japanese restaurant and café, opened on Bedford's Southside with the intent of "not only offering the local community of artists and young people a place to dine, but also providing a creative space where they can gather and socialize."[16]

The aesthetics and products in local stores—including prices, style, and presentation—that foster feelings of ownership and belonging among some residents can exacerbate the cultural displacement and exclusion of others.[17] Henryk, a member of the Bohemian cohort, illustrates this when discussing a new grocery store located at the base of a waterfront condo that is geared toward investment-attached customers: "It's expensive. It's also too fancy. . . . Going [there] when it looks so fancy, it just doesn't feel, I don't feel like that's my place. I don't know if it's the way it looks or the prices, just it feels weird."

In Portland, Oregon, sociologists Daniel Sullivan and Samuel Shaw studied how important these retail shifts could be. Tracking the change in businesses on Alberta Street, they found that Black-owned businesses decreased as the area gentrified and was rebranded as an arts district. Their interviews with Black residents revealed that new businesses helped set up "symbolic boundaries" that felt exclusionary to longtime residents. On Alberta Street in Portland and on Bedford Avenue in Williamsburg, fewer long-term businesses mean that necessities can be more expensive or harder to find, that local immigrant languages disappear from neighborhood signage, and that long-term residents have fewer reasons to be in public space. Through retail gentrification, the histories and cultures of existing resident groups are either manipulated to appeal to a broader audience or effectively erased from the public spaces of the neighborhood.

The consumption and cultural offerings that made Williamsburg unique are now replicated through a combination of gentrification and globalization, creating far-flung urban neighborhoods with very similar images, symbols, and retail offerings.[18] Worse than simply the homogenization of urban cultures, these neighborhoods hold more appeal for global elites than for existing residents. As Williamsburg became known as an international destination, the retail was ceasing to function for most locals, turning the once self-sufficient neighborhood into a playground for tourists, visitors, and the wealthiest of residents. When places around the world become "Williamsburgs," existing residents become culturally displaced from their neighborhood's public spaces.

The actions of local business owners have consequences for a neighborhood's reputation. A clothing designer who opens a pop-up shop helps to solidify Williamsburg's renown as a destination for fashion. A bakery owner who renovates his shop into a café changes the aesthetic of the street. Taken together, changing businesses alter the appearance and status of the neighborhood.

By tracing the retail trajectory of Williamsburg, we can understand how local actors and businesses influenced the neighborhood's identity away from its industrial and immigrant past toward a luxury consumption-based present. The narratives of local business owners and employees reveal how these players purposefully shape the symbolic atmosphere of a neighborhood. In this chapter, storeowners' perspectives are supplemented by accounts from residents who discuss what the neighborhood's retail meant (or didn't mean) to them. These perspectives are supported with archival data from Cole's reverse telephone directories, as well as my own ethnographic obser-

Figure 4.4. Retail landscape of Bedford Avenue, circa 2000. The businesses in this photo include an Italian bread bakery, two Polish butcher shops, and a laundromat. "Pralnia," the Polish word for "laundry," is prominent on the store's signage. Photo by Jerome Krase.

Figure 4.5. Repeat photography of the same landscape on Bedford Avenue, March 2014. By 2008 all of the previous businesses had left their storefronts, except for the bakery, which soon became a café. In this photo the laundromat and two butcher stores have all been replaced by restaurants. Photo by Lukasz Chelminski.

vations on the street.[19] The Cole's directories, which list businesses and residences by address, provide a more quantitative context of the changing retail landscape of Bedford Avenue through cycles of disinvestment and gentrification while also allowing for a triangulation of ethnographic and interview data.[20]

Bedford Avenue

Bedford Avenue is the main shopping and transportation street in the highly gentrified portion of Williamsburg. It was never the center of production during the neighborhood's industrial history, but it was and is the center of local commerce. Bedford has changed dramatically over the past few decades and serves as a useful reference for charting the neighborhood's retail changes.

In the 1970s a one-mile stretch of Bedford Avenue from McCarren Park to the Williamsburg Bridge was home to eighty-nine businesses and storefronts that served the needs of locals. There were grocery stores (including vegetable stands, butcher shops, bakeries, and bodegas—the New York City equivalent of a convenience store), bars, restaurants, clothing stores, and services such as laundromats, carpenters, plumbers, some light manufacturing, and a pharmacy (see figure 4.6). By 1981 the street hit a low point in retail, but still had fifty-nine businesses in the same one mile. In interviews, Old Timers on the Northside note that Bedford Avenue lacked retail variety in the 1980s, but those with a necessity attachment claimed that they could get what they needed and that the Southside and Greenpoint neighborhoods offered additional retail options as well.

Through the mid-1990s, the majority of the stores on Bedford continued to serve working-class Old Timers, with some newer establishments geared toward the Bohemian clientele opening up. For a time, Polish butchers, Italian bakeries, and Dominican grocers existed alongside vegetarian bistros and art galleries. Part of Williamsburg's identity as a hip locale relied on the presence of cafés, bars, and restaurants, which nearly tripled from eight to twenty-one in a ten-year period between 1990 and 2000. However as commercial rents rose, many Old Timer businesses, and later Bohemian ones, were priced out.

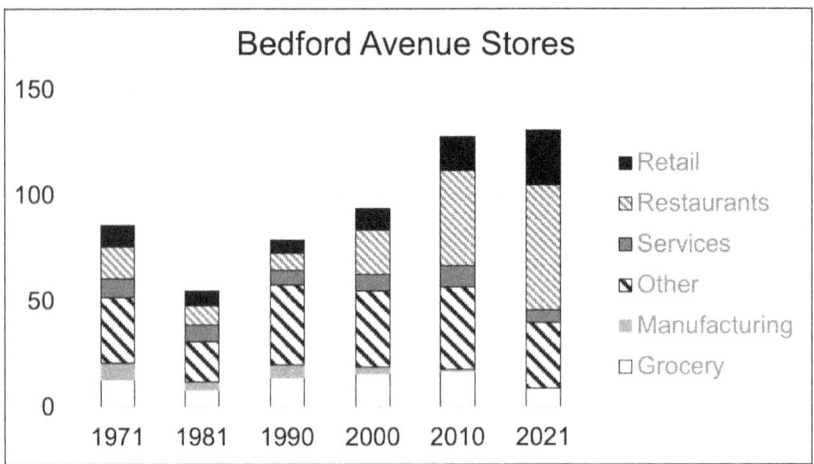

Figure 4.6. Bedford Avenue store counts and types over time from 1971 to 2021. Data collected by author from Cole's reverse phone directories. Observations for 2021 were completed in person by the author. Chart created by author.

Now the corporatized version of Williamsburg is a destination for its amenity-filled hotels, highly rated restaurants, popular music venues, and upscale boutiques. Even with the closure of some businesses during the pandemic, Williamsburg's retail has continued to gentrify. An ethnographic survey of the street in December 2021 showed that in the most recent decade, restaurants, cafés, and bars have come to dominate the commercial landscape, accounting for 45 percent of all storefronts on Bedford Avenue. Along the one-mile strip, there were also seventeen clothing or jewelry boutiques and four upscale beauty or skin care–related businesses. Pivoting to capture the health and wellness market, new businesses on Bedford include Kava Social, a mocktail bar and self-touted "best sober scene in New York," and Soul Recovery, a studio that offers floatation therapy, an oxygen bar, and a treatment that involves freezing temperatures to release bodily toxins. As gentrification has progressed in Williamsburg, the side streets have become consumption corridors of their own, with boutique shopping, a bathhouse, and several wine bars—all catering to a much broader scene than just neighborhood or New York City locals. Understandably, Old Timer, Bohemian, and Condo Dwelling residents have very different perceptions of the neighborhood's retail changes.

Resident Reactions to Change

There is an assumption that long-term residents would most strongly lament the loss of their old neighborhood as it gentrified. Old Timers were disappointed in some changes, and appreciated others; instead, it was the Bohemians who expressed the most dismay over Williamsburg's retail gentrification. Old Timers did not typically mention businesses when describing what their neighborhood used to be like. When probed about it, most indicated that local retail was a mode of accumulating the necessities of life, not an attraction in itself. Bohemians often referred to the neighborhood as "empty" when they first arrived, claiming that there was "nothing there" and then typically pointed to the opening of one or two businesses (relevant to their own identity) as signaling the beginning of Williamsburg. When Condo Dwellers described the neighborhood, they almost never needed probing about businesses, revealing that shops, restaurants, and nightlife are intrinsic features of their experience of Williamsburg. These amenities, and the convenience they bring, are among the top reasons investment-attached newcomers felt comfortable moving to the formerly "gritty" neighborhood.

Over coffee one morning at the Swinging Sixties Senior Center, a group of Latina women in their seventies reminisced about Williamsburg's changing retail scene. Amanda, a former schoolteacher, recalled how the neighborhood businesses used to cater to the lower-income residents of the neighborhood, and expressed disappointment that those offerings were no longer available. Rosa countered that she was impressed that Williamsburg had attracted new businesses like "coffee shops, and wineries, and beer shops, bars," but also expressed disappointment that she can no longer get some necessities: "There are still a lot of senior citizens in this area and there's no such thing as a store for senior citizens to walk in and buy a pair of pants, not anymore."

When discussing changes to businesses on the Southside, Maria described not just necessities but also entertainment offered in the local retail landscape of the 1970s:

> We had a shoe store, we had fruits and vegetables, . . . we had mom-and-pop shops. . . . You could find almost everything you wanted, kids'

clothes, women's clothes, everything was reasonable. We had a Woolworth years ago, the discount stores, record shops, soda shops, little candy stores, an arcade.

Two Former Residents spoke to the fact that not only did their neighborhoods have what they needed in the 1970s and 1980s, but that the businesses were run by immigrants and migrants like themselves: "That was the interesting thing," Arnold recalled. "You could do all your business in Spanish. Everything we needed was there. And as the neighborhood evolved a little more, even professional services were there." Gosia echoed that Northside businesses served ethnic and working-class populations: "The stores on Bedford Ave. consisted of mom-and-pop shops. There were two Polish stores, a little Italian coffee shop, a Laundromat, liquor store, and one bodega."

The Old Timers' accounts are confirmed by the archival retail data. The neighborhood was not a destination for visitors, but it provided most of the necessities for residents. Still, when Bohemians began arriving in the early 1980s, they found a residential neighborhood with "nothing" in it, at least nothing that served their identity attachment to Williamsburg. Similar to their accounts of crime, being in the neighborhood before certain landmarks helped legitimize their status as urban "pioneers." James remembered that when he moved into the neighborhood in 1983, "There was a rancid diner, two pet shops, and a Hasidic notary public. . . . Kasia's [Polish restaurant] opened after I moved to Williamsburg. If you got there before Kasia's, things were really old-school." This comment affords James and his friends a level of authenticity: they were in the neighborhood before it was cool. The perceived scarcity of retail was a marker of urban authenticity for Bohemians—they had chosen to live in gritty conditions, a neighborhood with graffiti tags on the walls, abandoned buildings, and only a few "awful" restaurants. But later James went on to talk about a job he had selling advertisements for a local paper, and he mentioned several more businesses: "I was walking around the Northside, Southside, doing that, bodegas, restaurants, Polish restaurants, hardware stores, and the local bars, Palestinian delis." There were suddenly many more businesses in the Williamsburg that James inhabited; they just weren't businesses that were particularly interesting for him and other Bohemians.

Kristy provided a similar narrative about how the neighborhood felt when she moved there in 1988. From my archival data count, just two years later, in 1990 there were eighty storefronts on Bedford Avenue, but as she remembered, "Bedford Avenue felt almost entirely abandoned. There were very few shops that were open. There were a couple of delis. I can't remember if the video store was open. I think Vinny's Pizzeria was there. . . . You definitely could not get the *New York Times* here." For identity-attached Bohemians, "abandonment" meant that there were businesses for necessities, but desired objects like the *New York Times* were missing. Allen recalled that people would go to a bakery for coffee because "there weren't alternatives." The absence of Manhattan levels of variety was interpreted and remembered as a void. He recalled when the L Café opened: "I sort of see that as that first cultural milestone of bringing together people, the cultural pull. . . . You would go there rather than the greasy diner across the street."

Bohemians who complained that "nothing was open then" and that "there was no food to buy" went on to admit that there were establishments that sold meat, fruit, vegetables, milk, and canned goods; there were bars, pet shops, laundromats, and at least one diner, even during the period when Bedford had the least amount of retail. But there was also a limit to the amount or type of retail that Bohemians welcomed as the neighborhood gentrified. Reflecting on Williamsburg in the mid-2010s, Allen lamented that brands had moved in: "I think last year we turned the next corner with the J. Crew and the Starbucks, because for a long time we kept the chains out." Courtney agreed: "It's kind of crazy to me that Apple is opening on Bedford, and I don't find that especially useful." Henryk noted that the retail was no longer for residents: "I think a lot of businesses cater to tourism, to outside people. I would even say more often the businesses right now cater to people who come here for a short time, half a day or a day."

Margot, a Former Resident, moved to Williamsburg in her twenties because many of her friends and their common hangouts were in the neighborhood. Reflecting on what Williamsburg had become by 2015, she said, "I almost feel that this is going through a second if not third phase of gentrification. It used to be catered towards individuals who wanted record stores, cool stuff, and now places have been kicked out and it seems like it's being replaced by chain stores." Margot and the

Bohemian residents above mourned the loss of the types of stores that they welcomed, establishments that initially made Williamsburg desirable for artists and students back in the 1980s, 1990s, and early 2000s. Bohemians and some Former Residents experienced a cultural displacement not unlike their Old Timer counterparts, who felt at home in their (im)migrant, working-class neighborhoods before the arrival of coffee shops and music venues.

What Bohemians and Former Residents viewed as a death of "their" Williamsburg turned out to be a boon for Condo Dwellers, who moved to Williamsburg for the short commute, convenience, and recession-era deals on luxury housing. Characteristic of many newer residents, Stephanie mentioned the restaurant scene as a major perk: "My husband and I have a date night every week. We probably go to a new restaurant every single week and we really only go out in Williamsburg, so that's, I mean, that's amazing."

Before all the chains arrived, early Condo Dwellers found Williamsburg lacking, compared to the convenience of Manhattan or the charm of Brownstone Brooklyn. To them, Williamsburg was a downgrade, a sacrifice they made because they could afford to buy apartments that they felt would appreciate quickly. The gourmet grocery stores hadn't yet arrived, the market for indoor children's play spaces hadn't emerged, and the waterfront parks were still under construction. Sarinda complained about the grocery store in her part of the neighborhood when she first arrived: "The [grocery store] was really old-school, . . . pretty crappy. I didn't know where we were gonna go grocery shopping." Josie moved into the neighborhood in 2010. That year, there were thirty-five restaurants and bars on Bedford Avenue alone (not counting side streets), seventeen businesses selling grocery items, and sixteen retail establishments like boutiques, bookstores, and jewelry shops. And yet, in her perception, "When we first moved here, there weren't great restaurants. Tops [a grocery store] was sort of crappy, it was old and oddly configured, it felt grungy. . . . It didn't feel like a full-on neighborhood. And now it does. There's all these amenities and that's really awesome."

By now, most of the retail has adapted to meet the aesthetics, needs, and deeper pockets of Condo Dwellers, and as a result they celebrate the convenience. Although they at first struggled to feel comfortable in "grungy" Williamsburg, investment-attached residents agreed that they can now get everything they need in the neighborhood. When asked to describe her neighborhood, Stephanie replied, "Convenient. . . . We have a supermarket right here, . . . we have, like, J. Crew and Urban Outfitters, and we don't shop at those places that much, but I guess it's nice, you know, that they're there. . . . But then the rents have gone up on the smaller stores." She liked having the J. Crew and Urban Outfitters around, even if she didn't often shop there, because they signaled something about the neighborhood she lived in—that it was worthy of corporate investment. The chains that Bohemians derided were barely commented on by Old Timers but were welcomed by Condo Dwellers, even when it was acknowledged that big-box stores threatened the existence of the small-scale retail that helped make Williamsburg popular.

Businesses on Bedford

The types of businesses and the decisions that store owners make about aesthetics, languages, and products create spaces that welcome or exclude different residential groups. In the sections that follow, we meet some of the storeowners of Bedford Avenue at a pivotal moment of change in the neighborhood—the early to mid-2010s, when the new buildings were beginning to fill with residents. The interviews below include newcomers who were attracted to the changes that had already taken place on Bedford as well as owners of established stores who changed their goods or aesthetics to reflect the shift in neighborhood imagery and demographics. No matter the tenure of the store, interviews with business owners and employees indicate how shops on Bedford have altered the retail landscape from one of everyday necessity to upscale recreation and personal care.

Retail Adaptations on Bedford Avenue

Studying Williamsburg in the late 1990s through early 2000s, Jason Patch noticed a "double landscape" that was emerging, one that was industrial but increasingly focused on consumption.[21] At the time, this landscape represented immigrant and artist communities, working-class and luxury; some signage included local ethnic languages and others communicated the aesthetics of French bistros and upscale diners. A decade later, it was less common to experience the "double landscape." Ethnic signage and stores catering to everyday needs were still present but much less visible. Longtime store owners who managed to stay had changed their businesses to attract new clientele: updating their décor and offerings, and eliminating non-English languages on signage.

As late as 2010 Vittoria, an Italian bakery, was visually an odd man out on Bedford Avenue, a relic from another time complete with linoleum floors, bagels stacked against the windows, and oversized muffins and cookies laid out on big yellow trays. Like the new cafés and bars, it was a social hub, but mainly for older adults who were Old Timers. One day at the end of the summer in 2010, Vittoria closed. Predictably, a chic café opened a few weeks later; unpredictably, that café was still Vittoria.

Vittoria has been a Bedford Avenue institution since the 1960s. Joseph, the current owner, inherited the business from his father. Watching the changes in the neighborhood, he estimated that he needed to make a change or go out of business, so he renovated. After the reopening, the walls were exposed brick, the floor was wood, and an antique scale sat on top of the counter next to an espresso machine. At the time, he planned on eventually opening a wine bar in the back room: "We're going for more of a café than a bakery—hoping to catch the younger people," he explained. I asked whether his clientele had changed since the big renovation. "Yeah, oh yeah. The regular mix have dwindled away." Joseph's attitude around this was positive; he was happy to be attracting visitors and newer residents, or, as he put it, "the cappuccino crowd."

The Northside Pharmacy was another longtime establishment at the corner of Bedford Avenue and North Seventh Street, a prime location right across from the subway entrance. The building's awning included the words "Apteka" and "Farmacia," signaling to Polish, Puerto Rican, and Dominican residents that they would be assisted by the employees. By 2013 the current owners could no longer afford the rent and a Dunkin' Donuts franchise moved in. One of the pharmacy owners, Halina, complained:

> Everybody who has to renegotiate a lease, . . . there's no way [they] can possibly stay. . . . Being an independent business owner staying in Williamsburg is really very tough. I see corporations coming. . . . It's only corporations that can afford to stay in those places. . . . It's just stun-

ning. Who would have thought this neighborhood would have gotten so expensive?

To be able to stay in the neighborhood, the pharmacists bought their own building; they couldn't afford to be on Bedford Avenue, so they moved to a nearby side street. With the move, the business became more upscale, selling high-end cosmetics in an updated storefront, a far cry from the crowded shelves and outdated fixtures of their previous location. The Polish and Spanish words for "pharmacy" are noticeably missing from the new storefront, and the pharmacy's website refers to the business as a "boutique apothecary." The business didn't lose customers because of the move, but Halina told me, "I am saying goodbye now once every three days to someone who is leaving—not just Williamsburg but Brooklyn, even New York. The rents are insane." At the same time, new customers are coming in:

> I don't know exactly where they're moving from. I think some of them are from the city [Manhattan], and I think there are a lot of people from Europe. Someone said, "Oh my god, this is just like the pharmacy we have in Paris." You definitely see less of the Polish, definitely less of the Spanish, more Americanized.

Like the pharmacy and the bakery, Ayman's corner store had also changed with the times on Bedford. Ayman is a Palestinian immigrant who had been working in Williamsburg since he came to the United States in 1994. He worked at his brother's deli, also on Bedford, until he took over the corner store in 2007. He described how his store changed to keep up with the neighborhood. According to him, Williamsburg used to be:

> warehouses, . . . factories. It was a lot of construction workers, a lot of factory workers. It wasn't so many people visiting like now, tourists from all over Europe and South America, it was just neighborhood people that, you know, that come all the time. Now it's a lot of different people.

Ayman was surprised at the prices people were willing to pay as the neighborhood gentrified. He described his inventory as shifting from "just normal products that people would buy all the time" to "organic, more organic, gluten-free, more healthy stuff, more expensive stuff." Ayman did not open a business in Williamsburg for any particular reason aside from the fact that he was already working across the street, but he would have liked to stay in the neighborhood indefinitely: "It's a great area, there are no problems here, no one will ever bother me, nice people, and I've known the neighborhood for a long time." He knew that would be almost impossible when his lease expired: "I have an old rental. It's like $7,000, but I know it can be a lot more. I have a little bit more than two years and I know I'll be out of here." Ayman's store was under new ownership by late 2017.

The corner store was a business of necessity, and in that way, it reflected the old Bedford Avenue. While it did carry expensive organic products, it also sold staples of everyday life that cost the same or less than they did in the larger, local grocery stores. Ayman opened his business as a way to provide for himself and his family. His goal was not to bring the community together, as many Bohemian businesses claimed, but his store was one of the most diverse mixing grounds of locals. The brief conversations that people had in Ayman's shop did not result in friendships, artistic collaborations, or other "community building" like the L Café or Supercore mentioned above, but it was one of the few businesses in the neighborhood where elderly Polish men, Latinx teenagers, and condo moms came into contact with each other. At some point everyone needs to buy a container of milk, whether it be organic, plant-based, or, as Ayman refers to it, "just normal."

The store owners in this section can be said to have an attachment of necessity to Williamsburg. They opened (or took over) businesses in the neighborhood because they already lived or worked in the area and retail rents were affordable. The businesses they chose to open catered to the daily needs of residents—bread, medicine, and groceries. These businesses survived through Williamsburg's initial stages of gentrification because of their ability to adapt.

Unlike the local shops that were priced out of Williamsburg, Vittoria, the Northside Pharmacy, and Ayman's corner store all shifted their aesthetics and products to attract Condo Dwellers. In all three cases, Old Timers still patronized these stores as well. The pharmacists know their established clientele by name and talk them through directions for their prescriptions. Ayman engaged customers in conversation and always seemed to know what was happening on the block. Despite Joseph's delight in the fact that he could now lure "the cappuccino crowd," his café continued to attract Old Timers as well. The symbols of gentrification—laptop users at the café or vegan treats at the corner store—do not outweigh the familiarity of the faces behind the counter for Old Timers. Unfortunately, adaptation is not a common outcome for retail establishments in Williamsburg, and Old Timers are less likely to visit the many new retail businesses in the neighborhood.

Capitalizing on Community: Entrepreneurs Attracted to the Williamsburg Identity

When this research began, many of the businesses that were created by and for the Bohemian community were petering out. While some indie art and music spaces lasted for a few years after the rezoning, much of that scene was in the process of moving to Bushwick or beyond.[22] In the early 2010s, a new generation of businesses began moving to the neighborhood, attracted by the aesthetics and reputation that the Bohemian community had cultivated.

One such business, Radish, was a prepared-foods shop that opened in May 2010 and closed in 2013. The décor was meant to evoke a nineteenth-century general store, with antique lighting fixtures, menus written on chalkboards, a coffee station set on top of a hundred-year-old stove, and goods stored in baskets along the wall. For three years the store sold house-made sodas, snacks, and takeout meals. Laura and Amy, two friends in their mid-thirties, chose Williamsburg as the location for a number of reasons. Amy already lived in the neighborhood and the rent was cheaper than anything they could get in Manhattan, but they were also searching for a place that had a sense of "community." As Laura explained it, Williamsburg had "more of a neighborhood feel. We have regulars we know their name or what they want. . . . It's a community store, very homey, where people feel like it's an extension of their kitchen." She added that because a lot of artisanal food was being produced in Williamsburg, "it's a good environment for that sort of creativity."

When asked about their customer base, Laura stated that they served "a broad cross section of the neighborhood. We're on the 'mommy network'; at lunch we have young professionals, real estate brokers, freelancers who work from home. Then at night we have commuters at dinnertime, and on the weekends, tourists." Her tally of customers described the newer inhabitants of Williamsburg but left out long-term residents and people who can't afford high-priced takeout. Laura also mentioned that her store filled a gap in the neighborhood because before opening, she would see "people coming home from work with Whole Foods bags, but they could be getting their takeout here!" In reality, there is no shortage of takeout food in Williamsburg, and the Polish bakery around the corner had been offering home-style meals to go for years. The gap that Radish filled was then more aesthetic, reflecting the new, luxurious, upper-class version of Williamsburg.

The owners of newer businesses were attracted to the new image of Williamsburg, and the wealthy clientele that come along with it. Robert, the owner of By Robert James, opened his first store in Manhattan's Lower East Side in 2007, before opening a second business on Bedford in 2012. His clothing line focuses on locally made pieces, with shirts in the $150–$200 range. When asked why he chose the Williamsburg location, he replied, "I just wanted to vend in Williamsburg. . . . I was reading some of the tea leaves maybe a little later than I should have. My realtor started pushing me to come here a while ago." After a minute, he seemed to remember his store's mission less candidly:

> One of the great, biggest tenets of this store is community. Building our own community, maintaining that, being a part of the community that we're already in, . . . especially for a neighborhood like this that has changed so much and . . . maybe the old timers kind of take an issue with the development and change. I think it's nice when everyone can kind of mingle together and remember that we're all the same.

At the time of the interview, Robert was in a temporary location, a pop-up store in a building that was about to undergo construction. He was lucky enough to find another storefront just a few blocks away, but the nature of pop-ups and the generally quick turnover of high-rent stores afford fewer chances for ties between store owners—with each other and their customers. Additionally, given the symbolic boundaries that new businesses present, the likelihood that an Old Timer or less wealthy resident enters a boutique with $200 shirts to have the chance to "mingle together" is already slim. The Williamsburg location of his store closed by 2018, decamping to another gentrifying Brooklyn neighborhood.

Among other curiosities to open on Bedford in the early 2010s was Goorin Brothers, a national hat chain founded in 1895. The store was carefully curated to resemble an early twentieth-century shop, with fedoras displayed atop antique suitcases and on shelves peppered with black-and-white photographs in vintage frames. The Goorin Brothers grand opening was the culmination of an eight-year endeavor to get a Williamsburg location. The CEO and head of stores had been scouting out spaces in Williamsburg for years before they decided on a storefront. According to the manager, Gloria, they wanted a location in the area because "even then [2005] they felt like there was an up-and-coming artist scene here. . . . They liked the bohemian feel. It was so much more laid-back than Manhattan. They wanted a shop here." While some might argue that the artist scene was already dissolving by 2005, and certainly by 2013 when the location finally opened, Williamsburg's renown as a hip destination was still meaningful as a selling point. The avant-garde reputation outlasted the actual period of time when large numbers of artists lived in the neighborhood.

Gloria acknowledged that most of the art scene had "moved out to Bushwick" by that point, as the rents had become unaffordable. The hourly employees at these businesses are also unable to afford living in the neighborhood. Gloria and many of her coworkers commuted for up to an hour each way. Their customer base is not necessarily local either: "We get a lot of people who are just coming to check out Williamsburg." Goorin Brothers moved into their storefront a few months after the previous tenant, Trojanowski Liquor, had left. The liquor store predominantly served a mix of locals and would acknowledge the neighborhood's various cultures with multilingual signage, like a chalkboard on the sidewalk with holiday greetings in English, Polish, Spanish, and Italian. While it made no claims to foster community, the liquor store was welcoming to, and reliant on, a local population. Goorin Brothers closed in 2021, as the pandemic temporarily reduced the number of visitors to New York, highlighting the precarity of businesses that fail to cater to neighborhood residents.

Imagination and Exploitation of "Community"

The newer entrepreneurs often claim that they actively seek to build or be part of the community. Laura and Amy refer to Radish as a "community store," Robert mentioned building and being part of the community where his store is located, and the Goorin Brothers' outpost was chosen because of the Bohemian community the owners were attracted to. The skyrocketing rents push out long-term and medium-term businesses that already had a familiarity with the neighborhood, as well as the Bohemians who contributed to the community that more recent businesses capitalized on. Old Timers are almost never included in the "community" that newer storeowners try to achieve, and the older stores that were able to adapt are actually more likely to be sites of interaction for residents of different class backgrounds and tenures in the neighborhood. The places of necessity—a pharmacy, a corner store, and a bakery turned café—were used by neighborhood residents regardless of class, ethnicity, or other demographics. Day-to-day interactions across these groups were more likely to occur in those spaces, if at all, but the owners made no claims toward fostering community.

The rhetoric around community at newer businesses is also in contrast to the efforts made by Bohemian-era businesses like art studios, bookstores, underground party venues, and restaurants/bars. These establishments stocked hyper-local periodicals, held events to showcase neighborhood artists and musicians, and had bulletin boards where people could advertise services like dog-walking and babysitting or post calls for new band members. The newer entrepreneurs in this chapter looked to Williamsburg to provide a "neighborhood feel" without contributing to it themselves.

In addition to independent and small-scale chains like the ones above, Williamsburg witnessed an influx of corporate and big-box interest in the 2010s. For these businesses, like J. Crew, Levi Strauss, and Sephora, the Williamsburg location doesn't always bring in enough traffic to justify the rent, but they capitalized on the existing cultural cachet of the neighborhood to reflect positively on their brand. The larger chains were aware of the stigma of being a "big-box" store in a neighborhood known for its individuality. In an attempt to be more covert, some have used alternate names like Space Ninety 8 (Urban Outfitters) and Brooklyn

Harvest Market (Key Food, a New York City grocery chain) or added unique touches—beer taps to fill growlers at the Duane Reade pharmacy chain, and a special menu of craft-brewed coffees at the Starbucks. But these nods to authenticity do not mask the fact that these corporations utilized the reputation of avant-garde culture while simultaneously contributing to its displacement as the condofication of Williamsburg progressed.

In recent years, Williamsburg's brand and reputation have shifted once again. No longer known as an artist enclave, Williamsburg has become synonymous with luxury consumption, making it an investment opportunity for high-end retail and services. In 2022 the median sale price of Williamsburg homes reached $1.28 million, with Northside median household incomes ranging from $83,000 to $156,000. The most recent additions to Williamsburg's retail landscape include stores like Showfields, "a lifestyle discovery store," clothing shop Ganni, which is described as "a state of mind more than a way of dressing," and Hotoveli, an appointment-only "avant-garde garment" boutique. In the ultimate shift from necessity to luxury, Hermés announced plans to open in 2023. It will fill a storefront in a new building, constructed in a lot that was adjacent to Tops, the grocery store that served the community for two decades but was labeled "crappy" and "grungy" by Condo Dwellers.

The Meaning of Retail

Williamsburg's transition from local community, to magnet of cool, to enclave of the wealthy has played out on the local shopping street. In the Williamsburg of the 1970s and 1980s, owners were selling necessities to the immigrant and working-class communities of the neighborhood. Historically, owners set up businesses because they had a personal connection or they noticed a missing necessity in the neighborhood. Early gentrifying business owners often cited a desire to create community, but their intentions are not necessarily inclusive of all resident groups. New business owners in the 2010s dutifully paid lip service to the "culture" and "community" of Williamsburg, but also admit to the neighborhood's popularity and, at the time, relative affordability as their motivating factors to open a business there. From the mid-2010s, an increasing number of businesses are owned by national and international high-end chains.

The aesthetics and products that are welcoming for wealthy Condo Dwellers and visitors can have the opposite effect for existing residents, even when it comes to potential benefits of retail gentrification. One touted advantage is better access to retail and services, especially well-stocked supermarkets, but even grocery stores can signal exclusion.[23] Recall Bohemian Henryk's evaluation of the new grocery store as "too fancy," which made him feel that he didn't belong there. The signals that attract wealthier residents can act as symbolic boundaries for Old Timers and even Bohemians, preventing them from making use of new amenities.

Because this type of retail shift is characteristic of gentrification globally, it is important to understand the roles that local businesses play in the symbolic changes of a gentrifying neighborhood. An aesthetic featuring exposed brick, bare wooden tables, and antique décor has become popular, even cliché, in Williamsburg and many other gentrified locales. Even the Dunkin' Donuts that replaced the pharmacy has a wood-paneled exterior and an etched wooden sign. The trend evokes nineteenth-century European bohemianism, erasing actual local history to create an "authentic" urban setting. These aesthetics harken back to a different time *and* place; Williamsburg's immigrant and manufacturing history is ignored in this strategy. The disappearance of necessity businesses includes the erasure of ethnic products and languages, leaving Old Timers without a sense of ownership over these spaces. The process is continued with the omission of their histories and cultures as the aesthetics of an imagined past saturate the neighborhood.

Identity-attached Bohemians maintain that there was "nothing" in Williamsburg when they first moved in, but the data presented here contradict that narrative. Descriptions by Old Timers and counts of local businesses show that in the past, Williamsburg's retail catered to the necessities of daily life. As shops that served the needs of older adults, poor and working-class people, and people of color disappeared from the main commercial strip, these populations had fewer reasons to be on Bedford Avenue and the surrounding area. Old Timers are then only occasionally present in the most gentrified parts of the neighborhood, making their presence noticeable and even suspicious.[24] There is a need for city governments to protect the rents of small business owners in gentrifying cities, and this must apply to purveyors of necessities. In a capitalist society, the future economic stability of former industrial neighborhoods and cities hinges on their ability to attract new residents, businesses, and visitors—but policy makers must approach this change in a way that does not exclude existing residents.

Despite the negative effects for Old Timers as Williamsburg transformed, Bohemians are the ones who expressed the most bitterness about cultural displacement around retail change. In the next chapter, we turn to residents' overall perceptions of gentrification and explore some important narratives that emerged. Retail comes up again as central to experiences of neighborhood change, including the notion that Williamsburg's branding has become too global and tourist-centered. As a result, Condo Dwellers and some Bohemians push for a return to a more local neighborhood.

5

Views of Change

Convenience and Erasure

January 2023. On my last ethnographic visit to Williamsburg, I noted that a medical clinic was moving into a building on the Northside. The clinic, associated with a New York hospital, was opening on a block that had previously been home to factories and, later, music venues within former factories. It was set to open on the ground floor of a twenty-one-story boutique hotel, bejeweled with upscale shopping and dining and capped off with the Turf Club, a rooftop bar with an Astroturf lawn. Medical services are relevant to a broader range of locals than another high-end designer shop or a bistro with carefully plated microgreens, so I optimistically viewed the soon-to-open clinic as a necessity-based addition to the neighborhood. However, as I found out later when searching for the space online, it's not really a clinic; it is Health Quarters, a venture capital–backed "healthcare consultancy platform." The website, perhaps anticipating critique, promises, "This isn't a luxury. It's care as it ought to be," and invites virtual visitors to meet its three new executives, "who bring a wealth of health care, real estate, and start-up knowledge." Indeed, these men come from health-relevant companies like the Au Bon Pain bakery chain and WeWork, a company that leases co-working spaces, but was mired in scandal in the late 2010s.

Health Quarters' Manhattan location is decorated with stylish light fixtures, luscious plants, modern couches, and trendy art. The company is essentially a lavish waiting room and an online booking platform, bringing together various health and wellness services in neighborhoods with high real estate values. Instead of a rare new business of necessity, Health Quarters appears to be a continuation of the neighborhood's commercial upscaling.

To understand the impacts of gentrification, we need to examine residents' daily experiences of neighborhood change. We must pay heed to all residents—the ones who eagerly await the opening of Health Quarters, the ones who will roll their eyes at its presence, and the ones who don't walk down that street anymore because there are no relevant businesses for them, no friends or family members left to visit on this unrecognizable block. While so much of the concern of gentrification is rightly on the residential displacement it causes, it's critical to also understand the experiences of navigating life among drastically changing demographics and landscapes. As we've seen, residents' attachment styles have impacted their participation in community organizations and local events, their perceptions of local crime, and their use of the neighborhood's retail and services. This chapter focuses on residents' perceptions of gentrification itself, and the important themes that emerge from their reactions to these changes.

Perceptions of Gentrification and Neighborhood Change

At the time of their interviews, most of the residents in this book were already familiar with the word "gentrification," and even if they didn't recognize that exact term, they knew the process and had feelings about it. Old Timers were candid when discussing gentrification and the changes that have happened in their neighborhood. Recalling the neighborhood before gentrification, they balanced the issues of city neglect and crime with memories of a vibrant community. With a necessity attachment to the neighborhood, they can do both. They fondly remember Williamsburg as a family-oriented neighborhood that satisfied their needs. Still, they felt that some of the changes that came with gentrification were positive—including improved infrastructure, parks, services, and a broader diversity of economic classes.

When asked about what had changed for the worse with gentrification, only two Old Timers complained about the noise or how crowded the neighborhood had become, though that is a common complaint among Bohemians and Condo Dwellers. For the majority of Old Timers, their main concerns with gentrification were necessity-based. First, the increasing rents not only presented a financial strain for themselves but also prevented their children from affording apartments in the neighborhood and acted as a barrier to new (im)migrant or working-class in-movers. Second, they lamented the disappearance of businesses and spaces that were affordable and relevant to their needs and desires.

Maria was beaming with nostalgia as she recounted the various organized and informal activities she participated in while growing up in Williamsburg. She acknowledged the physical markers of disinvestment in her neighborhood but maintained that it was a fine place to live. To some extent, she even enjoys the area's popularity:

> We played out front, we played in the park, we were cheerleaders, we had a lot of activities, clean fun. . . . It was good in a sense. It wasn't good when you saw the graffiti, it wasn't aesthetically pleasing, but our basic needs were here. . . . When everybody started coming over . . . from Manhattan, . . . it sort of brought this flair, this fun, this difference. . . . The fact that you see people enjoying Williamsburg's Southside, it gives me pride.

But her tone changed as she remembered Latinx social clubs that have been displaced during the course of gentrification: "Now they've converted all these social clubs into sidewalk cafés. It's disappointing because I wanted my grandbabies to experience that. . . . That really hurts because you felt like you had this sense of home and then you had it taken from you." Mike was also worried about the disappearance of social institutions due to increasing rent, and was upset at rumors that the building housing the Swinging Sixties Senior Center might be sold: "They're kicking people out. It shouldn't be like that. They're trying to get rid of this [senior citizen] center."

Mike and Renaldo, both retired factory workers, noted the increase in city services as positive aspects of change, but were skeptical that they would have improved without gentrification. As Mike stated, "Now [that] you've got people with money, the neighborhood changes. And the cops are around more, the garbage men come around more. When it was poor people, they didn't care." Renaldo added, "It's not for the people who lived here for years. When it started to change, I think the approach was, 'Let's get rid of the people that live here.'" This was a common theme in gentrifying locales. Williamsburg's Old Timers were aware that the investment that has flowed into Williamsburg was not necessarily for them but rather in response to, and to attract more, wealthy new residents.[1]

This wasn't just a refrain of older adults in Williamsburg. Younger people with a necessity attachment to the neighborhood felt similarly. Like the older residents who appreciated certain updates to infrastructure and businesses, Old Timers who grew up in the 1990s and 2000s shared that they enjoyed visiting some of the new businesses. Still, this was often tinged with remorse about long-term institutions that had closed, the local culture that had been diluted, and the precarity of their tenure in Williamsburg, given rent increases.

In his twenties, Paul liked that he could go on dates in the neighborhood and save on subway fare. He listed a few restaurants and a movie theater that he had been to, but he also saw a lot of turnover in his building, where he shared a one-bedroom apartment with his parents and sister. He worried that when his parents move back to Puerto Rico, he will not be able to afford splitting the rent with his sister. Likewise, George appreciated that friends from other neighborhoods wanted to go out in Williamsburg: "It's nice that people will come to the neighborhood now because there's some of these options. . . . That's definitely a benefit of it, having a place where people are like, 'Oh, I wanna go dine there.'" Yet he also expressed frustration at the overemphasis on consumption: "Now there's just this big focus and emphasis on nightlife, you know, big business, chain stores, and just extracting money."

In contrast to Old Timers, the early Bohemians spoke about what was lacking in pre-gentrified Williamsburg. A neighborhood resident since 1981, Carol offered an assessment of the neighborhood that reveals how invisible the long-standing populations were to newcomers: "Nobody came here. I would never say I lived in Williamsburg because people would always think I meant Virginia." According to Kristy, "In those days everybody lived in Manhattan. . . . There really wasn't anything happening." But this "nothingness" was fetishized and referred to as a "magical" quality of Williamsburg, something to be discovered. Artists and musicians especially recalled parties in abandoned warehouses, music performances at the overgrown waterfront, and a "sprinkling of artists" throughout the neighborhood. Morgan, Rob, and Henryk all remembered Williamsburg in this way: "It was really magical"; "a magical time"; "It was really beautiful scenery"—a backdrop to the adventures of their twenties.

Bohemians expressed a bitterness that the subculture that they strongly identified with has not only been eradicated through gentrification but was used by real estate developers to market the neighborhood. Owen, a Former Resident who participated in the bohemian culture, recalled a conversation he had with the co-owner of his gallery in the 1990s. Already aware of the tenuous relationship between art and neighborhood change as it had played out in Chelsea and the East Village, he wanted to avoid that dynamic in Williamsburg: "We're not gonna perpetuate the process of gentrification. How are we gonna do that? Well, we're going to create art institutions that actually reach out to the local community and bring them in in a way that the East Village never did, . . . tone it down because we don't want to gentrify." James was also explicit about the connection: "Art is a stimulus for gentrification. . . . Art causes gentrification." This was one of the most notable differences between Bohemians who stayed in Williamsburg and those who left: artists who stayed did not speak as much about their possible roles in gentrification. Having remained in the neighborhood and personally seen the processes unfold, Bohemians who still live there were more likely to place blame on private real estate interests and the city.

Compared to necessity-attached residents, those with an identity attachment were much less likely to recognize benefits to gentrification. They were also more likely to express cultural displacement and a sense of betrayal toward the condos, crowds, and corporate stores that now characterize much of Williamsburg. When asked about neighborhood change, Bohemians were quick to mention what they thought of new residents.

Morgan spoke harshly about the waterfront buildings and the people moving into them:

> It's ugly, crowded. The people are entitled and uninteresting. Everyone is concerned with how they look and status, and it makes me mad that they're able to have whatever they want in my neighborhood and the people that I care about can't stay here. And I really don't appreciate bringing in the least interesting population into my neighborhood. . . . I don't like being around them. It's a huge sense of loss.

Erin also echoed this sense of loss, remembering when most people she met in Williamsburg were artists: "It used to be, like, yes we have jobs and we're working, but we were all artists and musicians as well,

... but now I'm meeting lawyers and investment bankers." Odin, a musician, compared Williamsburg of the 1990s to that of the 2010s:

> There was an artistic community, and the environment was conducive to artmaking. And now it's transformed into an environment that's not so much about the inhabitants anymore, really full of people who can afford to pay the highest rents in New York. . . . Most of the artists have moved out because the cost of space just skyrocketed. . . . Everything's being taken over by corporate interest.

Morgan owned her building, but Odin and Erin were renters. While these Bohemians were communicating that rising rents were a significant disadvantage of gentrification, the focus was on the loss of the artist community broadly and a dislike for newer residents. Bohemians infrequently expressed concern that Old Timers would be physically displaced by increased rents.

One of the most frequent complaints that the Bohemians made about advanced gentrification is that Williamsburg has become a crowded destination. Paradoxically, given their memories of desolation and "nothingness," Bohemian residents lamented the loss of their "sleepy" or "quiet" neighborhood, something they recalled as a retreat from their jobs and social lives in Manhattan. The crowds that now congregate around the subway, fill bars and restaurants, and throng to waterfront food and music festivals are a significant drawback for Bohemians like Susan, in chapter 2, who yelled at concertgoers from her front door.

Naturally, the Condo Dwellers have a very different view of gentrification. Unless venturing to Williamsburg for dinner, a party, or other special event, the majority of Condo Dwellers did not spend a lot of time in the neighborhood in the 1990s or 2000s. A handful of new residents in this book didn't even come to the neighborhood until they were looking to buy real estate in the 2010s. Condo Dwellers described Williamsburg in the 2000s and even 2010s as lacking. The qualities that lent the neighborhood a "magical" and "bucolic" vibe to their Bohemian predecessors held no such appeal for Condo Dwellers. They depicted Williamsburg's past as dirty and dangerous, countering the Old Timer nostalgia for a rich social life as well as the memories of a creative enclave among Bohemians. On visits to Williamsburg in the late 2000s,

Caithlin felt that "there was really nothing going on" in much of the neighborhood, Ali perceived Williamsburg as "largely abandoned," and Josie found it to be "unsafe and dirty." Since Condo Dwellers perceived Williamsburg in this way, they found many benefits to gentrification, while their list of negative outcomes was much more limited. With an investment attachment and a desire to see their real estate continue to increase in value, Condo Dwellers praised gentrification for making the neighborhood beautiful, attractive to corporate investment, and above all convenient to their lifestyles.

Convenience was the most frequently cited benefit of gentrification for Condo Dwellers, coming up multiple times within one interview, and it was especially mentioned in the context of parenting. People who previously hadn't considered Williamsburg as a place to raise children felt that the infusion of luxury housing, corporate retail, and amenities helped mark Williamsburg as a place that was ideal for family life. Visiting the neighborhood in the early 2000s, Stephanie did not feel safe. When she decided to move to Brooklyn from Manhattan to raise her children, Williamsburg wasn't on her radar, but it ended up being the best neighborhood for her husband's commute, and they moved there in 2008. Reflecting on this decision, Stephanie focused on what she perceived as positive changes:

> I think the neighborhood has become more convenient for us. It used to be that you would have to go into Manhattan for everything. . . . [Gentrification] has brought more convenience into the neighborhood, in terms of the stores that are available. We have some very high-end shopping now. We just have a variety of different things that we didn't have before. With gentrification, the simple fact that there are more people living here, and probably more people with money, we've gotten things like the ferry, I would say probably we got more services.

Tina found not only the amenities convenient, but also the location: "And everything's so convenient. . . . Everyone wants to hang out here. . . . It's really convenient for everyone to meet at my place. And then if you want to go out, there's something across the street." Ella and Ashley both expressed surprise at how infrequently they leave the area: "I very rarely go to Manhattan except for working occasionally." "I haven't been into Manhattan except for three times in the past year, which is, for me, phenomenal." At first displeased with the area's retail, Sarinda now believed that "this neighborhood will become basically self-sufficient for us," something that Old Timers had felt in the past, but no longer do.

The convenience that Condo Dwellers admired revolves around the retail and amenities that were never provided for Williamsburg residents in the past, including ferry service to Manhattan, manicured waterfront parks, and maintained and well-lit sports fields. Gone are the longtime grocery stores and bodegas that were not up to investment-minded standards, replaced with boutique versions of standard New York City grocery chains, a Whole Foods, and upscale corner stores stocking small-batch kombucha and seven-dollar chocolate bars.

When asked about the negative aspects of gentrification, some investment-attached residents said they were aware that physical displacement was a problem facing Old Timers, but tempered that with the speculation that those who owned property benefited from gentrification and that Old Timers could also enjoy the neighborhood's new amenities. The city's renewed interest and investment in Williamsburg were seen as a benefit by some Old Timers, but many studies have shown that there are negative effects of gentrification even for residents who stay put—including broken social networks, increased policing, loss of representation and ownership in public spaces, and even poorer health outcomes.[2]

Other Condo Dwellers only noted that established businesses were shutting down, overlooking the fact that residents were also displaced. Milo lamented the loss of dive bars, while Caithlin was upset to have seen her favorite coffee shop and other businesses get pushed out: "The major con is that small businesses are being destroyed." Ella denied that Old Timers would miss anything: "When you talk to people who have been here forever, they don't think it was so great, it's yuppie kids who lament things." She's only half wrong. The "yuppie kids" were the ones who lamented the most, but Old Timers also missed much about a more necessity-focused Williamsburg.

One additional disadvantage that Condo Dwellers identified was that the neighborhood was becoming too crowded and touristy. They said that they appreciated Williamsburg's slower pace, referring to it as "charming" or even "village-like" compared to Manhattan, but they were disappointed that the neighborhood was starting to lose that charm by the mid-2010s. This example once again illustrates how attachment style influences perceptions of people who inhabit the same spaces simultaneously. With an investment attachment and desire for convenience, Condo Dwellers found the increased activity and media attention beneficial up to a point, while identity-attached Bohemians felt that the neighborhood had lost the village-like charm far earlier, and Old Timers simply didn't think of the neighborhood in that way.

To make meaning out of residents' differing perceptions of the same neighborhood, it is useful to turn to three themes that emerged out of these experiences of gentrification. First, Bohemians and Condo Dwellers each perceived Williamsburg as a "void," though at different points in the gentrification timeline and with different reactions to the lack of activity. A second important theme is the notion among Condo Dwellers that Williamsburg has recently become a "family-friendly" location, this in spite of the fact that there has always been a high proportion of families in the neighborhood. Finally, Condo Dwellers and Bohemians have both expressed disappointment at how Williamsburg's global recognition turned the neighborhood into a tourist destination, and desire to return the neighborhood back to a more local focus.

Filling the Void

Bohemians, Condo Dwellers, and Former Residents alike spoke of a time when "there was nothing there," "nothing was open," and there was "nothing going on." Whether referring to the 1980s, 1990s, or as late as 2010, incoming cohorts of residents felt a void in Williamsburg. In the past, Old Timers did not view the neighborhood in that way. More recently they have noted a decreasing number of businesses and institutions that are "for them," as when Lillian remarked that there was "nothing here for us" at Williamsburg Walks.

The majority of Bohemians in this book were white Americans who moved to New York after college and had initially lived in the East Village, or had planned to before rents became unsustainable due to the Village's own exploding art scene. Their perceptions of a void are at least partially informed by comparing Williamsburg to Manhattan art scenes. Bohemians found themselves in a residential, deindustrializing neighborhood with, in their view, "nothing" in it. Being in the neighborhood before certain landmarks helped legitimate Bohemians' status. The notion of being in Williamsburg when there was nothing there lent them more authenticity than those who came after them. Paired with their recollections of crime, the rhetoric of a void was integral to their identity as urban pioneers who discovered the neighborhood. This claim allowed them to express disappointment when their discoveries were no longer their own.

Carol maintained that at the time, "nothing was open.... You couldn't really shop in the neighborhood." She referred to herself as "sort of like the original gentrifier" and was upset when she began to see so many kids in Oberlin College t-shirts, her own alma mater. When her husband, Allen, moved in a few years later, he bemoaned the fact that you couldn't get the *New York Times* or the *Village Voice* in the neighborhood. They would drive to the East Village (about fifteen minutes away) for dinner or to go out on weekends. James remembers "Williamsburg 1.0 or something.... There was nothing out there. There was one gallery, then there were two.... Stores were boarded up."

By the late 1980s there were a few restaurants and galleries, as well as party and art scenes that appealed to new residents and visitors. The excitement of "discovering" the nascent scene of Williamsburg was expressed by incoming cohorts from the 1980s through the mid-2000s. Residents invoked an "explorer" motif by repeatedly using the word "discovery." Over the course of three decades, they discovered Williamsburg or some aspect of it—a restaurant, a bar, an accessible stretch of waterfront. In the 1980s Morgan was taken with both the built and natural environment: "The waterfront was phenomenal, just a magical sort of space. There was an abandoned aspect too. A lot of it really struck my imagination. It was very inspiring." Kristy discussed the excitement of "discovering" what seemed to her to be an empty neighborhood: "I don't think anyone, nobody knew about it yet, it was uncharted territory at the time.... Bedford Avenue felt almost entirely abandoned." This narrative of discovery and being the first to live in an "up-and-coming neighborhood" continued into the 2000s. According to Erin, "It wasn't a draw in that way, in 2002, it was just a place to live.... Back then it felt like we were still kind of part of somebody discovering it." Bohemians took pride in this discovery, but the underdeveloped aesthetics and unpredictability that gave Williamsburg its cool reputation were a turn-off for future Condo Dwellers who visited.

Ella used to patronize a popular Thai restaurant with her husband and children in the 1990s. She remembers thinking, "God, I would never, ever, ever consider living in Williamsburg. There's nothing there. It's dead." More than a decade later, Sarinda didn't want to move to Williamsburg from Fort Greene: "Coming from there to here felt very different. . . . It just felt a little more haphazard." Josie was not impressed with Williamsburg when she first visited in the mid-2000s, but she and her husband came back in 2010 to check out the new condos: "It felt like more of a neighborhood, like there were all these shops," which made her feel more comfortable, but "it was winter. . . . It was dark early when we'd come to see some of these condos and we were like, 'Oh god, this feels scary.' Now everything's developed, it doesn't feel scary at all." In addition to the physical environment feeling uninviting, Josie was disappointed with the lack of amenities at the time. Ashley felt similarly when she and her husband came to Williamsburg in 2010. Like early gentrifiers two decades earlier, they found themselves leaving the neighborhood at first for necessities and restaurants, but now, Ashley said, "I feel like I can find everything here. That makes us happy."

While most Condo Dwellers mentioned the "small-town feel" as a draw, they also found Williamsburg at first to be inconvenient and lacking in retail amenities that they had previously had access to. Within the next few years, dozens of big-box stores and several national bank chains opened. After these changes, the addition of ferry service to Manhattan, the creation of a new park, and several other features, Condo Dwellers used the word "convenient" most frequently when asked to describe the neighborhood.

Now that gentrification had advanced in the neighborhood, the Old Timers were the ones feeling the lack. George, a forty-something Dominican American, countered the gentrifier perceptions with his own memory of Williamsburg:

> So many great things have come out of Williamsburg, and it gets lost in this dynamic of "Oh, it was all completely crime-ridden and it was all just blight" and everything. There hasn't been a focus on maintaining some equity, some of that original character and feel, that's important. It's been

skewed completely to high-end.... It has taken away some of that quality of culture. A lot of that has been lost.... Those are some of the things that I feel sad about . . . when you look at Williamsburg now, that could have been maintained.

The notions of nothingness, vacancy, void, pioneering, and discovery are key in the progression of gentrification. In-movers utilize them to ignore and erase the long-term cultures, institutions, and residents. Geographer Neil Smith likened gentrification to colonization and expansion, asserting that "the frontier discourse serves to rationalize and legitimate a process of conquest."[3] Waves of incoming residents have perpetuated the narratives of blight, disorder, and "nothing," and these themes are reflected in media reports and the actions of city government. These claims are important for the justification of redevelopment: displacement isn't a concern if "nothing" was there before. If crime, disorder, and blight make up the bulk of what is reported and believed to be happening in a specific neighborhood, then gentrification appears to benefit everyone. Like Bohemians and Condo Dwellers, city government officials maintained that Williamsburg was blighted and had "nothing" going on through the 1990s and early 2000s, as evidenced by their multiple proposals to locate trash incinerators and power plants in the neighborhood before deciding to rezone for luxury development. This trajectory helped to set up mayor Michael Bloomberg's growth agenda for the city.[4]

A Family Neighborhood

Williamsburg's newest residents gushed about how family-oriented the neighborhood had become. In the late 2010s it gained a reputation for catering to young families, and several media outlets reported on Williamsburg's transformation into a family-friendly locale. What changed Condo Dwellers' perceptions of Williamsburg from undesirable to family-friendly? And what constitutes Condo Dwellers' understanding of a family neighborhood?

For Old Timers, Williamsburg was always a family neighborhood. Theresa remembered the Northside as "very family-oriented," and Amanda recalled that "there were so many children around." Repeating a classic New York City trope from the 1960s and 1970s, respondents maintained that neighbors looked out for each other's children. Even Rosa, who was less integrated into the neighborhood as an adult, reported that when she was a child, "everybody was like a big family" and that her elderly neighbor "would watch to see us come home from school. That was like a family looking after the kids."

Maria shared the community feeling of familial ties on the Southside as well: "Having people watching over you, because there was a sense of that, a tone of community. . . . It was like, people knew you and they could see you, they respected you, they cared for you, they watched out for each other's children." George felt lucky to have grown up surrounded by his extended family and close friends: "There's like a big support system there." Paul also describes the familial nature of the neighborhood when he was a child in the 1990s: "It was pretty cool. . . . Everyone basically knew everyone."

To necessity-attached Old Timers, Williamsburg has always been a family neighborhood with institutions and networks catering to family life, but these networks were often invisible or ignored by newcomers. While all of the Old Timers mentioned family networks or the presence of children in their descriptions of what Williamsburg used to be like, only two of the twelve Bohemians did so. Few Bohemians reported having substantial interactions with any existing residents when they arrived in the 1980s or 1990s. Since Bohemians were not embarking on parenthood themselves, children in the neighborhood and institutions like schools and daycares likely went unnoticed by this artist/student population.

When Bohemians began having children, they repeated a similar narrative that we see reflected in their memories of "the first restaurant" to open, "the first artist" to move in. They implied that they were also pioneers of parenting in Williamsburg. Carol talks about raising kids in the 1990s: "I did find the Williamsburg Nursery school; my son was the first child to be in the preschool program. That was the beginning of the Williamsburg kid stuff." Bohemians with younger children noticed more children in the neighborhood in recent years. Courtney, who had then lived in the neighborhood for about twelve years, said, "It's kind of amazing how many little children are in this neighborhood now," and Anna observed "way more people with babies than even a couple years ago."

In contrast to Bohemians, many of the Condo Dwellers had children soon after moving to Williamsburg. Parenting has therefore been an integral part of their experiences in the neighborhood. They feel that Williamsburg has only recently become a place fit to raise children. When Josie and her husband first started looking to buy an apartment, they searched in Park Slope: "Initially we were looking there because we were thinking that we wanted something that was family-friendly." After being unable to find something they liked in their price range elsewhere, the couple resigned themselves to buying in Williamsburg in 2010. By the time of her interview, four years later, she saw the neighborhood differently:

> Now it feels more family-friendly. . . . Since we moved in, so many indoor play spaces have opened up for children. . . . It feels like a family neighborhood. . . . I'm so thankful we didn't move there [Park Slope]; like, all you could be there was a parent, but here you can still be an adult and go out and have drinks with a friend but still have the family stuff.

Local media sources reference the trend as well, with one neighborhood blogger writing, "In the decade or so since I've lived in Williamsburg, the neighborhood has changed a great deal and experienced a tremendous baby boom."[5]

If we examine the proportion of children over time, the numbers tell a different story than a recent boom. Figure 5.1 shows the percentage of Williamsburg residents under five years old from pre-gentrified 1970 through condofied 2020. Using Brooklyn as a comparison, we can see that pre-gentrified Williamsburg, particularly the Southside, very much was a family neighborhood with a higher proportion of children than the borough overall. Things evened out between Williamsburg and Brooklyn by 1990, with the Southside still showing a higher proportion of youngsters. After decreasing between 1990 and 2000, the proportion of children under five has remained relatively the same through two decades of rapid gentrification, while the Southside's rate has decreased slightly. Looking at table 5.1, we can see that in terms of raw numbers, the Southside has held constant, with approximately 1,200 children under five for the past twenty-five years. In Williamsburg overall, the population of children increased by 850 during a period of advanced gentrification from 2010 to 2020, but this is more a factor of a population explosion than a baby boom specifically; there were 13,000 more residents by the time of the 2020 census.

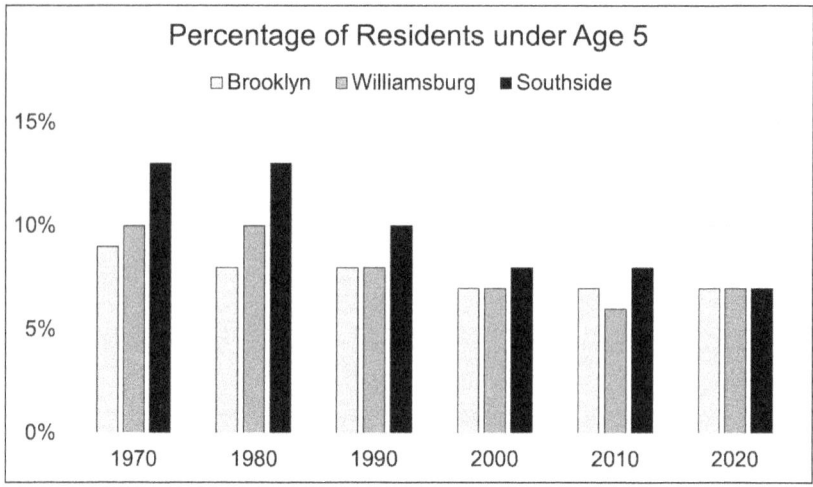

Figure 5.1. Percentage of Williamsburg residents under the age of five, compared with rates of Brooklyn and Southside only, from 1970 to 2020. Data collected from US decennial census on Social Explorer. Chart created by author.

These numbers indicate that Williamsburg has always been a family neighborhood, particularly on the Southside. The narratives that the "kid stuff" started with Bohemians or that Williamsburg is only now becoming a family neighborhood suggest that children had simply become more visible in the neighborhood through gentrification. This could be a combined effect of the following four reasons: differences in childcare practices between Old Timers and Condo Dwellers, an increase in retail and institutions geared toward children, media promotion of these changes, and the higher visibility of the children of gentrifiers among other gentrifiers.

TABLE 5.1. Total Number of Children under Five Years Old in Williamsburg and on the Southside Only, 1970–2020

	1970	1980	1990	2000	2010	2020
Williamsburg	3,070	2,064	1,897	1,667	1,755	2,741
Southside Only	2,168	1,514	1,458	1,229	1,256	1,262

Source: Data collected from US decennial census on Social Explorer. Table created by author.

First, the visibility of childcare has increased in Williamsburg. In previous decades the children of working parents would be taken care of by relatives or a neighbor who might be watching several other children, or they might attend one of the community-run preschools. Among the wealthier residents of Williamsburg, caretaking is often performed by individual nannies for each household, the new Montessori daycare, and a handful of preschool centers. The fact that nannies are dealing with one or two children gives them more mobility compared with someone watching four or five children in their home. Individual caretakers can bring children on strolls in the neighborhood or go to the park to socialize with other kids (and nannies), and they may even be performing errands for the family.[6] This more public form of child rearing, coupled with new nursery schools, makes childcare more visible, leading the average observer to infer that there are more children being cared for.

In recent years, blogs and online forums have become a popular way for Williamsburg parents to connect with each other, with some of these online groups organizing regular meetups and events. The meetups typically take place in neighborhood restaurants and cafés, where (for the most part) mothers, children, and strollers congregate. Sometimes, seating at these locations spills out onto the sidewalk, making their presence even more evident to passersby, who take note of the "baby boom" in their neighborhood. These groups have organized outdoor family movies, Halloween costume parades, Easter egg hunts, and Santa brunches. In the past, these events and parties would have occasionally been planned by community associations but also would have taken place in the context of neighborhood ethnic or religious institutions, something that Bohemians and Condo Dwellers would be far less likely to participate in. Now that these events occur in public parks and restaurants, children and family activities are more visible.

The upscaling and specialization of local institutions are a second reason why Williamsburg is considered a more family-oriented neighborhood. In the past, basics like diapers, formula, baby food, and children's clothing would have been purchased at the pharmacies, grocery stores, and clothing stores in North Brooklyn. With the simultaneous increase in wealth and specialization of neighborhood retail, children's boutiques, toy stores, and even commercial indoor play spaces have become a significant presence in the retail landscape. Symbols of parenthood have also become an important part of Williamsburg's economy, from handmade greeting cards congratulating new parents, to signs outside upmarket lingerie stores announcing that they carry nursing bras. Additionally, the continually expanding waterfront parks are a place where childhood plays out publicly. Efforts by gentrifiers to regulate public spaces aside, the waterfront parks are technically accessible to all residents. New playgrounds and water features have increasingly made the parks a draw. Throughout the day, caregivers and parents of all religious, ethnic, and class backgrounds bring children to these parks, and in warm months visitors from outside the neighborhood are also attracted to these amenities. These retail and public institutions have helped to elevate the presence of children in the neighborhood and contributed to Williamsburg's new reputation.

Media attention has also highlighted Williamsburg as a family neighborhood. Dozens of blogs and Instagram accounts by local parents have proliferated in recent years, most of them run by Condo Dweller moms. Williamsburg's kid scene has also garnered attention from larger sites like Mommy Poppins, which has neighborhood guides written by local parents in various US cities. Of the roughly seventy neighborhoods in Brooklyn, Mommy Poppins has guides for about fifteen, most of them for gentrified or gentrifying neighborhoods. The site identified "35 Best Things to Do with Kids in Williamsburg," including a self-guided tour of graffiti murals that have by now all but disappeared from the neighborhood. Once again, the *New York Times* factors in as a promoter and chronicler of local change. A few years into Williamsburg's condofication, the paper published an article entitled "Williamsburg, Toddler Town" in its real estate section. The reporter interviewed a string of new parents, coming to the conclusion that "families are discovering that Williamsburg is much more than a playground for the post-college, skinny jeans set." The folks in the article list off various child-focused amenities in the neighborhood, but are also delighted that the neighborhood's nightlife affords them opportunities to reclaim moments of feeling "sexy and single-ish." In this way, they draw a distinction between Williamsburg and other family-oriented neighborhoods, in line with Josie's comment earlier that in Park Slope, a parent was "all you could be." When the article was written, in 2011, Williamsburg was still transitioning from hipster-cool to condo-corporate and so with this came compromises. One parent remarked that their neighbors were unhappy about a bar that played loud music in the summer; the same person caught himself just short of a "get off my lawn" moment, about to antagonize neighbors who were hanging out in front of his building. In a moment that exhibits the investment-attached approach of Condo Dwellers, the compromise of the neighborhood is summed up as, "if Williamsburg could mature into a neighborhood where kids can grow, then you've won." This ignores the fact that generations of children have grown and thrived in Williamsburg even without members-only toddler play spaces.

Years later, a 2019 article, also from the *Times*' real estate section, "South Williamsburg, Brooklyn: Where Families Are Out in Force," detailed the onward march of gentrification past Grand Avenue, the dividing line between the North and Southsides. On the Southside, condo development is anchored by Domino Park on the former site of the Domino Sugar refinery. The article celebrated the park and its contribution to family life in the neighborhood, but in reality, tracts on the Southside have witnessed a decrease in population of young children as gentrification has progressed. The perceived Williamsburg baby boom is just one more example of the erasure of Williamsburg's history and longtime residents from the neighborhood's identity.

Connected to this erasure is the final reason why gentrifiers are only now labeling Williamsburg as a family neighborhood. Bohemians noticed more children in the neighborhood by the mid-2010s, which indicates that they weren't previously as aware of the children of Old Timer families. With the arrival of whiter, wealthier families into the neighborhood, Bohemians were more likely to notice the presence of children.[7] It is not the numbers of children or families that contribute to gentrifiers' perceptions of Williamsburg as a family neighborhood, but rather the increasing number of families *like their own*. Recall Anna, who mentioned above that she recently saw "way more people with babies" in her neighborhood. Anna has lived across the street from New York City public housing since 2003, and around the time she moved in, there were over eight hundred children under five years old in the census tracts near her home, comprising 7 percent of the population. By 2015 that number had dropped to 456 children under five, or 3.9 percent of all residents. The percentages dropped similarly in the three tracts that Anna would walk through between the subway, the local shopping street, and her home. The increase in babies she is noticing is actually an increasing number of children of Condo Dwellers.

Sarinda mentioned that she runs a website of parent resources in North Brooklyn: "I'm definitely more focused on the sort of young families, second-generation type people living here." In this statement, the newcomer families are the second generation, assuming that the first generation were the Bohemians. Even the owners of the indoor play space, Frolic, repeated the common falsehood. Frolic was located on the ground floor of the Edge waterfront condo building and had a membership plan that cost $1,000 a year in 2013. When the play space was closing, one owner was quoted on a parenting blog reflecting on her contribution to the Williamsburg kid scene: "We were here when Williamsburg was just becoming a neighborhood for families."[8] The space had opened in 2012. In these narratives, Old Timers, lower-income residents, and families of color go unnoticed; their histories in the neighborhood are erased as Williamsburg is just now becoming a family neighborhood in the eyes of wealthy in-movers.

Regardless of the real numbers, the common perception among Bohemians, Condo Dwellers, and even some Former Residents is that Williamsburg is *now* a neighborhood where people move to settle down in. If the neighborhood has always had a lot of children, then it is not the presence of youth that signals Williamsburg as a "family" neighborhood for Condo Dwellers, but rather the visibility of specific children and institutions. When gentrifiers say that it has *become* a family neighborhood, it is code that Williamsburg has been sufficiently upgraded to a point where wealthy people feel safe, that it is convenient for their lifestyles, that it seems more like established gentrified neighborhoods, and that there are other people there like themselves.

From Local to Global and Back Again

A final common trend in accounts of gentrification was whether or not the neighborhood felt "local"—a term that held different meanings across cohorts. For Old Timers, the neighborhood had been local in that it provided residents with daily necessities. Many had worked in local factories, and social life happened at neighborhood institutions like churches, ethnic clubs, and bars. Occasional ethnic or religious festivals may have attracted nearby co-ethnics and other outsiders, but there typically weren't many reasons for non-locals to hang out in the area until the late 1980s. Despite this, Old Timers rarely mentioned that pre-gentrified Williamsburg felt quiet or that there was a slow pace of life. A handful of them briefly commented on the "Manhattanization" of Williamsburg, but mostly in terms of the architecture. Only one Former Old Timer, Gosia, expressed disappointment about the shift away from the local: "I get a little frustrated how crowded it is and overwhelming.... Now it just feels like the city, Manhattan, where you don't know anyone."

Although most Bohemians described their early experiences in Williamsburg in terms of a void, they also relished the quiet neighborhood they moved into, at least retrospectively. Allen remembered the area in simpler times: "I just [thought] of it as kind of a backwater, very quiet." Kristy appreciated the "nice combination of quiet working class and industrial," while Erin recalled spending time on her porch: "I felt like that part of the neighborhood was a little bit relaxing. We actually had a front porch; we would hang out outside a lot.... [It was] bucolic and peaceful and quiet." At that time Williamsburg wasn't even on the radar of most New Yorkers, let alone international tourists, but Bohemians (particularly artists and musicians) were invested in making Williamsburg an attraction. They knew that an art scene would not be sustainable in a strictly local community, and some wanted fame. Whatever the motive, they had to attract outsiders to keep their galleries and performance spaces afloat. Bohemians spoke of promoting the neighborhood in the early days of gentrification, and some admitted that they wouldn't have "jazzed it up" as much if they had known what would follow. Though the artists and creatives of this cohort found Williamsburg to be almost provincial, their lifestyles, parties, concerts, and galleries attracted like-minded others from around the city, and beyond. Eventually Williamsburg became a global avant-garde destination. Years later, Carol resents that after gentrification, "I feel like I live in a city, but I used to feel like I lived in a neighborhood."

As evidenced earlier, Condo Dwellers rejected the "quieter and slower pace" even as late as the mid-2000s. They had a distaste for the "vinyl siding" houses and what they perceived as visible signs of disorder. The newest residents enjoyed the shopping that this global destination has attracted. They cheered on announcements of new restaurants opening. Yet they also claimed to have moved to Williamsburg for its "village-like" qualities, at least compared to Manhattan. Ashley and her husband decided on Williamsburg because they "wanted a little community or a village life, . . . something a little bit more charming." Caithlin described the area as a "mix between suburban and urban."

Gentrifiers consistently commented on how quaint Williamsburg was when they first moved in, whether that was in 1980 or 2011. Bohemians and Condo Dwellers obviously have different perceptions of what is charming or quaint, but the idea of a quieter, more local Williamsburg also means different things to them. For Bohemians, the appeal of slower-paced 1980s and 1990s Williamsburg was connected to their ability to participate in an identity-affirming avant-garde subculture, even if certain lifestyle desires like the *New York Times* or cafés were not yet accessible. These early gentrifiers could feel that they lived in a neighborhood within the city, surrounded by a network of other artists and like-minded creatives. Condo Dwellers moved into a very different version of Williamsburg, but still found it slower-paced than Manhattan. Their focus has been on building up amenities like schools and public parks that bolster their investments. Since real estate values are a primary concern, they are focused on the elevation of Williamsburg as a luxury residence. In order to protect this asset, some Condo Dwellers are using their political and social capital to reclaim Williamsburg's "local charm," or at least their definition of it.

By the mid-2010s, Condo Dwellers found Williamsburg to be overwhelming on the weekends. Food markets, music festivals, and dozens of popular restaurants and bars invited hordes of tourists and visitors, especially in the summer months. Attractions like these were often Condo Dwellers' reasons for visiting Williamsburg before they lived there, but as locals themselves, they now reacted negatively to the tourists who poured into their neighborhood each weekend. For those with investment attachments, the upscaling of local retail aided their end goals of living in a convenient neighborhood; crowds of tourists did not.

In recent years, tensions have emerged around Smorgasburg and Brooklyn Flea, a flea market where vendors sold crafts, antiques, vintage clothing, and other wares. These events, both owned by the same two people, rented a concrete section of waterfront park space beginning in 2011. By 2013, residents were holding meetings to complain that these events were bringing too many tourists and visitors into the park, which abuts some of Williamsburg's earliest high-rise condos. A *Brooklyn Paper* article about the conflict quoted several residents who railed against this use of public space. One resident, an equity trader and financial consultant, complained about bringing his child to the park; as a result of the events, he felt that "basically, we no longer have a park on the weekends." A second resident who weighed in was an interior designer and was listed as a real estate agent in the neighborhood. On her public-facing real estate profile, she mentioned that she "loves the local feel of the neighborhood, from the street art and street fairs to the boutiques and coffee shops," but in the article she was less generous toward the neighborhood fairs: "I try to avoid North Seventh on the weekend. . . . The influx of people is crazy."[9] Amidst complaints, the flea market eventually decamped to DUMBO, Brooklyn.[10] Smorgasburg remains in the park during the warmer months, at least for now.

It can be argued that consumption-based events that take up public space and draw thousands of people to the neighborhood each weekend are not necessarily a boon for any locals. However, when we take the outrage about these fairs into context with anecdotes from chapter 2, a trend becomes apparent. Recall that newer residents complained about who was using the newly opened McCarren Park pool and also tried to organize to prevent barbecue pits from being set up in Cooper Park. The desire to remove the food and flea markets from the waterfront parks can then be seen as more in line with actions to generally control who participates in Williamsburg's public life, and how. Although they both found Williamsburg initially lacking for their lifestyles, some Condo Dwellers and Bohemians now find the neighborhood to be too popular for their tastes. For Bohemians, this has been framed in terms of an identity attachment, a nostalgia for the version of Williamsburg they loved and a dislike of what it has become. In contrast, Condo Dwellers attempt to re-center Williamsburg around a more "local" vibe as a way of exerting control over the neighborhood's amenities.

Erasing the Past at Domino Park

These conflicting perceptions of Williamsburg bear out in one final example—the renovation of the old Domino Sugar refinery. Domino is a former site of production and industrial pollution, it is a participant in our country's exploitative history of sugar production, and it holds the memories of generations of working-class laborers.[11] Along with other factories in the area, Domino was an important source of jobs for Brooklyn's (im)migrant populations. At its height, the refinery employed 4,500 people, but that number began to shrink as the company opened plants in other cities and demand shifted toward corn syrup.[12] When the Williamsburg refinery closed in 2004, there were just over two hundred workers left. The property, including factory buildings, was purchased by a developer for $55 million in 2004, but then sold again to Two Trees management in 2012. The eleven-acre parcel is now being redeveloped into a mixed-use complex of residential, office, retail, and park space. If the Health Quarters concierge wellness service epitomizes the extent of the Northside's gentrification, then the redevelopment of the Domino Sugar refinery is carrying the torch to the Southside.

The Domino developer, Two Trees, is known for spearheading gentrification in Brooklyn's DUMBO neighborhood. The company owns more than a dozen high-end residential buildings throughout the city. Still in-progress, the Southside complex will eventually have housing, retail, and 600,000 square feet of office space. Much of the boutique office space will be housed in the former refinery building. "Rustic enough" with industrial charm, the landmark building has been celebrated as the "crown jewel" of the development.[13] In negotiations with the Community Board and then mayor Bill de Blasio, Two Trees agreed to rent a quarter of the 2,800 apartments at below-market rates and foot the bill for developing Domino Park, a public space that opened in 2018. For these concessions, the developers were allowed to build higher. The first residential tower is forty-five stories, the second-tallest in the neighborhood. The mayor hailed the deal as a win for affordable housing; in turn, the owners of Two Trees donated $100,000 to Campaign for One New York, a nonprofit that was run by the mayor.

In contrast to the sleek Health Quarters office, which will likely be used by a particular slice of Williamsburg's population, Domino Park is at least a benefit for the broader Williamsburg community. The park is filled with amenities including playgrounds, a dog run, a volleyball pitch, and even an outpost of the Billion Oyster Project—an organization that is trying to assist in cleaning up the East River by restoring the waterway's original, natural filtration system. Architectural elements of the park include gantry cranes, syrup tanks, and other artifacts from the site's industrial history. A section of playground equipment even mimics the process of refining sugar. The industrial aesthetic and vintage Domino Sugar sign add touches of authenticity that harken back to the neighborhood's history without contextualizing it among the people and cultures that continue to exist in this neighborhood.

In 2014, years before the park opened, a green construction fence was built along the perimeter of the property. As construction began, Two Trees commissioned a mural to be painted on one portion of the fence. Developer-led artwashing like this can help build goodwill with the community while distracting from the negative impacts of profit-motivated projects, like physical and cultural displacement.[14] Artwashing is part of Two Trees' gentrification playbook. The "Art and Community" section of the multibillion-dollar real estate agency's website shows off several public art projects that it has sponsored in DUMBO and Williamsburg, alongside the claim that it "believe[s] in the transformative power of art." Despite the developer's questionable motives for financing the mural, the art itself served as an important testament to life on Williamsburg's Southside, and it countered many of the narratives of gentrifiers presented in this chapter.

The Southside mural was painted by Los Muralistas, a group of local artists that formed in 1990 and are part of the community organization El Puente. The group designed and completed the project with the help of neighborhood high school students. Titled *Los Sures*, the mural expressed themes of resistance, pride, and neighborhood life. People of all ages were portrayed in both mundane and heroic poses. One part of the mural showed two young men sitting on steps with a quote: "I feel most welcome in Los Sures when I see people in front of their homes." With this quote the mural reminded onlookers that although Williamsburg did not always have waterfront parks, there was still a rich neighborhood life, and all residents have the right to continue participating in that. A second image depicted an older man holding a photo of people

Figure 5.2. *Los Sures* mural on the construction fence surrounding the old Domino Sugar factory construction site, September 2017. Photo by Erin Nekervis.

working at Domino. During our interview, Renaldo had divulged that this was him. Beneath the photo was a quote: "I miss my sugar house. I'm glad I was part of history working in the factory."

The mural was symbolic for all three of Williamsburg's attachment groups. It was centered on the necessity-attached Southside Old Timers. When others saw Williamsburg as a void, the Old Timers saw a neighborhood, not without its troubles, but nevertheless full of family, work, religious celebrations, and cultural pride. Where gentrifiers saw disorder, Old Timers felt at home with the neighborhood's public life. Generations of Old Timers grew up in Williamsburg, a neighborhood that typically had a higher proportion of children than other Brooklyn spots. These themes were depicted on the mural. Taken together with the neighborhood's history, demographics, and the accounts of Old Timers, we can see that their narratives conflict with the perceptions of gentrifiers.

Bohemians grappled with confronting their own role in gentrification. They were keenly aware that art played a role in the gentrification of Williamsburg, but they also felt used in that process. They saw how public art has been used to soften the blow of neighborhood change, with corporations and condo buildings utilizing murals and cheeky Williamsburg-specific advertisements. The *Los Sures* mural, and some of the last vestiges of industrial Williamsburg behind it, reminded Bohemians of how their identity as artists and the art they produced were both used to sell the neighborhood. At a time when Condo Dwellers viewed Williamsburg as dilapidated and dangerous, Bohemians found excitement and inspiration. When construction is complete, the industrial building that Old Timers worked in and Bohemians romanticized will be repackaged as sanitized authenticity for Condo Dwellers and tech companies looking to rent unique office space.

Finally, for those with an investment attachment to Williamsburg, the mural was representative of what did and did not fit with the direction they wanted the neighborhood to go in. Condo Dweller attempts to make Williamsburg more "local" were indicative of their attempt to exert control over public spaces. A temporary, tokenized mural of

Figure 5.3. Part of *Los Sures* mural featuring Renaldo, a worker at the Domino Sugar factory, September 2017. Author's photo.

Puerto Rican and Dominican cultures was fine, but those same folks hanging out at the McCarren Park pool or barbecuing in Cooper Park were sources of tension. The renovated factory building was authentic, while the grocery store that factory workers shopped at was grimy. Where Condo Dwellers saw convenience and progress in Williamsburg's new amenities, Old Timers missed their own institutions and sometimes felt excluded or unsure about navigating newer ones. While locals selling horchata or empanadas during Williamsburg Walks were viewed as problematic, a taqueria owned by a millionaire was welcomed in Domino Park.

That taqueria, Tacocina, is the park's only food vendor, installed by Two Trees and granted a ten-year lease. The owner, Danny Meyer, is the restauranteur behind Shake Shack, a burger chain that has outposts around the United States, Asia, the United Kingdom, and the Middle East. A reporter from the food blog *Eater* gave Tacocina a poor review and in an interview asked the management company why it did not tap a local Southside food vendor instead. A representative from Two Trees responded that the developers "engaged in outreach to the Latino community during the staffing process for Tacocina."[15] Existing residents were deemed adequate for lower-wage, service industry jobs but not as entrepreneurs for the park's restaurant.

Gentrifiers said that they preferred a more local version of Williamsburg, but much of the existing local community was excluded from that calculation. Instead, "local" meant a neighborhood for themselves, one where they set the norms for public spaces, one with conveniences and amenities but without tourists and crowds. For the investment-attached developers and Condo Dwellers, the *Los Sures* mural served its purpose as a veneer of appreciation for the local culture while the neighborhood rapidly transformed. This testament to life on the Southside was not taken down at once but, perhaps more symbolically, it was slowly stripped away as a luxury building rose behind it. Renaldo's identity as a factory worker has now been erased from the neighborhood twice.

6

The Myths of Gentrification

What Attachment Style Can Tell Us

The debate around gentrification's benefits and disadvantages began shortly after the term first came into use in the 1960s. Urban scholars identified integration and social mixing as potential benefits in the 1970s and 1980s. Those notions have been broadly criticized by later research, but are still widely promoted in policy and the press.[1] Arguments have been made around gains for local economies and improvement of neighborhood amenities, with proponents pointing to initially low displacement rates to label dissenters as reactionary. At the turn of the twenty-first century, the *Howard Law Journal* published a widely cited, if critiqued, article entitled "Two Cheers for Gentrification" in which legal scholar J. Peter Byrne outlined economic, political, and social benefits of gentrification that in his view "substantially outweigh[ed]" negative impacts.[2] Fifteen years later, when gentrification had spread further and wide-ranging negative impacts were clear, the *Economist* magazine published "In Praise of Gentrification," extolling the virtues of a wrongfully demonized process that is benevolently restoring the ills of disinvestment, segregation policies, and white flight.[3] The arguments set forth in pro-gentrification pieces like these are parroted in urban "revitalization" schemes that are used to reshape neighborhoods around the world. In light of this ongoing myth making by city government, media, and pockets of scholarship, this chapter explores claims about gentrification's merits, using final examples from residents' attachments in Williamsburg.

A Note about Attachment Style

The aim of this book was to make sense of conflicting perceptions and experiences of daily life by considering residents' neighborhood attachment styles. Length of tenure in a neighborhood has long been a primary category used to understand experiences of gentrification. As documented in the introduction, length of tenure can influence various aspects of neighborhood life, including feelings of connectedness or cohesion. Similarly, an individual's race, ethnicity, (im)migration status, socioeconomic standing, and even whether they rent or own their housing will fundamentally shape their experiences of daily life at the neighborhood level and, of course, beyond. While these factors can all have an impact, grouping individuals along these categories sometimes obscures important nuances for experiences of gentrification. Attachment style allows us to analyze how an individual's relationship to the physical, cultural, and social aspects of a place mediate their daily experiences of neighborhood life.

The necessity-attached have generally lived in Williamsburg the longest, although there are many Old Timers who arrived or were born there well after the first Bohemians arrived. The residents of Williamsburg struggle with wide-ranging effects and pressures of gentrification, including the threat of physical displacement, the unaffordability of daily necessities, the breakdown of social networks, and the displacement of local institutions. Old Timers tended to be more vulnerable to these consequences, but Bohemians were the ones who expressed the most bitterness about how Williamsburg had changed.

For the necessity-attached, Williamsburg was a place they moved to because of work, family connections, or a supportive (im)migrant network. While these are parts of their identities, their attachment to Williamsburg wasn't unique to the neighborhood itself. They could have just as rationally moved to other New York neighborhoods with working-class and (im)migrant populations, like Greenpoint, Ridgewood, Washington Heights, Harlem, or the Lower East Side, and many of their co-ethnics did move to these places instead. Their necessity attachment didn't prevent them from being critical of the impacts of gentrification, but it did make it easier for them to identify some advantages.

With an identity attachment to Williamsburg, Bohemians expressed the most discontent with gentrification. The idea of Williamsburg, or what it used to be, loomed large in their personal identities. Whether they created art, played music, partied in abandoned factories, or lived in lofts, these experiences were often specific to Williamsburg's avant-garde scene. Parts of their own identities were tied to a particular iteration of the neighborhood that no longer exists. As the neighborhood was stripped of its bohemian flourishes, identity-attached residents lost their symbolic ownership and felt that their own cultural contributions were exploited to market Williamsburg to investment-minded in-movers. As a result, Bohemians were much less likely to acknowledge any benefits coming from gentrification, almost exclusively expressing disappointment about neighborhood changes.

The distinction between the perceptions of necessity-attached residents and those of identity-attached residents is important to our understanding of the impacts of gentrification. If we assume that longer tenure causes more distaste for gentrification, a myth on its own, then we are at risk of ignoring the aspects of change that are significant to different groups of residents, overlooking their desires for balanced neighborhood improvements. Indeed, some Bohemians had been in the neighborhood longer than Old Timers, or moved to Williamsburg before some of the necessity-attached residents were even born. Instead of relying on generalizations, those who work to shape the futures of urban neighborhoods need to be in communication with existing populations. The following sections take attachment style into account while considering four myths that planners, scholars, city government officials, and real estate developers have promoted as positive aspects of gentrification. The supposed benefits—safer neighborhoods, improved amenities, benefits to the local economy, and increased diversity and integration—are appealing but inaccurate justifications to utilize public funds to support private interests via state-led gentrification.

Unpacking the Myths of Gentrification

MYTH 1: GENTRIFICATION MAKES NEIGHBORHOODS SAFER. As discussed in chapter 3, the connection between gentrification and crime is complicated. There is no conclusive evidence that gentrification decreases crime, and certain crimes become more prevalent as a neighborhood gentrifies. Despite the murky relationship, the notion that lower crime rates follow development is often assumed in state-led efforts. An influx of new residents and investment can cause neighborhood norms to change, demands for surveillance to increase, and more frequent 311 calls and police presence that can lead to harassment of existing residents. In these ways, gentrification can make neighborhoods less safe for some. I argue that instead of making places safer, the narratives of gentrification act to destigmatize neighborhoods, recasting them as desirable for wealthier residents.

As gentrification progressed in Williamsburg, neighbors perceived conditions differently, influenced by their attachment styles. Old Timers and Bohemians witnessed a time of relatively high crime rates in Williamsburg. While Old Timers acknowledged that the neighborhood had crime, they felt mostly insulated from the danger through family networks and religious and social institutions. Old Timers may have even benefited from certain criminal activities that provided protection or resources in a neglected neighborhood. In contrast, the impression that Williamsburg was dangerous served identity-attached Bohemians in multiple ways. To them, life in Williamsburg was unpredictable and exciting. Respondents took pride in the fact that friends and family thought Williamsburg was gritty. The blighted aesthetics held meaning for Bohemians, who found that it added authenticity to their identities as artists in an urban landscape, a space that was dangerous enough for adventure but not threatening enough to dissuade them from living there.

By the early 2000s, all three resident groups were present to observe graffiti, abandoned factories, and outdated housing stock. Old Timers felt that the neighborhood had gotten safer, while Bohemians still found corners of grit and edge. The aesthetics that Bohemians found inspirational did not hold any romantic value for Condo Dwellers. To them, Williamsburg was a place that could be cool to go to for a party, concert, or dinner, but they perceived it as dirty, unsafe, and empty as late as 2010. With an investment attachment to the neighborhood, Condo Dwellers focused on their perception of how it has improved since.

Crime rates, especially for violent crimes, dropped throughout New York in gentrified and non-gentrified neighborhoods alike through the 1990s. Williamsburg was already becoming a safer place before the new investment. However, the neighborhood didn't feel safe to Condo Dwellers until the appearance of expensive housing and corporate businesses. For these investment-attached newcomers, gentrification was viewed as a process that increased neighborhood safety.

In this book, residents with an identity or investment attachment to the neighborhood were more likely to sensationalize crime and danger at the local level, a narrative that alternately serves the "urban pioneer" trope and the justification for gentrification. When Williamsburg was viewed by outsiders as a dangerous, crime-ridden area, it was devalued; the stigmatization was a dominant narrative about the neighborhood reflected in news and city government's plans to build municipal services like waste transfer and recycling on the waterfront. The entrance of gentrifiers changed the reputation of Williamsburg. Despite the fact that Williamsburg was home to concentrations of several large immigrant communities with their own ethnic and religious festivals, it was not worth reporting the neighborhood's cultural accomplishments before the Bohemians arrived. Later Williamsburg became known as a family-friendly neighborhood, after Condo Dweller families moved in, even though there was a high population of children and families in Williamsburg in the 1970s, 1980s, and 1990s.

Gentrifier and media accounts of Williamsburg heightened the presence of disorder pre-gentrification, and then celebrated the neighborhood's emergence first as a cultural destination, and later as a convenient and family-friendly neighborhood. When we consider these personal stories alongside media representation and the actions of a city that devalued the neighborhood, we can see that an agenda of gentrification has been promoted while long-existing neighborhood life and populations have been erased from the story. This rhetoric acted to destigmatize Williamsburg as it began to conform to middle- and upper-class norms, contributing to the advancement of gentrification. Beyond physical displacement, areas at risk for gentrification are also at risk of a process of cultural displacement and surveillance that erases or minimizes existing experiences as norms shift to accommodate investment-attached individuals, corporations, and real estate developers.

MYTH 2: EXISTING RESIDENTS BENEFIT FROM IMPROVED AMENITIES. As Old Timers readily identified, gentrification can bring a plethora of new amenities to a neighborhood. Williamsburg now has more park space, medical services, and municipal attention than it did two or three decades ago. The presence of parks, transit, retail, and a diversity of institutions within a walkable distance to home contributes to an individual's sense of living in a "complete neighborhood" that serves daily needs with opportunities for recreation and socializing.[4] On the surface, the upgrades and additions of these amenities appear to be unmitigated improvements stemming from reinvestment, but only if everyone has equal access to them. There are three reasons why residents of a gentrifying neighborhood might not have access to new amenities or may choose not to utilize them.[5]

First, neighborhood amenities will always vary in relevance for locals based on their lifestyles, age, and family composition. These are benign reasons that people would avoid or not use neighborhood institutions: for example, a child-free couple will not make use of a daycare center; outside of volunteering, a thirty-something is unlikely to access a community center's older adult care program. While not necessarily relevant to them personally, the diversity of neighborhood services and amenities can still contribute to their sense of living in a complete neighborhood that responds to the needs of all residents. In this case, there is nothing preventing individuals from accessing these, aside from their own needs, preferences, and life choices.

Ideally a lack of desire or need would be the only reason an individual would not access a local amenity, yet in neighborhoods experiencing conflicts like gentrification, there are additional barriers to utilizing resources. A second reason individuals may not take advantage of new amenities is a sense that they do not belong in a space. Feelings of cultural displacement are well documented in the urban gentrification literature, but it has increasingly been identified as an issue by urban institutes, think tanks, and even the US Department of Housing and Urban Development.[6] In the context of changes to a neighborhood's amenities, cultural displacement can make existing residents feel excluded from these new spaces. In Williamsburg, necessity-attached residents reported appreciating improvements to municipal services or public space like transit, libraries, and parks, but their appreciation is tinged with a knowledge that the improvement was introduced into the neighborhood only after the in-movement of newcomers. While they may benefit from the improvement, they are also aware that it was not "for" them. As neighborhood spaces become upscaled or symbolically owned by certain groups, others may feel hesitation or discomfort. The change in aesthetics, the signaling of ownership, the feelings of exclusion instead of belonging all deflate how beneficial these new amenities can be for existing residents. For example, not everyone will feel comfortable in the upscale waiting room of Health Quarters, the boutique clinic described in chapter 5, lessening its impact as a beneficial source of health care in the neighborhood. Feeling that improvements are not for you or that you do not belong in the upgraded spaces can diminish feelings of connectedness, especially when coupled with pressures around physical displacement or the social isolation that arises when longtime neighbors, friends, and family members have been physically displaced from the neighborhood.[7]

A third reason why some residents may not access or utilize neighborhood amenities is that they are actively excluded. This dynamic is of course not just limited to areas that are gentrifying. Dominant groups leverage power to enforce social norms or exert control in all types of neighborhoods. Recall from chapter 2 that Old Timers exercised their own power over public space by petitioning the city to close the McCarren Park pool in 1984. Today, investment-attached Condo Dwellers pressure local politicians and community organizations in attempts to enact their own norms. As discussed in previous chapters, they have mobilized to have concerts and food festivals exiled from the waterfront, pushed back on barbecue pits in a public park, and wrung their hands over the presence of non-white teenagers at the local pool. These exclusionary actions challenged the rights of some residents to participate in the neighborhood.

Residents of different socioeconomic, cultural, and generational backgrounds and attachment styles might have different ideas about the norms of public life. In gentrifying neighborhoods, this manifests as noise complaints, new rules posted in parks, or a suspicion of neighbors who engage in the sidewalk life of playing dominoes or chatting on stoops.[8] These examples all reflect the desire of newcomers to impose their own social norms and control public spaces, resulting in minimized use by existing residents. While new amenities like parks, pools, and improved services are often named as positive contributions of gentrification, they are not necessarily accessible and welcoming to all residents and can instead invite exclusionary and even harmful interactions.

MYTH 3: GENTRIFICATION BENEFITS THE LOCAL ECONOMY. Investment associated with gentrification typically brings more businesses into a neighborhood. Pro-development policies argue that in addition to increased retail, existing residents in a gentrifying neighborhood also benefit from more employment opportunities.[9] Among his cheers for gentrification, J. Peter Byrne argued that the in-movement of middle-class and wealthier newcomers would improve the local economy in three ways. First, existing residents will find employment in new businesses that crop up to serve newcomers; second, existing residents can take advantage of the new businesses appearing in the neighborhood; and finally, long-term retail will "welcome newcomers with money to spend."[10] The assumptions made in these arguments are that existing residents will benefit from new retail, that existing retail will benefit from new residents, and that a growing retail and service sector will provide jobs for locals. These vague promises persist, but they are not reflected in the experiences of residents in Williamsburg or other gentrifying places.

Does gentrification create jobs? According to decades' worth of academic literature, middle-class jobs, especially in production, decrease during the process of gentrification.[11] The jobs that are created by incoming new retail are more likely to be lower-wage positions. While some of these jobs will be filled by local residents, those who are subject to market-rate housing will not be able to pay their increasing rent or property taxes with minimum-wage service and retail sector jobs. Instead, employees in these jobs will end up commuting from far-off neighborhoods where they may still be able to afford rent, split among several roommates or family members, just like the manager of Goorin Brothers hats from chapter 4.

Do existing businesses benefit from new residents? Occasionally long-term businesses, particularly ones serving ethnic food, gain notoriety and may benefit financially from gentrification. Others might manage to hang on for a while by providing a necessity that serves a broad range of customers, such as a hardware store in a neighborhood that has not yet attracted a Home Depot, or a bodega that begins to sell organic products before a health food store opens. Still other businesses successfully adapt, like some of the long-term businesses discussed in chapter 4 that were able to update their products and aesthetics to catch a new clientele without alienating necessity-attached customers. But these were the exception, not the rule. Whether or not existing businesses welcome new residents says nothing about the likelihood that newcomers will patronize existing businesses. In the case of Williamsburg, we've seen that many early gentrifiers found the local retail lacking and would commute to Manhattan for some goods and services. Investment-attached residents who moved in during Williamsburg's state-led condofication found the existing grocers "grimy" and "gross," preferring to order goods online until stores like Urban Harvest or Whole Foods opened. This only served to strangle the existing retail that was already struggling with rent increases.

Aesthetics prevented investment-attached gentrifiers from patronizing local grocery stores, contributing to their dissolution, but other local businesses have been more actively protested by gentrifiers. As early as 2012, newcomers in the slower-to-change southeastern corner of the neighborhood rallied against two Puerto Rican music stores—San German Records and Johnny Albino Music Center—that had each been on the street for nearly half a century. Documented in an article by *DNA Info*, a New York-based digital news magazine, gentrifiers had filed complaints with 311 and the Community Board, claiming that the music coming from the stores was a violation. These grievances resulted in visits from the police and eventually fines for the business owners, who had not previously had this issue. In these examples, investment-attached newcomers with differing social norms either refused to patronize existing businesses or actively objected to their presence. The argument that long-term retail will benefit from an influx of new residents is at best flawed.

Finally, is it true that existing residents benefit from new retail? Old Timers did not report having trouble obtaining necessities in Williamsburg before gentrification, and they also identified businesses and institutions for recreation. At the same time, Bohemians interpreted these conditions as a void because they were not as concerned with necessities. They frequently repeated some variation of "There was nothing there." By the early 2000s, the neighborhood was dotted with Bohemian-focused businesses—quirky coffee shops, dive bars, thrift stores, and art and music venues, alongside locally owned bakeries, butchers, pharmacies, hardware stores, groceries, and pet shops. Advanced gentrification has certainly mushroomed Williamsburg's retail scene in the past decade, to include upscale dining, chain stores, and international luxury brands, but the number and variety of businesses do not speak to their appeal to a diverse range of residents. The identity-attached and necessity-attached alike said that they experienced discomfort in some of the newer stores, and they found fewer businesses catering to their needs and desires.

Businesses oriented toward necessity and Bohemian identity are now few in number in the wealthiest corner, and the retail gentrification has been steadily increasing in less gentrified pockets as well. Some of the older businesses did more than just provide necessities. Ethnic businesses in Williamsburg have stocked newspapers in Polish, Spanish, and Italian, and conducted business in these languages too. Bohemians and Old Timers have lost businesses that were relevant to them.[12]

The shift from necessity to luxury has also impacted residents' navigation through the neighborhood, further solidifying who does and does not "belong" in gentrifying spaces. The closure of the Northside's Social Security office stands out as an example. The branch served primarily lower-income and older adult residents who needed various forms of assistance. This important neighborhood amenity disappeared after the one-story building was purchased for $4.5 million in 2012. The storefront has been vacant since 2013, aside from briefly being occupied by the Dream Machine, an immersive exhibit referred to as an "Instagram playground" because of its popularity for selfies and social media posts. The building has changed hands a few times, but one developer attempted to attract retail businesses with the following description: "Positioned adjacent to the new Hoxton Hotel, with 180 rooms, 93 N. 9th Street will be exposed to many locals and tourists drawn to all the hotel has to offer including three in-house restaurants." They even provided an artist's rendering to help future retailers imagine who will be on the street. Two dozen people are pictured walking on the block; none of them are families with children, older adults, or folks using any kind of mobility assistance. The intended clientele are clearly the guests of the hotel and Williamsburg residents who can afford, and desire, to eat in the hotel's upscale restaurants. Missing from this calculation are the residents who previously would have navigated their way to the Social Security office, to the animal hospital that used to be next door, or to work at the various light manufacturing businesses around the corner that were open through the 2000s. The replacement of these institutions of work and necessity changes who uses the street. As discussed in chapter 4, changing retail can shift residents' paths of movement through their neighborhoods. The danger inherent in this is that when they do appear in public spaces, their presence is viewed suspiciously.

Supporters of gentrification promise that investment will bring benefits to the local economy for existing residents and businesses. Instead, these state-led efforts can lead to lower-paid, retail sector jobs that create a further socioeconomic polarization between locals. Existing businesses can be simultaneously burdened by increasing rent and a shrinking customer base and are sometimes vulnerable to increased surveillance as investment-attached gentrifiers come to dominate neighborhood norms. Finally, retail gentrification results in fewer relevant businesses for necessity- and even identity-attached residents, leading to their further isolation and lack of belonging in the neighborhood.

MYTH 4: GENTRIFICATION INCREASES DIVERSITY AND INTEGRATION ALONG RACIAL AND CLASS LINES. While there is evidence that gentrification has increased racial and ethnic diversity in urban neighborhoods, the benefits to merely increasing these are debatable and are sometimes reflective of displacement processes.[13] The benefits of economic diversity could be more straightforward as middle-class tax bases might improve neighborhood infrastructure and institutions, but tax breaks and various loopholes decrease these benefits. The underlying and insulting assumption inherent in these arguments is that the mere presence of white, wealthier, or more highly educated residents will improve neighborhoods. Does the diversity that comes with gentrification benefit existing residents, and does this lead to meaningful integration?

Existing literature has found that the integrative impacts of gentrification are varied in their results. In a review of gentrification and integration in the context of the Fair Housing Act, law professor Olatunde C. A. Johnson outlined the ways in which gentrifiers with economic, political, or social capital *could* improve neighborhoods by bolstering public schools, sustaining local business, and advocating around parks and other amenities.[14] Johnson argues that, theoretically, compared with integration programs that move people from cities to suburbs, the in-movement of wealth to urban neighborhoods via gentrification has the potential to benefit existing residents without displacing them, although she acknowledges that these are not typical outcomes.[15] In his pro-gentrification piece, J. Peter Byrne argued that the process "is good on balance" for existing residents in terms of economic, social, and political outcomes, but like the more critical Johnson, he provides examples that are mostly hypothetical and are not supported in the empirical literature.

The supposed boon of tax revenue in gentrifying or "economically integrating" neighborhoods does not always pan out. In New York the 421-a tax abatement program incentivized developers to build more housing, requiring a percentage of it to be affordable. The affordable housing, if it is built, lags far behind the market rent housing, leaving plenty of time for existing residents to be displaced while waiting for the few units of affordable housing that may never come. Additionally, the abatement costs New York City $1.77 billion annually in missed tax revenue that could be used to make much-needed improvements to infrastructure.[16] While Williamsburg has seen public investment to transit and private investment to public amenities like pools and parks, these have not been direct improvements from property tax, and as mentioned above can be problematic in their own ways.

Public schools are one commonly named beneficiary of gentrification, the assumption being that the increased economic and racial diversity improves educational experiences for all students. Yet a study of schools in New York City indicated that wealthier parents in lower-income neighborhoods are the most likely to exercise school choice, sending their children to schools beyond the ones they are zoned for.[17] The reality is that the schools may not immediately reap the benefits of a wealthier tax base, and they don't necessarily see a marked increase in racial or class diversity among students. If integration means anything more than spatial proximity, there is little evidence that it occurs in gentrifying neighborhoods.

As Williamsburg gentrified, residents of various ethnicities, incomes, and ages have come to simultaneously occupy the same public spaces, transit hubs, and even some businesses. Yet when asked about their social circles and what they did for recreation in the neighborhood, the residents in this book did not speak of meaningful interactions across attachment styles or more traditional categories like tenure, class, ethnic, or racial lines. Early gentrifying Bohemians (including those who no longer live in the neighborhood) were the only ones who mentioned attempts to bridge gaps between Old Timers and themselves. At the end of chapter 2, Morgan detailed an Old Timer block party that, in her recollection, welcomed participation from in-moving Bohemians. That collaboration quickly faltered when artists tried to co-opt the block party for their own identity-attached goals of increasing Williamsburg's reputation as an art scene. Former Resident and artist Owen recalled a time when he was optimistic that the artist class was making meaningful connections in the community:

> So yeah, we did have this exhibition of this Polish guy and he did his paintings and he . . . saw it strictly as an opportunity to show some paintings in his neighborhood and sell some. We thought, "This is great, we're breaking through!" Well, not really, because there was no desire to foster a dialogue. It was just like, you're here and this is awkward.

In both cases, necessity or identity attachments created conflicting expectations for these interactions. Out of place in these respective contexts, Bohemians expected to utilize a community event for identity purposes and a Polish artist aimed to benefit financially without forging any deeper connections, a necessity approach in an identity-focused space. These anecdotes describe a neighborhood dynamic where there were moments of overlap or outreach, but also where an individual's attachment style and understanding of the neighborhood got in the way of genuine connection. In the picture painted by Bohemians and Old Timers, inter-cultural and inter-attachment encounters occurred, but for the most part they were brief and superficial.

As discussed in chapter 2, investment-attached Condo Dwellers have occasionally worked with identity-attached residents on events or issues where existing neighborhood organizations have been useful. When it comes to Old Timers, there was no mention of sustained interaction from either side. In her account of gentrification in Massachusetts and Chicago, Japonica Brown-Saracino identified some newcomers as "social preservationists" who viewed old-timers as contributing to authentic experiences of neighborhood life, and who therefore work to limit the displacement of certain existing residents.[18] In Williamsburg, the presence of Old Timers does not afford authenticity for the investment-attached. Several high-end businesses and residences in the neighborhood take on an industrial aesthetic—with exposed brick, iron accents, and Edison bulbs. Sometimes former churches or factories are redeveloped into upscale housing like the Gretsch building, a former instrument factory, and the Austin Nichols House, previously Austin, Nichols and Company grocery wholesalers, or Spire loft, which dropped the church's name but retained the vaulted ceilings and stained-glass windows. What is being preserved through this aesthetic is a romanticized version of Williamsburg's industrial, ethnic, and working-class past, but carefully curated as history, with the existing remnants of that culture increasingly removed from public spaces.

Instead of increasing meaningful diversity, integration, or cross-cultural relationships, gentrification contributes to the homogenization of urban neighborhoods and the cultural displacement of existing residents. Rather than fostering integration, the first-wave cultural gentrification reinvented the neighborhood into one that was symbolically owned by artists. With state-led gentrification, not only have the Polish, Puerto Rican, Dominican, and Italian cultural influences been muted, but the avant-garde artistic culture of the neighborhood has also disappeared.[19] Neither the cultural gentrification nor the state-led condofication has fostered an environment where different groups of individuals interact and are influenced by each other. At best, there has been proximity without familiarity; at worst, the proximity has been antagonistic.

A Rising Tide?

The overarching theme of these four myths of gentrification is that the process is a rising tide that lifts all boats, but instead of uplifting neighborhoods and residents, development is carried out in an uneven way. There are many other challenges impacting cities aside from gentrification. Some people sarcastically or perhaps earnestly "wish" for gentrification in neighborhoods that continue to suffer from disinvestment or high crime rates. The insult with this type of change is that if a place does gentrify—if more investment flows into a neighborhood, if a diverse amount of retail, parks, and other amenities are built—it is not for the benefit of existing residents. If they can no longer afford to pay rent or property taxes, then they no longer have access to daily use of these amenities; if they manage to remain in the neighborhood, they can

Figure 6.1. Anti-gentrification posters on a Southside construction site, March 2018. Author's photo.

face cultural displacement and increased surveillance. They may benefit from some aspects of reinvestment and revitalization, but as the norms change, they may find their presence increasingly unwelcomed. As neighborhoods come to be symbolically owned by groups with different attachment styles, the neighborhood begins to function differently for existing residents.

Through state-led gentrification, city policy courts developers with incentives that fail to prioritize community needs. The affordable rental "kickbacks" to the community are Band-Aids on a housing crisis. Sometimes the rent on "affordable" housing is well out of reach for low-income and even middle-class residents, and the need far exceeds supply—87,000 applications were submitted for 104 units in one of the new Domino buildings. Luxury condos are proposed by developers and approved by the City Council without thoughtful consideration of the ripple effects they will have. A recent development in the eastern portion of Williamsburg will have 186 units; reportedly a third of them will be affordable, though how affordable we do not know. To make space for the building, developers demolished a supermarket. Remaining grocery stores are at least half a mile away, a distance that is inconvenient for many but especially difficult for older adults, people with physical disabilities, and families with small children who will need to accompany them on the walk. Dissent in the form of graffiti soon appeared on the construction fence surrounding the lot: "Luxury isn't cool, it's violence." In this view, state-led gentrification finds its place as just the newest planned aggression toward poor, non-white, and immigrant populations following redlining, urban renewal, disinvestment, stop and frisk, and other policies that have failed urban citizens.

Gentrification brings increased rents, it replaces necessity businesses, it decreases belonging while increasing surveillance, and homogenizes neighborhoods while displacing local cultures. Following decades of segregation and austerity, improved infrastructure and amenities are rarely distributed equally in gentrifying locales.[20] The most historically and systemically disadvantaged residents will have less access to any proposed benefits. When it comes to the rising tide of gentrification, not everyone is in a boat. For many vulnerable residents, the forces of rapid change are more of an encroaching flood.

Conclusion

Williamsburg's Global Reach: Lessons Learned?

In 2013 the pop culture blog *Gawker* asked readers to name the "Williamsburgs" of their own cities. The website's description laid bare what Williamsburg was, and what it was not: "What is your city's Williamsburg? What's its hippest—or formerly hippest—or sometimes just youngest—neighborhood, the one with the art galleries and the boutiques and the lines for brunch?" It published the results a few months later, with submissions including the usual suspects, neighborhoods in Portland, Berlin, and Melbourne, but also the Williamsburgs of Budapest, Krakow, Cape Town, Saskatoon, and Lincoln, Nebraska. Three years later, the Where Is Williamsburg? app identified "Williamsburgs" in cities around the world and asked users for feedback on its accuracy; the choices were "agree," "disagree," and "meh." A description of the app assures users, "Built on data curated by other people exactly like you, this app will ensure that you are never too far from home." The brand of Williamsburg proliferated around the world in the 2010s. At the same time, the reach of gentrification has continued to expand into increasingly peripheral neighborhoods. Two examples of state-supported gentrification provide insight into how the spread of "Williamsburgs" leads to the reproduction of urban inequality.

The Union Market district of Washington, DC, is too new to have been labeled a "Williamsburg of DC" in 2013. While *Gawker* readers had identified H Street as the Williamsburg of DC, it had clearly moved nearly a decade later. One review of the Union Market district on Trip Advisor starts with "If you miss Brooklyn and you are in DC . . ." A skyline of high-rise, amenity-filled buildings has risen in a space that was mostly warehouses, distributors, and parking lots as late as 2019. By the time I visited in April 2022, it had all the typical trappings of the state-led gentrification playbook: newly constructed housing, upscale eateries, small-batch distilleries, and an industrial-aesthetic event space in a former auto body shop. The neighborhood even featured a handful of Williamsburg-based businesses, including an ice cream shop that got its start with a truck on Bedford Avenue in the 2000s and a sister restaurant of a steak house that borders the Southside. There were also several upscale national and international chains that one sees in Williamsburg, including Blue Bottle Coffee and the Dutch clothing company Scotch and Soda.

The fast pace of the condofication in Union Market is alarming. The development relied on state support for zoning, land use accommodations, and concessions to developers. In 2016 the zoning commission referred to this as the "redevelopment of an underutilized parcel."[1] Proponents of the plan asserted that it would provide housing near transit, helping DC to become a more walkable, sustainable city. At the same time, the City Council approved $82 million in city funds to build parking for new residents, as well as subsidies for developers.[2] Critics focused on the lack of truly affordable housing and the impact that rapid gentrification would have on surrounding working-class neighborhoods where housing prices have increased dramatically.[3] In the fall of 2021 promoters of the Union Market district relied on the state again, for the forced removal of the area's unhoused population, clustered under the shelter of the metro overpass.[4]

On a sunny morning in 2022, the neighborhood was populated by dozens of young people strolling with their pandemic puppies. It felt shiny, new, and sanitized. It exemplified the issues with this kind of rapid change. The hastily built luxury condos were nowhere near capacity, with units being rented out as pseudo-hotel rooms at the time. Restaurants, bars, and coffee shops had popped up in the spaces that were occupied by distributors and wholesalers just a few years or even months before, with remaining purveyors counting their days.[5] The end result: a homogeneous neighborhood that looks like so many others, and achieved through similar means—the cultural and physical displacement of existing populations, state prioritizing of corporate profits over people, the forced removal of unsheltered people, and the disappearance of working-class jobs and housing.

About a year after my visit to DC, I recalled the condofied neighborhood while finishing edits for this book. Referencing a map of the

Union Market district, I noticed a coffee shop called Unido within the neighborhood's La Cosecha food hall, which features upscale Latin American cuisines. The name sounded familiar. I was in Panama at the time and drank coffee at an Unido a few days earlier. A quick Internet search confirmed that Unido is a small Panamanian coffee chain with ten locations sprinkled throughout the country, mainly in the capital, and, sure enough, with two locations in Washington, DC. Of course, there was also a location in Panama City's Casco Viejo, a historic district that was declared a UNESCO World Heritage Site in 1997 and has more recently been the site of a transnational brand of gentrification.[6]

The small, peninsular neighborhood of Casco Viejo is starting to change. Crumbling old buildings and statues celebrating independence bump up against cocktail bars with Brooklyn prices and coffee shops like Unido, while an explosion of Airbnb rentals is tightening the local housing market. There are tourists and "digital nomads" inflating the cost of living, but local families are still very visible, flooding into the neighborhood for religious celebrations or hanging out on the streets on warm nights. In the spring of 2023 it felt like the balance was about to tip. Two large banners staked on the site of a new housing project confirmed that hunch: "No a La Gentrificación" and "Sin Habitantes, No Hay Patrimonio." What kind of heritage can a UNESCO site have if all of the existing culture and people are displaced?

A blog post that, naturally, refers to Casco Viejo as a "Williamsburg" has the following to say about changes in the neighborhood:

> As a local tour guide explained to me, just fifteen years ago guidebooks only mentioned Casco Viejo in order to warn tourists not to step foot there—it had deteriorated into a dangerous, dilapidated slum. But then somewhere in the past decade, things started to shift. . . . A whirlwind of artists, visionaries, and all around It People started swirling through those colonial streets. Today, Casco Viejo is the Williamsburg to downtown Panamá City's Times Square. While the rough edges, thankfully, have yet to be smoothed out entirely, the Casco is ground zero for Panamá City's boutique hotels, hip eateries and happening nightlife.[7]

We repeatedly hear the uncritical narrative that there was "nothing there" in a neighborhood before it gentrified, and what was there was unsavory—crime, poverty, homelessness. Before the "It People" were lured in by the UNESCO status, the area was dangerous, dilapidated. Now it's hip but, just as Williamsburg was described in chapter 3, still dangerous enough, with the rough edges providing authenticity and excitement.

The specters of danger, grit, and nothingness that permeate gentrifiers' accounts of Williamsburg in the 1980s and 1990s, even into the 2000s, are echoed about countless other "Williamsburgs" around the world. These themes, perpetuated by media, are then utilized by politicians to justify state-led redevelopment. Exaggerations of what the neighborhood was, or wasn't, help to paint gentrification as a social good. There was nothing in Williamsburg until the artists arrived; there was nothing in Casco Viejo until the "It People" showed up; in DC the removal of unhoused populations and working-class jobs from the Union Market district allows it to now be proclaimed "a destination for creative enterprise and authentic experiences." Erased from the "Williamsburgs" are the people, the existing residents who counter these stories with their own recollections of vastly imperfect neighborhoods that still managed to serve many of their needs and provided a backdrop to their family memories, their jobs, their social networks, their daily lives.

The myths that are told about the fruits of gentrification are predicated on disparaging and erasing existing communities. Gentrification is not a new process, and it does not show signs of halting anytime soon. It is imperative, then, to understand it from various perspectives. By utilizing the lens of neighborhood attachment style, distinguishing between groups of gentrifiers, and including former residents in the sample, this book adds new layers to understandings of gentrification and contradicts some assumptions. It also uncovers questions for future research and suggests changes that need to be made in approaches to neighborhood development.

Paths of Future Research

Williamsburg serves as one of the most high-profile instances of cultural and then state-led gentrification. While it stands out in its notoriety, it is also emblematic of the "toolkits of revitalization" that are copied in other cities around the world.[8] It felt necessary to catalogue this pivotal moment in the neighborhood's history given its influence in the 2010s. Yet the depth of detail here can compromise the case's utility toward understanding patterns of gentrification broadly. What new avenues of future research have been created by the intricacies exposed in the case of Williamsburg? How can the lessons learned here be applied in other contexts for future research? And perhaps most importantly, how can the in-depth findings from interviews, content analyses, and ethnographic observations inform the work of local groups that are actively resisting gentrification, but lack the time or staffing for intensive data collection and analysis?

Future gentrification research should aim to include people who have been displaced. This book differs from most accounts of neighborhood change by including the viewpoints of people who no longer live in the neighborhood. This is uncommon in urban research for the very practical reason that people who have left can be hard to track down.[9] While only ten Former Residents were included here, a few themes from the data are worth exploration in future research. First, within the sample of Former Residents, attitudes toward gentrification were similar along initial attachment styles. The few Former Residents who had necessity attachments to Williamsburg held perceptions of the neighborhood that were similar to those of Old Timers. They recalled the neighborhood's past as rough but vibrant, remembered the retail of the 1980s and 1990s as having served their needs, and felt a cautious appreciation of how the neighborhood had changed, if coupled with resentment that this wasn't "for them" or the Old Timers who remained. Likewise, identity-attached Former Residents had responses that aligned with those of Bohemians on most topics, including their past experiences in community events or organizations, their narratives around crime and the void, and their view of gentrification in almost entirely negative terms. The only marked variation is that identity-attached Former Residents and Bohemians who still live in Williamsburg differed on who they blame for gentrification. Of the Former Residents, four were directly involved in the neighborhood's avant-garde culture in the 1990s and early 2000s. The Bohemians, many of them also directly involved in the art scene, point the finger at city policy, specifically the 2005 rezoning. Identity-attached Former Residents are more likely to look toward the cultural gentrification that they facilitated as the primary driver of change. This pattern provokes questions about how narratives of gentrification differ within a subpopulation that has indisputably impacted the neighborhood's trajectory. State-led gentrification in Williamsburg and in countless other neighborhoods has ridden the coattails of a local artistic subculture. How can a city simultaneously foster the arts while insulating existing residents? How can a meaningfully diverse art scene be nurtured while protecting neighborhoods from large-scale condofication efforts? Future research focused on artists and the patterns within their varied perspectives could lend insight into the relationship between art and gentrification. In general, the perspectives of former residents can and should be included in gentrification research. The picture of neighborhood change is incomplete without the perspectives of the displaced.

Landlords are a second key and underexamined population for future studies to focus on. When I interviewed local business owners, a few told me that frequent building sales were driving rent increases, that the retail turnover was due to new landlords wanting to extract the maximum amount of capital. Yet others offered a different reason—that evictions of existing retail tenants were not caused by new landlords looking to quickly capitalize on their investment, but rather longer-term landlords who understood the demand for added or different retail spaces. The initial claim, that new building owners wanted to extract higher rates, is logical, but it doesn't seem to tell the full story. A brief examination of deed transfers along the Bedford Avenue retail corridor showed that the rate of transfers reached its peak in the 1980s, with a significant slowdown in the first decade of this century.[10] As gentrification was picking up, fewer buildings were being sold. In the decade when the city announced the 2005 rezoning, only 37 percent of buildings on Bedford Avenue changed hands. These rates had been above 50 percent for all three prior decades. The trends in deed transfers suggest that the surge of businesses that opened as state-led gentrification set in (ninety-four new businesses between 2000 and 2010) might be due to existing landlords, as some respondents claimed.

Retail turnover isn't just about rental prices but potentially also aesthetics and place making. The building owner who favors the boutique over the bodega is making an individual decision that is both a cause and an effect of broader neighborhood changes. Little by little, the signs and symbolic ownership of the shopping streets shift, as individual decisions have a tangible effect on the atmosphere created by local shops. Future studies could continue this inquiry by interviewing landlords about their preferences for renting retail space, what signals they use to determine when the local market is "ready" for new types of business, and how they view their role in a changing neighborhood. Understanding this would provide an important insight into how decisions about retail space promote gentrification.

Finally, a critique of qualitative projects like this one is that they sacrifice breadth for depth. The opposite is of course true for quantitative work, but I would add that most quantitative studies of gentrification have the added pitfall of relying on preexisting data. While there is no shortage of insightful and creative quantitative studies of gentrification, the reliance on preexisting data means that approximations are used: 311 data serve as a proxy for surveillance or demand for policing, or questions about trust, belonging, and willingness to help neighbors are stand-ins for an individual's connection to their community.[11] These variables can give us broad understandings of the relationships between gentrifying places and neighborhood effects, but they are not direct measurements. We have no way of knowing which residents are calling 311 or whether someone who doesn't necessarily trust their neighbors still feels quite connected to the community through participation in local institutions. This means that most quantitative studies on the topic do not capture finer-grain issues like neighborhood attachment, complex aspects of belonging, symbolic ownership, and cultural displacement.[12] For the purposes of comparative research, the qualitative findings presented here could be operationalized into survey questions and administered on a much larger scale to gather firsthand data measuring experiences of gentrification.

Based on the findings in this study, survey questions might ask about experiences and perceptions of crime, membership in community organizations, how access to groceries and other retail has changed over time, types of amenities and services that residents currently utilize as well as what is missing, relationships with neighbors, use of services like 311, participation in local events, and attitudes toward gentrification overall. Attachment style could be operationalized in different local contexts by capturing why residents moved to a given locale, and scaled questions that ask their feelings about the neighborhood and how they view themselves in it. In addition to exposing new patterns along these themes, comparative research could also uncover trends in neighborhood conditions that increase or decrease feelings of cultural displacement or symbolic ownership, important aspects of gentrification's impact on everyday life.

A validated survey on the topic of cultural displacement would be informative beyond academia, as a tool for community organizations and policy makers trying to minimize the negative effects of gentrification. Quantitative data on the subject could be utilized to determine which aspects of change are beneficial for existing residents and could point to policies that need to be enacted in the face of gentrification. For example, interviews with Old Timers and Bohemians in Williamsburg emphasized the importance of pre-gentrified retail to feelings of belonging for residents who are not physically displaced. It follows then that in addition to rent stabilization and the creation of affordable housing, local leaders need to also protect existing retail and institutions like churches, senior centers, or ethnic clubs that make up the daily social lives of residents. Data of this kind could also be useful as new amenities and public spaces are built in a neighborhood. Understanding the needs and desires of existing residents is a necessary step in making public spaces that are meaningful, responsive, and democratic, as discussed in chapter 2. Building spaces that are welcoming, accessible, and relevant for various groups of residents necessitates input from beyond the most vocal or visible residents, or the biggest campaign donors.

What Can Be Done?

Gentrification, particularly the state-led variety, quickens the pace of change, but urban neighborhoods are still in flux without it. Despite a brief dip during the pandemic, city housing is in high demand. Rents have surged past pre-pandemic rates in many metro areas. As a result, the cultural and social impacts of this process continue to move further into outlying urban neighborhoods. Politicians promote gentrification and real estate development as part of a growth agenda that attracts tax revenue and tourist dollars. They are unlikely to turn their backs on this strategy anytime soon. Aware of the state's role in gentrification, we cannot reliably look to government officials as sources of support or to enforce protections that safeguard existing residents. Resistance must come from solidarity and coalition building within neighborhoods. Given these conditions, how do we build urban futures in ways that are just, sustainable, and equitable for all residents?

- Fighting for True Affordable Housing. Cities around the world are facing crises of affordable housing, leading to physical displacement of existing residents and preventing the in-movement of new non-wealthy residents. Too often, the only solution offered by politicians is to pave the way for developers to build more, but what is built is hardly ever affordable enough, and units do not trickle down. The fight for true affordable housing and rent control measures is an ongoing necessity in cities, and it must go beyond precarious and privately owned affordable housing. Citizens and community organizations need to constantly advocate for fairer housing policies through rent strikes and demands for public and publicly subsidized housing. Community land trusts, often relying on public and private funds, are another strategy for maintaining affordable housing, and can also be conduits for political, racial, and economic empowerment.[13] Rather than passing subsidies along to developers, who may or may not be held accountable in developing "affordable" housing, these funds should go to public housing initiatives. Securing sustainable housing is not just a measure to prevent physical displacement. The shifting norms in rapidly gentrifying neighborhoods can create stress and peril for existing residents.

Enacting rent control and providing public and affordable housing in a neighborhood can create more of a balance, preventing incoming groups from dictating social norms and gaining symbolic ownership over the neighborhood.

- Commercial Rent Protections. Existing neighborhood retail provides goods, services, socialization, and a sense of belonging for residents. Maintaining a proportion of existing retail establishments as new commercial options are introduced can create an environment where businesses of necessity and recreation are provided for residents of all backgrounds and economic levels. This is an important step in maintaining the visibility of existing residents and preventing the cultural displacement of these groups. Even in cities with a fair amount of residential rent control, these protections are almost never extended to retail units, although New York City did have commercial rent control from 1945 to 1963, and a Brooklyn City Council member introduced a bill for commercial rent regulation in 2019.[14] One argument against retail rent regulation is that landlords may pass over independent businesses in favor of corporate tenants who could pay higher rates. This type of rent control legislation would need to include regulations to monitor such treatment, and perhaps the creation of city-owned retail spaces, as in some buildings owned by the New York City Housing Authority.[15]

- Increased Mechanisms for Community Input. There needs to be more opportunity for advancing or curtailing urban policy at the local level. In the late 1990s, residents of Williamsburg and Greenpoint created community-based plans for the North Brooklyn waterfront that aimed to retain the local character by developing the waterfront with low- and mid-rise housing and protecting what remained of local industry. As discussed in chapter 1, the plan was approved by the city, but then bulldozed over by the Department of City Planning's rezoning.[16]

In the broader New York context, Community Boards are advisory branches that hold public hearings and vote on proposed initiatives like changes to zoning, land use, and real estate development. However, the outcomes of Community Board votes are merely considered by the City Council and mayor, who retain the final say. This will look different in every city, but it is critical that residents can more directly weigh in on policies and plans that greatly impact their lives. This could be achieved through more direct voting on significant neighborhood plans, or the establishment of local panels that carry more power than an advisory committee.

- Guidelines for Publicly Supported Events. When organizers ask for city support in terms of permitting, logistics, and/or funding, there should be guidelines in place to ensure that these spaces are accessible to all. Some events may not be of interest to all residents, but physical ability, language, age, socioeconomic status, or other individual characteristics should not present barriers to participation. Without this effort, high-profile public space events like Williamsburg Walks can come to symbolize who does and does not belong in a neighborhood. Alternatively, events that include outreach to the community and relevant programming could at best foster integration and at minimum mitigate the loss of symbolic ownership for existing residents.
- Increase Funding for Community Organizations. As neighborhoods see additional capital flows through reinvestment, increased funding needs to be redirected to community organizations. While often imperfect, these organizations are less top-down than city government and will have a better read of what residents desire and need locally. Increased funding for these organizations can help them promote and maintain the visibility of existing populations and advocate for the rights of existing communities to remain, physically and culturally, in the neighborhood.
- Campaign Reform. Many of the above initiatives would benefit from the support of political leadership, but when it comes to gentrification these figures frequently side with developers. In the long term it is necessary to build city governments that are more sensitive to the needs of constituents. In New York, real estate is habitually the industry that contributes the most to political campaigns at the state, city, and more local levels.[17] Too often elected officials sell out their constituents and entire neighborhoods to developers who promise to build a small fraction of below-market-rate apartments and some park space. Policies like ranked choice voting and an overhaul of campaign financing are a start for creating a more even playing field for new candidates, with fewer favors to be returned while in office. Still, most of the immediate actions

listed here will need to be made in opposition to city politicians, not with their assistance.

There Was Nothing There

In the fall of 2020, two large and very illegal Halloween parties were busted in New York City as the pandemic raged on. One was in eastern Williamsburg, the other in the Westchester Square neighborhood of the Bronx, both drawing people from well beyond those neighborhoods. The sheriff who helped break up the Bronx party said that he realized something was amiss when he noticed people wearing costumes "in the middle of nowhere." Reporting on it the next day, a local newscaster said, "The party planners picked neighborhoods like this one, industrial, empty so their parties could go largely unseen and unheard." This logic of finding a desolate area would make sense when planning a party for over 550 people during a pandemic, except that this party was not in an "empty" area. The census tract down the street from the venue has a population density of 195,863, higher than many tracts in Manhattan. I taught in the area from 2018 to 2022 and exited the subway at the same stop where the partygoers would have disembarked. The neighborhood was always bustling with food vendors, children running back and forth in the playground, teenagers celebrating their freedom from the school day, families and older folks waiting in line for a shuttle to the nearby hospital complex, and dozens of businesses of necessity as well as fast-food and sit-down restaurants.

The party was not "in the middle of nowhere" but rather in a highly populated, lower-income, and predominantly Latinx, Asian, and Black neighborhood. The comments from the sheriff and the news reporter are reminiscent of the descriptions of pre-gentrified Williamsburg(s). When existing populations and businesses are labeled in this way, we can imagine that gentrification is not far off. Parts of the Bronx have already been reshaped by state-led condofication efforts. The narratives of the Westchester Square neighborhood being empty and "the middle of nowhere" should alert us that it is a likely candidate for future gentrification projects and real estate speculation.

The use of attachment style in this book sheds light on the stories we tell about gentrification and how attachment to a neighborhood helps to orient those narratives. In Williamsburg, attachment style impacted how residents organized, claimed space, and came to symbolically own their neighborhood; it mattered for how they perceived social disorder, their use of and expectations for neighborhood retail, and their perceptions of the neighborhood's past and future. The tracing of Williamsburg's contemporary history alongside the perceptions of residents who have lived there over the course of four decades highlights how the wounds of disinvestment are interpreted in disparaging ways by in-movers, media, and the city. These narratives neatly set up a justification for state-led gentrification, a mechanism for politicians to provide incentives and breaks to the real estate developers who buoy their political campaigns. In its wake, existing populations of residents experienced surveillance, a diminished sense of belonging, and cultural and physical displacement. Looking at the complexities of gentrification and neighborhood attachment in other contexts will help us to expose the myths of state-led change, preparing residents, community organizers, and progressive urban leaders in their fights for equitable cities.

Unimaginative strategies for urban growth give rise to Williamsburgs around the world. Popular neighborhoods increasingly have predictable mixtures of cocktail bars, breweries, public art, coffee shops, and boutiques. If the retail, amenities, and luxury housing of Williamsburg's gentrification are recognizable elsewhere, so are its problems. The emptied warehouse districts and loss of jobs, the clearing away or incarceration of unhoused people, the Airbnb takeover of housing, the physical displacement through skyrocketing land value, the pricing out of subcultural or artist scenes, the erasure of existing residents and cultures through the repeated narrative that there was nothing or nobody there—these are observed globally as well. The goal of the Where Is Williamsburg? app, to never be too far from home thanks to data from users "exactly like you," is a promise of homogeneity, predictability, and consistency, an urban-lite experience that makes global cosmopolitans feel safe and comfortable. Developers, politicians, and corporate entities are all too eager to oblige these ideals.

The spell of homogeneous cities and displaced populations can be broken. Neighborhoods must be revitalized with public investment, housing security, and input from existing residents. Historically divested places need to be rebuilt in restorative ways that focus on uplifting existing communities. We must drop these narratives of "empty nowheres" and the privileging of gentrifiers' perspectives at the expense of everyone else. If we fail to protect and honor existing cultures, residents, jobs, institutions, and histories, then there really will be nothing there.

Epilogue

An "L-pocalypse," a Pandemic, and a New Mayor

The 2005 rezoning of Williamsburg was a high-profile example of how state-led interventions can transform neighborhoods. In the preceding chapters we've seen how these interventions can play out in the everyday realities of urban residents. The bulk of data collection for this book was completed by 2018, but since then there have been two more interventions in Williamsburg worth noting. The first was a proposed transit suspension at the state level, and the second was the COVID-19 pandemic. In the meantime, the citizens of New York elected a new mayor, who wavers when it comes to gentrification.

In January 2016 New York's then governor Andrew Cuomo announced that major repairs needed to be made to the L train because of damages sustained four years earlier during Hurricane Sandy. In the initial proposal, the MTA estimated that it could take anywhere from three to seven years to make all of the repairs, depending on the plan for suspending train service. City Council members and then mayor Bill de Blasio met with community groups in North Brooklyn to discuss the closure and in the late spring of 2016 they decided on a plan to completely shut down the L for eighteen months starting in 2019, later shortened to a fifteen-month estimate.

Panic ensued as the 2019 shutdown approached. There was outcry from neighborhood groups, and wealthy, mobile residents began moving out of rentals and selling units because of what came to be known as "The L-pocalypse." Rent began to dip in Williamsburg for the first time in decades. Bohemians and Condo Dwellers alike had said they wanted a more local, neighborhood vibe, but Williamsburg was about to get a little too local. Some residents along the L train in Manhattan even sued the governor, and businesses in the neighborhood formed a coalition to resist the shutdown.[1] Facing pressure from these groups and realtors who donated millions to his 2018 gubernatorial campaign, Cuomo backtracked at the last minute and decided to go ahead with a slowdown of service rather than a full suspension. The fears of an L train shutdown exposed how reliant the Williamsburg economy had become on outsiders. At that point, few businesses in Williamsburg were focused on the needs of the surrounding community. There were grocery stores, pharmacies, cafés, laundromats, and a few other businesses that served residents, but for the most part Williamsburg's economy revolved around upscale restaurants, boutiques, hotels, and "experiences" like concert halls, clubs, and events that attract people from around the city and the world. When the businesses of a neighborhood no longer serve the local community, their success is dependent on visitors and attracting them becomes a priority.

The L train concerns seemed almost quaint when the COVID-19 pandemic hit New York in March 2020. Early in the pandemic, an Instagram account that promotes Williamsburg businesses began posting the names of dozens of independently owned restaurants, bars, and boutiques that had permanently shuttered. While the large chains could afford to stay in the neighborhood through the lockdown, places like Apple and Sephora temporarily boarded up their storefronts, a visual vote of no confidence in their neighbors.

After more than a decade of studying Williamsburg, I didn't think that the neighborhood could surprise me anymore. I was proven wrong in the summer months of 2020. As I walked through the neighborhood, I saw bands of young twenty-somethings skateboarding down a street that was closed to car traffic; the Department of Transportation had closed several that summer. Gaggles of teens stood on corners eating falafel and laughing loudly, wearing flannel shirts tied around their waists and more baggy jeans than I'd seen in a few decades—1990s styles had come back just in time for hipster Williamsburg 2.0. The scene made me recall a popular hashtag from the early days of the pandemic: #NatureIsHealing, referring to reports that a decrease in human activity and CO_2 emissions in the spring of 2020 led to shifts in the animal kingdom—more birdsong in cities, appearances of bobcats in the Bronx and coyotes in San Francisco, even a (false) account of dolphins appearing in Venice, Italy. With many of Williamsburg's wealthy residents having absconded to their country homes, or at least country Airbnbs, I wondered: Was Williamsburg's gentrification healing?

It wasn't, of course. Within a few months, rents were quickly climbing past their pre-pandemic rates, and purchasing an apartment or home is still out of reach for the majority of New Yorkers. Yet in the summer of 2020, the public spaces of Williamsburg were symbolically owned by a crowd that looked like a more racially diverse version of the Bohemians of the 1980s and 1990s. Suddenly Williamsburg's Northside was visibly quite different from the version populated by Condo Dwellers, tourists, and the businesses that have cropped up to serve them. COVID-19 was likely the first time that Condo Dwellers felt a lack of control to dictate the spaces of their neighborhood; many left temporarily, and in their absence, teenagers, the children of parents who did not or could not leave, symbolically owned Williamsburg.

Condo Dweller Stephanie had lived in the neighborhood for more than a decade before the pandemic hit and was distressed by its immediate impact on Williamsburg. She and her children moved to a summer home that she owns on Long Island for most of the spring and summer of 2020. On occasional visits back to Williamsburg, she felt that it was more treacherous than it had previously felt: "We came back in June for a month, and I was very annoyed by it. . . . A lot of fireworks, and I couldn't sleep. It felt a little more dangerous." Later in the summer, with restaurants opening back up with outdoor dining, she reflected that it was starting to feel "more European," but the flight of families like her own concerned her for Williamsburg's longer-term future.

Evan had also lived in the neighborhood for about a decade but headed to Maine with his children to wait out the spring of 2020 at an empty home owned by a family member. Upon his return in the summer of 2020, he felt that Williamsburg was regaining "a feeling of grunginess again" and complained about the use of public space during the summer: "We had a lot of issues with people coming in, partying, being up late, playing music. . . . A lot of unruly, unlawful behavior." The "grunge" and "unruly behavior" were sources of excitement and authenticity for early gentrifiers decades ago, but they produce anxiety for Condo Dwellers, unsure at that point of what the future would hold for their Williamsburg investments.

Discussing how the pandemic had affected Williamsburg, Bohemian resident Carol lamented that businesses had closed, but she also talked about how she was interacting with the city differently with the new, slower pace of things. Carol said that she hadn't felt as connected to Williamsburg over the last few years. She half-jokingly hoped that the crisis would plummet New York rents low enough for the reemergence of an art scene: "Maybe it will make things cheap, like Detroit," this in spite of the fact that she rents out an apartment in the building she owns. Since Carol had an identity attachment to the neighborhood and complained of more recent changes, it made sense that she saw the lockdown-related slowness not as an inconvenience, but rather an opportunity for Williamsburg to reclaim its artistic past.

My survey of Bedford Avenue on a frigid winter night in 2021 revealed that 10 percent of the storefronts had been recently closed, but new businesses were opening, including an upscale art gallery and a hotel. It's too soon to tell exactly how the long-term effects of the pandemic and other macro factors will affect gentrifying neighborhoods. New York City's unemployment rate has slowly decreased in the two years since vaccinations have been widely available, but rapid inflation and increasing rents have left the city with record levels of homelessness. Crime rates have also fluctuated, with instances of violence further exaggerated in media reports and on neighborhood social networking sites. These trends pose additional questions for the future of cities. Will poor, working-class, and even middle-class residents be further displaced to less expensive suburban areas? How would the increasing racial and economic diversification impact everyday life and politics in suburbs? If signs of disorder continue, what steps will wealthy New Yorkers take to securitize and maintain ownership over their gentrified enclaves?

In addition to short-term interruptions, like the L-train suspension, or longer-term issues, like COVID-19, local politics also have important consequences for day-to-day life in cities. As made evident during Michael Bloomberg's tenure, mayors can play an important role in facilitating or curbing gentrification. Bloomberg was focused on development and "upgrading" New York City to attract investment. In 2012 Bill de Blasio campaigned on a platform that included attention to the city's housing crunch. At the time, gentrification critics were frustrated with broken promises around the construction of affordable housing and looked to de Blasio to enforce the construction of affordable units that were planned for Bloomberg's rezoning projects. While de Blasio's administration was more focused on affordable housing, financing thirty thousand units in 2020 alone, the lottery system for those apartments is competitive, and still often leaves out the city's most economically vulnerable populations.[2] One recent affordable housing lottery in Williamsburg's Southside had only three affordable units, with an income minimum of $68,572 for a one-person household. For reference, my salary at the time as an assistant professor in New York City would have been too low to qualify.

Meanwhile, the New York housing market continues to shoot up. In the spring of 2021, real estate company Douglas Elliman reported that the median home price in Brooklyn had reached $900,000. A few weeks later, the *New York Times* editorial board interviewed mayoral candidates and asked eight of them this question: "Do you know the median sales price for a home in Brooklyn?" Tellingly, many of the candidates were extremely far off in their answers. Several guessed in the $80,000–$100,000 range. Eric Adams, who went on to win the election in November 2021, guessed $550,000, a number that is already unmanageable for most New Yorkers, but still far below the actual median. In the article where it reported on the candidates' guesses, the *Times* included a quote from political consultant Monica Klein: "It's hard to imagine these men solving a problem they don't know exists."

Klein's comment highlights an ongoing tension in the disconnect between residents' experiences of housing anxiety and leadership's lack of awareness and empathy around the problem. It remains to be seen whether Mayor Adams, a year and a half into his tenure at the time of writing, will increase truly affordable housing for the New Yorkers who need it most. In a controversial speech in January 2020, Adams renounced gentrification to an audience of long-term residents in Harlem. In a neighborhood that has increased from 1.2 percent white in the 1990s to 13.5 percent in 2020, Adams declared, "Go back to Iowa. You go back to Ohio. New York City belongs to the people that were here and made New York City what it is." He went on to discuss tensions not just around housing, but also cultural displacement: "Folks are not only hijacking your apartments and displacing your living arrangements, they displace your conversations and say the things that are important to you are no longer important, and they decide what's important and what's not important." In an open letter in the *Daily News* a few days later, Adams walked back his statements significantly: "I welcome all people of good will to New York City—no matter who they are and where they come from," with the caveat that newcomers should invest in their neighborhood. But later on in his campaign, New Yorkers found out that Adams might not live in the city himself, or even the state. In a video that went viral, Adams gave a tour to news reporters of an apartment he claimed to live in, in Bed-Stuy, Brooklyn. But on social media and in the news, many speculated that the apartment was actually inhabited by his son, with Adams living in New Jersey. Despite his comments about cultural gentrification, physical displacement, and investing in the neighborhood, Adams may suffer from the same lack of empathy and awareness of previous mayors and the other 2021 candidates.

In his former post as Brooklyn borough president, Adams supported a rezoning in Gowanus, a Brooklyn neighborhood with a profile similar to Williamsburg's. Formerly a center for manufacturing and production, Gowanus slowly deindustrialized while becoming populated by artists and early gentrifiers as early as the 1970s. Like Williamsburg's rezoning nearly two decades earlier, the Gowanus plan went back and forth in the City Council with input from local organizations, planners, and politicians. The neighborhood is currently home to a Whole Foods, several craft breweries, an infamously polluted canal, and public housing that has fallen into steep disrepair. A week after the mayoral election, the rezoning was approved by the City Council. In the coming years, eight thousand new apartments will be added to the neighborhood, with a third of them projected to be affordable housing. The deal also promises a cleanup of the Gowanus Canal and a $200 million investment in the existing public housing, the Gowanus Houses and Wyckoff Gardens. However, affordable housing, infrastructure improvements, and environmental cleanups have all been part of previous rezoning deals and administrations have failed to enforce these concessions to existing communities. Within just three months, Eric Adams accepted nearly $500,000 in campaign contributions from the real estate industry, including Thor Equities, a prominent developer in Williamsburg.[3] Given this track record, it feels unlikely that he will prioritize people over profit and demand that developers build truly affordable housing. We must continue to look beyond politicians to community organizations, and coalition building within neighborhoods to resist displacement and demand equity and justice in the planning of urban housing. If not, we will continue to create exclusive enclaves throughout New York and wherever else "Williamsburgs" pop up.

ACKNOWLEDGMENTS

This book is simultaneously a love letter and a breakup playlist. It is a cautionary tale of the far-reaching consequences when the city supports and leads gentrification, a phenomenon that has only increased in my time studying Williamsburg. It is a call for resistance and solidarity in the face of unending greed. It is a reminder to consider how we describe people and places, because those narratives matter. It is a plea to think a little more deeply about your interactions with your neighbors. It is about approaching all residents of the city from a place of compassion. I hope that this book finds its way into the hands of Williamsburg residents, community organizers, and people who love cities and who imagine urban futures that are just, sustainable, equitable, and accessible for all.

I owe a great deal to the people who have encouraged and critiqued this project throughout the years. It's hard to believe that I first started studying Williamsburg in 2008 while at Brooklyn College. That fall, I enrolled in urban sociology with Jerome Krase and methodology with Timothy Shortell. Since I was a first-generation college student, very unsure of academia, their support meant the world. They ushered me into my first conference presentation and later my first publication along with the guidance and patience of Judith DeSena. I am forever grateful for that mentorship, and I try to model it with my own students today.

A much earlier version of this book benefited greatly from comments, enthusiasm, and debate with my professors at the City University of New York Graduate Center: Phil Kasinitz, Sharon Zukin, and John Mollenkopf. They each contributed to my development as a scholar in fundamental ways. This project has also benefited from comments and feedback from Richard Ocejo, Melanie Lorek, Steven Tuttle, and Jason Patch. I am appreciative of the anonymous reviewers of this manuscript and to Ilene Kalish at New York University Press for pushing me to make this book something I am truly proud of.

I thank the residents of Williamsburg who freely gave of their time and shared their memories and experiences with me. On days when I felt tempted to give up on this project, my commitment to getting their stories right pushed me ahead. Thanks especially to Dennis Farr, who will always be the most insightful critic of Williamsburg's gentrification, and to the memory of Helena Olszewska. Some of my earliest understandings of the nuances of gentrification came from translated conversations with her.

My dear friends have been so patient with my absence for months at a time as I've been engrossed with this work. Thank you for always checking in, making space, and doing this life thing together. Especially thanks to Leo Gomez, who has been along for this entire ride and is probably looking forward to never hearing the name "Williamsburg" again. A massive amount of appreciation to Lukasz Chelminski. I absolutely would never have moved to Williamsburg without his influence. I am thankful for his friendship over the years, his endless recon on gentrification, and the fact that over fifteen years he has read just about every page of every iteration of this work.

My years as a PhD student at the CUNY Graduate Center were some of the most formative of my life. It was there that I settled into the joys of research and teaching and became further inspired around social justice. I am blessed by the close friendships forged in that environment, and grateful to CUNY for attracting all those brilliant and radical people. We studied together and commiserated; we danced and cried; we marched in the streets and locked arms; we held each other through breakups, and we celebrated love. You all make life richer.

My family has been a constant source of encouragement and motivation. Both of my parents worked incredibly hard so that I could have all of life's opportunities. My father's model of persistence has come in handy in the world of academia. My mother was my first teacher in life and nurtured my curiosity from the very beginning. My sister, Chelsea, can always make me laugh and keeps me humble no matter what.

Finally, I have endless love, gratitude, and respect for my partner, Kevin Andrus. Throughout the years of working on this project he has given constant emotional and intellectual support. He has championed this book from the beginning and has made it possible in so many day-to-day ways. Thank you, Kevin, for making every day beautiful just by being yourself. And to our wonderful Mila, thank you for your impeccable timing, and the immense joy that you bring.

METHODOLOGICAL APPENDIX

ETHNOGRAPHY

I reluctantly moved to Williamsburg in May 2008. My boyfriend at the time was from Poland and an apartment was available in a building where he had family connections. I had a vague understanding of gentrification back then, enough to not want to move to the neighborhood, but it was hard to argue with the steeply discounted rent. For the following decade I had a front row seat to the neighborhood's dramatic transformation.

That summer, I enrolled at Brooklyn College and took my first urban sociology class, which inspired me to begin this project. The following year I went on to the CUNY Graduate Center, where I continued this work for the better part of a decade. Though the school was in Manhattan, nearly all of my classmates and friends lived in Brooklyn, most along the L train somewhere near Williamsburg, Bushwick, or Ridgewood (technically in Queens but an honorary Brooklyn neighborhood). Whether it was study groups, dancing, bar hopping, grading sessions, or house parties, it was in Brooklyn. According to family lore, my grandfather used to refer to Brooklyn as "the armpit of the world" to chide my grandmother about her birthplace, but if Brooklyn was the armpit of the world in the 1940s, it felt like the center of the universe in the 2010s.

During my tenure in Williamsburg, I lived on the North and Southsides and in one apartment that was really in Bushwick but marketed as Williamsburg. Over the course of ten years, I attended countless meetings of various community organizations, City Council hearings, and events like the Puerto Rican Day Parade, Our Lady of Mount Carmel's Giglio Feast, and of course Williamsburg Walks. I walked endlessly throughout the neighborhood, noting physical changes in the retail, residential, and natural landscapes over time as well as the shifts in the populations using these spaces. In these years, I carried a notebook with me everywhere, constantly making observations, jotting down ideas and the contact information for people I met who would eventually become participants in my study. While in Williamsburg, I was always in ethnographer mode, which probably made me less fun at parties.

Throughout my research I was aware of my social location as a white woman working on a professional degree and how that affected the information that people shared with me. My whiteness gave me a level of access to the Polish and Italian Old Timer community, while my inability to speak Spanish sometimes prevented me from having conversations with Puerto Rican and Dominican residents. I was undoubtedly viewed as a gentrifier and outsider by the majority of Old Timers, which may have also affected the experiences they shared with me. Bohemians were generally the most forthcoming with me. Some were sampled through my participation in community organizations, but others were people I met in the neighborhood through social circles or commercial spaces that we simultaneously inhabited. My personal social network, as well as my interests and lifestyle, helped me access this group of residents. When it came to interviewing Condo Dwellers, I recruited some participants from a local parenting forum, almost entirely occupied by mothers. Childless myself at the time, I may not have had access to this forum if I did not present as a woman.

While conducting this study, I participated in the local community by volunteering at a senior center, joining protests for affordable housing, giving presentations of my findings at community events, and attending demonstrations in the neighborhood and at the courthouse when one of the senior centers was threatened with eviction. I moved out of Williamsburg in May 2018, after exactly ten years in the neighborhood, but I continued to make ethnographic trips over the following years, especially to track the COVID-induced changes to the neighborhood in 2020 and 2021, and as late as 2023.

SAMPLE AND RECRUITMENT

Since this work is an ethnography, the sample for this research was never intended to be random. Old Timers in this study were predominantly working-class to middle-income and were first- or second-generation (im)migrants from Puerto Rico, the Dominican Republic, Poland, and Italy. Bohemians were frequently college-educated, white, middle-class Americans, typically not from New York City but often from suburbs in the northeastern United States. The Condo Dwellers were mostly wealthy professionals and white Americans or immigrants who came to Williamsburg after living in Manhattan as well as other international cities. Former Residents are a diverse group because they are composed of a mix of people who have lived in the neighborhood over time, including second-generation Dominican and Polish professionals, artists and musicians, and even relatively new residents who were pushed out by swiftly rising rents.

Participants were recruited from community groups and other local organizations, neighborhood events and businesses, and online forums used by residents. They were also snowball sampled from original respondents, which was especially important for accessing Former Residents. The sample broke down as indicated in table A.1, with a minimum of ten members for each attachment category.

TABLE A.1. Sample Broken Down by Attachment Cohort and Race/Ethnicity

	Hispanic	White ethnic	White American	Any other background	Totals
Old Timers	9	7	1	0	17
Bohemians	1	1	10	0	12
Condo Dwellers	2	1	7	1	11
Former	2	1	6	1	10
Totals	14	10	24	2	50

Note: These are the ethnic and racial groups that are most predominant in Williamsburg. Most Old Timers were first- or second-generation (im)migrants from Poland, Italy, Puerto Rico, and the Dominican Republic. "White American" refers to individuals who categorized themselves as "white" when asked about their racial/ethnic background and were not first- or second-generation (im)migrants. One Former Resident identified as biracial (African American and white), and one Condo Dweller was a British Indian woman who moved to New York from London.

Though not a random sample, the participants in this study are fairly representative of Williamsburg's racial and ethnic composition. At the time of my research, the zip-code that comprised most of Williamsburg was 24.8 percent Hispanic, 64.1 percent white non-Hispanic, and just under 4 percent Black. In 2015 the two tracts at the East Williamsburg border averaged out to 19.7 percent Black, but most tracts in the highly gentrified areas reported less than 6 percent. Since the focus of this study was the effects of gentrification on daily life, the sample was concentrated on the area that had undergone the most rapid change. Outreach to churches and community organizations on the eastern edge of the neighborhood did not yield any interviews. As gentrification continues to spread into East Williamsburg, additional research needs to be completed to capture residents' experiences of change in that portion of the neighborhood.

Although a significant population in Williamsburg, the nearly sixty thousand Hasidic Jewish residents and business owners were not sampled for this project. Living in a dense residential and commercial district just south of the Williamsburg Bridge, they play important roles in the real estate and sociopolitical fabric of Williamsburg, but the community is insular and local businesses cater to most daily needs.[1] Kosher supermarkets, bakeries, clothing shops, and bookstores line the streets, and medical services, religious institutions, restaurants, and pharmacies are all oriented toward the Hasidic population. While some change has occurred, the community actively resists gentrification.

One infamous example of this resistance was the "bike lane wars," a years-long showdown between hipsters and Hasidim. In the late 2000s, the city's Department of Transportation (DOT) painted hundreds of miles of bike lanes throughout the city, including a route that connected Greenpoint and Williamsburg to other Brooklyn neighborhoods. Part of the bike lane passed through the Hasidic neighborhood, which caused tension with the community. Local news outlets reported that the Hasidic residents complained about the disruption in parking patterns, the unwelcome traffic through the neighborhood, and, allegedly, the immodest dress of women cyclists. Within a few weeks, the DOT sandblasted the South Williamsburg strip of bike lanes at the behest of Hasidic leaders, but the lanes reappeared shortly thereafter, painted by bike-lane supporters. Both sides ratcheted up the conflict, the Hasidic residents by harassing cyclists, and the hipsters by planning (if not executing) a naked bike ride through the neighborhood.

This example illustrates both the local power of the Hasidic community and their active resistance to the encroachment of gentrifiers. As a result, residents have not experienced cultural displacement on the scale of most other Williamsburg locals. A study on the relationship between gentrification and the Hasidic community, though it would be rich and worthwhile, would necessitate different research questions and an entirely different focus of study; for this reason, the Hasidic population is generally absent from this book.

INTERVIEWS

The core of this research is based on fifty interviews with neighborhood residents, which lasted anywhere from thirty minutes to three hours. Interviews were also conducted with ten business owners. Most of these interviews were collected between 2014 and 2017. The epilogue includes three interviews with residents conducted in the summer and fall of 2020; two of those participants were included in the original research and one was new and not included in the count of fifty.

In each interview, respondents were asked the same set of questions, with a slightly different script for Former Residents. Participants were asked about how they came to live in Williamsburg, their consumption and recreational patterns in the neighborhood, their descriptions and feelings about how the neighborhood has changed, experiences of crime in the neighborhood, and whether they participated in community events and meetings. A full list of questions for residents and business owners, along with some probes used, can be found below. Of course, many other questions arose throughout individual interviews. The earliest interviews did not include a question about safety in the neighborhood; that question was added after criminal activity came up in multiple early interviews with Bohemians.

Resident Interview Script
1. How long have you lived in Williamsburg? (Probe to find out housing situation, i.e., homeownership, family/friend connections, rent stabilization.)
   If not born in Williamsburg: What was your impression of Williamsburg before you moved there?
2. How did you come to live in Williamsburg?
3. What was Williamsburg like when you moved here/when you were growing up?
4. Could you describe your neighborhood today?
5. Was there ever a time that you felt unsafe in the neighborhood?
6. Where do you buy groceries? Other necessities . . .

7. Is there anything you feel you need that you cannot get in Williamsburg?
8. Do you ever go to other neighborhoods for groceries or necessities? Which ones? For what?
9. What do you do for fun/recreation in Williamsburg? (Probe: restaurants/bars, socialization, public parks, etc.)
10. Have you ever participated in community events? Could you describe your experiences of these events? (Probe: festivals, Williamsburg Walks, Taste Williamsburg.)
11. Do you know anyone who has moved away from Williamsburg? To where? (Get contact info if possible.)
12. Demographic information: age, education, occupation, racial/ethnic identity, family (marital status/children).

Additional Questions for Former Residents
When did you leave the neighborhood? (How long did you live there?)
How did you decide to leave Williamsburg?
Where do you live now? What is it like?
Do you still visit Williamsburg? What do you do there? (probe: visit people, recreation, specialty foods, etc.)

Business Owner Interview Script
1. Can you describe your business to me? (Probe: what kinds of products/services are sold and what is the price point?)
   If a long-term business: How has your store changed over time?
2. How long have you been in business on Bedford?
   If a long-term business: How did you manage to stay?
3. Why did you choose to open a business in Williamsburg?
4. Can you describe your customer base?
   If a long-term business: Has your customer base changed over time?
5. Do you have relationships with other store owners in the neighborhood?
   (Probe: were you ever part of the Northside Merchants Association?)
6. Have you ever participated in any of the community festivals?
   (Probe: Williamsburg Walks, Giglio Feast, block parties . . .)
7. What are your future plans for your business?

VISUAL SOCIOLOGY

In addition to always having a notebook with me, I also always had a camera. As a result, this book includes scenes from Williamsburg's transition through the 2010s. Visual methods are an important part of urban sociology, a way of tracking what public space looks like, how people use it, and how it changes over time.[2] The images included in this book invite readers unfamiliar with Williamsburg to get a taste of how the physical neighborhood impacts everyday life. A specific visual method employed in this work is repeat photography—comparing photographs of the same spaces in Williamsburg over time.[3] While only one set of repeat photographs is included in this text, the process of documenting the same places over the years was essential in my analysis. Repeat photography was especially important for understanding residents' visibility and use of public space, the erasure of Old Timer cultures and languages, and shifting symbolic ownership over time.

RETAIL DATA: COLE'S CROSS-REFERENCE DIRECTORIES

Studying Williamsburg's retail change in the early 2000s, Jason Patch utilized business directories to help triangulate otherwise qualitative data, allowing for accuracy and more robust descriptions of neighborhood trends and characteristics.[4] This is especially essential for scholars of gentrification. The method offers a way of looking back on what was, while minimizing the influence of nostalgia and other subjectivities that arise in interview responses. Patch accessed business directories to map out and label Williamsburg businesses as "gentrification related" or "non-gentrification." In the early 2010s, I was participating in Sharon Zukin and Phil Kasinitz's Local Shops Project, where I learned to use the same directories using a different categorization scheme. In their study, Kasinitz and Zukin compared main commercial streets on Manhattan's Lower East Side and Brooklyn's Bedford-Stuyvesant, making distinctions between types of businesses, including personal care, restaurants, and art galleries, among others.[5]

In 2015 I logged many hours at the Science, Industry, and Business branch of the New York Public Library, poring over their Cole's cross-reference directories of Brooklyn. The Cole's directories have catalogued residential and business listings by street address since the 1940s. I compared the retail listings for Bedford every ten years from 1970 to 2010. Each business listing for a one-mile stretch of Bedford Avenue was recorded for every tenth year (1970 and 1980 were not available, so 1971 and 1981 were used instead). The stores were then coded by category, including retail, restaurants, services, manufacturing, grocery, and other. In the rare cases when the type was not identifiable, the store was coded as "unknown." In December 2021 I returned to Bedford to take my own inventory of the street, walking from the Southside to the Northside and noting each business, later categorizing them as I had done before with the Cole's data.

After the names and types of stores were recorded, I arranged the businesses in an Excel spreadsheet to analyze how long each one had remained in the neighborhood. From these data on tenure, I was able to calculate the percentage of new and continuing businesses from decade to decade. These data provide a more quantitative context of the changing retail landscape on Bedford Avenue as cycles of disinvestment and gentrification affected the neighborhood. Distinguishing between types of businesses provides a finer understanding of not only *when* Williamsburg's retail began to change, but also how specific shifts affected the neighborhood's identity over time.

CONTENT ANALYSIS: THE *NEW YORK TIMES*

Previous research has indicated the important role that media can play in gentrification.[6] I reference the *New York Times*' reporting on Williamsburg throughout the text, especially in chapter 4. A content analysis of *New York Times* archives was performed for these data. I searched the *New York Times* archives for appearances of the word "Williamsburg" for every five years between 1980 and 2000. After confirming that the article was about the Brooklyn neighborhood (and not the historical tourist attraction in Virginia), I coded the articles in terms of content—using categories like crime, arson, decay, transportation and infrastructure, housing, community, arts, or consumption/food.

OTHER DATA SOURCES
Crime Data: CompStat
The statistics on crime included in chapter 3 come from CompStat reports from the New York Police Department website. The reports include current crime statistics for various categories as well as total counts and rate comparisons for previous years. The reports list rates of various types of criminal activity. Police precincts are large in New York and are not based on neighborhood boundaries. Williamsburg's Northside is part of the Ninety-Fourth Precinct, along with Greenpoint. The Southside is part of the Ninetieth Precinct along with East Williamsburg into Bushwick. As a result, the crime rates provided are for a broader area than just the neighborhood itself. Additionally, these data reflect only crimes that are reported, something that can be impacted by race, gender, presence of police as well as relationships with police, and, of course, reporting practices among individual officers.

Demographic Data: Social Explorer
Most of the demographic data presented in this book, especially in chapters 1 and 5, are pulled from the US Census Bureau's American Community Survey and decennial census, both available from the database Social Explorer.[7] Unless otherwise noted, the Williamsburg data are focused on ten census tracts in the areas of the neighborhood most impacted by gentrification. Because census and American Community Survey questions changed over time, these are best estimates.

Deed Transfers: ACRIS
In the conclusion I discuss the role of landlords in retail change. There was disagreement between business owners about the cause of retail evictions. Some business owners asserted that existing landlords were refusing to renew leases, while other owners believed that evictions were due to building sales and new landlords. To assess this contradiction, I accessed the website of the New York City Department of Finance to determine the rate of deed transfers, indicating changing ownership on Bedford Avenue. The DOF maintains a digital archive of property records for city lots available online through ACRIS, the Automated City Register Information System.[8] From there it is possible to view all sales

and changes of deeds for a parcel of land by looking up addresses on a digital tax map.

In Williamsburg the deed transfer rates reached their peak in the 1980s (see table A.2), with a significant slowdown in the first decade of this century, meaning that as gentrification was picking up, fewer buildings were being sold. The trends in deed transfers suggest that the surge of businesses opening in Williamsburg (ninety-four new businesses between 2000 and 2010) was not the result of a sharp increase in building sales, but potentially existing landlords responding to neighborhood change. This preliminary finding highlights a potential path for future gentrification research.

TABLE A.2. Deed Transfers on Bedford Avenue, 1970–2009

	Number of deed transfers	Percentage of housing stock transferred
1970–1979	98	55%
1980–1989	100	56%
1990–1999	90	51%
2000–2009	66	37%

Source: Data collected from New York City Department of Finance online records.

NOTES

INTRODUCTION

1 Distinguishing between different groups of gentrifiers is a contribution of this book. See other examples of this distinction in Ocejo (2014) for an analysis of stages of gentrification in New York's Lower East Side; and Blasius, Friedrichs, and Rühl's (2016) proposed classification scheme for different types of gentrifiers.
2 See Lloyd (2005); Sullivan and Shaw (2011); Deener (2012); and Ahrens (2015).
3 See Susser (1982); Curran (2004); Marwell (2007); Patch (2008); and Krase and DeSena (2016), among many others.
4 The *New York Times*, a leading recorder and driver of gentrification in New York and beyond, had only twenty-seven mentions of the term before 1980, and nineteen of those mentions were in 1979 alone. In comparison, hundreds of academic articles and books had already been devoted to the topic, with Neil Smith's influential "Toward a Theory of Gentrification" published in 1979.
5 For thorough accounts of the main arguments in gentrification research from the 1960s through the 2000s, see Lees, Slater, and Wyly (2008); Brown-Saracino (2010); and Lees and Phillips (2018).
6 In interviews, multiple residents referred to themselves as Old Timers. Even younger people in their twenties referenced being "part of the Old Timer crowd" to mark themselves as different from gentrifiers. I defer to their terminology here, despite wanting to move away from assumptions of neighborhood tenure. The phrase "old timer" is used as a category in several studies of neighborhood change, most prominently in Brown-Saracino (2004, 2009). In her account, an old timer identity is focused on tenure, family ties, rootedness in social networks, and demographic factors. These locals are viewed as authentic by newer "social preservationists," who look to protect old timers from physical or cultural displacement. In this book, Old Timers are categorized as such based on their attachment to the neighborhood, and they are not viewed as a community to be preserved by gentrifying residents.
7 See Jacobs (1961).
8 See Glass (1964: xvii) for the original use of the term.
9 See Ley (1996); and Blasius, Friedrichs, and Rühl (2016).
10 In the 1960s the neighborhood of Gowanus, Brooklyn, then 43 percent Puerto Rican and 15 percent Black, was experiencing piecemeal gentrification. The new residents nicknamed themselves "the Brownstoners" and formed the

Boerum Hill Association, a neighborhood name created by the gentrifiers. They succeeded in distinguishing Boerum Hill from Gowanus by drawing neighborhood boundaries that excluded concentrations of minorities, publishing histories of the neighborhood, and holding house tours for visitors. See Kasinitz (1988) for more details.

11 See Porter and Barber (2006); and Davidson (2008).
12 See Jacobs (2005).
13 Lehrer and Wieditz (2009) give an early theorization of condofication in Toronto, a topic revisited by Keil and Üçoğlu (2021).
14 In this book I refer to Williamsburg's gentrification as "state-led" and as "condofication." These terms are used somewhat interchangeably, as condofication necessitates state support, and the state-led gentrification in Williamsburg resulted in a condofication of the neighborhood physically and culturally.
15 Easton et al. (2020) provide a review of existing literature on tracking displacement.
16 Williamsburg is similar to many other gentrified American neighborhoods, but New York has a unique housing market. With strong rent control laws and extensive public housing (approximately six thousand units in Williamsburg), many residents are insulated from the private housing market, allowing them to avoid or delay physical displacement. Although physical displacement still looms as an issue they might eventually face, the lack of immediate pressure allowed many participants to focus on experiences of cultural displacement—or the daily effects of living in a gentrifying locale. This provides a unique case to study cultural displacement, or how gentrification is experienced by residents who remain physically in place.
17 There have been a multitude of studies conducted around cultural displacement and gentrification in recent years. This focus was encouraged by a 2009 article in which Mark Davidson warned against a sole focus on physical displacement, which, he argued, obscured important cultural shifts and tensions that emerge in a gentrifying neighborhood. He advocated for a phenomenological approach to considering the various impacts of gentrification on the lived experiences of residents, even in the absence of physical displacement. See Elliott-Cooper, Hubbard, and Lees (2020) for a review of some of the cultural displacement literature.
18 See Fried (1966).
19 See Marcuse (1985: 207; 1986) for the development of the concepts of displacement pressures and indirect displacement—two concepts that are still relevant in discussions of cultural displacement today.
20 See Stabrowski (2014) for a discussion of "everyday displacement" between Polish tenants and their (often co-ethnic) landlords.
21 The concepts of "necessity" and "luxury" will be further explored in chapter 4. See also Levy and Cybriwsky (2010); and Krase (2017).
22 See Taylor (1992).
23 See Tuttle (2022).

24 In his *Distinction: A Social Critique of the Judgment of Taste*, French sociologist Pierre Bourdieu (1984) theorized about how our tastes and dispositions are shaped by social positions. Holding the social position of avant-gardes or creatives affected how the Bohemians dressed and acted and what types of music they listened to or businesses they patronized; just as the social positions of working-class or immigrant affected these things for the Old Timers.
25 See Zukin (2010), esp. chap. 1, "How Brooklyn Became Cool," which deals specifically with this process in Williamsburg.
26 Lloyd (2005: 106).
27 Ocejo (2014: 99).
28 See Tissot (2015).
29 Dozens of recent gentrification studies have focused on how class and racial identities can define an individual's experiences of neighborhood change. In some cities, patterns of gentrification-related displacement have compounded existing trends around residential sorting. Hwang and Ding (2020) found that, in Philadelphia, displacement further increased inequality and stratification around race and class. Huq and Harwood conducted a study on the everyday violence enacted by corporate landlords on tenants in Chicago. Paying close attention to the interaction between socioeconomic status and immigration status, they found that "harassment, intimidation, and dilapidation" of the living environment existed for months prior to eviction (2019: 718). Their results explored how gender, class, race, and immigration status can lead to threatening conditions for renters. Beyond physical aspects of displacement, the exclusionary practices around gentrification have shown to produce cultural displacement, as well as psychological and health stressors. Conducting focus groups with lower-income Puerto Rican older adults, García and Rúa (2018) showed how class and race intersected to impact their experiences of aging in Chicago. Residents felt that new businesses were for white residents, and they did not always feel comfortable visiting them. Interviews with Black men in Washington, DC, revealed how racialized exclusion created psychological and health stressors for them while navigating daily life in gentrifying neighborhoods (Holt et al. 2021).
30 Polish psychologist Maria Lewicka conducted a review of forty years' worth of literature on place attachment, cataloging its use in studies from gated communities to national parks. See Lewicka (2011).
31 See Taylor and Townsend (1976); and Stokols and Shumaker (1981).
32 See Kasarda and Janowitz (1974: 338).
33 See Altman and Low (1992).
34 See Guest and Lee (1983) for a focus on the sentiments involved, and Woldoff (2002) on the relationship between attachment and collective behavior.
35 See Scannell and Gifford (2010).
36 See Firey (1945).
37 Ladewig and McCann (1980); Cox (1982); Ringel and Finkelstein (1991).
38 See Mesch and Manor (1998).

39 See Shumaker and Taylor (1983).
40 See Hunter (1978).

CHAPTER 1. THE NEIGHBORHOOD

1 In 2020 the park was renamed the Marsha P. Johnson State Park in honor of the gay liberation and AIDS activist.
2 Campo (2013) explores the unplanned uses of the Williamsburg waterfront in the period between deindustrialization in the 1960s and 1970s, and the opening of the East River State Park in 2007. Campo shows that the abandoned waterfront was actively used by neighborhood residents during this period before the formal park was developed.
3 See Stabrowski (2014); and Kostrzewa (2020).
4 In fact, these businesses may have been premature. Both City Pilot and Rough Draft were both closed by 2019.
5 See Baker and Coumans (2020) for more details.
6 For more in-depth accounts of Williamsburg's manufacturing history, see Lederer (2005); and DeSena (2009) .
7 In the 1960s John and Leatrice MacDonald coined the term "chain migration" to characterize a form of (im)migration based on existing social relationships and networks, like family members moving to be together or individuals who hear about work or other opportunities thanks to a social relation who has already (im)migrated. See MacDonald and MacDonald (1964) for more details.
8 The two census tracts that contain the Williamsburg Houses grew from an average of 3.7 percent Black in 1950 to 15.8 percent in 1960 during the Second Great Migration. Today the same two tracts, on the East Williamsburg border, average out to 19.7 percent Black, while all tracts in the most highly gentrified parts of Williamsburg report less than 5 percent Black residents, according to the 2019 five-year estimates of the American Community Survey.
9 See Greenberg (2008).
10 See Mollenkopf and Castells (1991) for further analysis of deindustrialization and the restructuring of New York's economy.
11 See Van Riper (1975).
12 For more details on New York's economic and political climate at that time, see Fowler (1976); and Wallace and Wallace (2001).
13 See DeSena (1999).
14 See Mollenkopf (1983).
15 See S. Sutton (2020); and Rucks-Ahidiana (2021).
16 Annual ridership on the L train nearly doubled between 1994 and 2005, from 17 million to 30.5 million. Despite a $443 million investment in the late 1990s and early 2000s, the line was already overwhelmed by 2006. According to the Transit Authority, Bedford Avenue and First Avenue were the most heavily trafficked stops. First Avenue would be the closest subway stop to New York's East Village,

where many of the earlier gentrifiers worked, attended school, and/or partied. See Donohue (2006).
17 See Hackworth and Smith (2001).
18 The full 188-page plan can be found at New York City's Department of Planning website. See "Community Board 1" (2002).
19 See "Benefits for Property Construction" (n.d.) to learn more about the New York City tax abatement system.
20 See Stabrowski (2015).
21 See Amsden (2009).
22 See "Federal Superfund Cleanup Underway" (1998).
23 See Mooney (2007).
24 See "Cuomo Announces Settlement" (2010).
25 See Kensinger (2022).
26 This description comes from the building's profile on Street Easy, a website of real estate listings in New York and other cities, www.streeteasy.com.
27 For more on the dynamics of the housing market and gentrification, see Mollenkopf (1981).
28 See Sampson (2012).
29 It is not a coincidence that the Polish and Italian Northsides were quicker to gentrify. Rucks-Ahidiana (2022) used the concept of racial capitalism to understand how the racialization of space is always interacting with class to explain trends in disinvestment and reinvestment. In a 2021 article on the same topic, she found that Black and Latinx neighborhoods are slower to gentrify than white ones, and existing white neighborhoods were more likely to gentrify with higher-income residents. Immigration status adds an additional factor for understanding experiences of gentrification. Mumm and Sternberg (2022) also applied racial capitalism to property assessment data, showing that areas with an increase in white residents saw an increase in property valuations, regardless of improvements in the material conditions of the neighborhood.
30 Williamsburg's Hasidic Jewish community, while significant, is not focused on in this book. See the methodological appendix for more details about the Hasidic community in Williamsburg.
31 These counts utilize the US decennial census from 1970 to 2000 and the American Community Survey five-year estimates for 2010 and 2020. The data were collected through Social Explorer. See the methodological appendix for more details.
32 In 2015, 80 percent of the population in the Northside tracts were over twenty-five. This indicates that while Williamsburg still averages 41.3 percent eighteen-to-thirty-four-year-olds, most of those residents are in their late twenties and early thirties, more likely to be coupled and established in their careers.
33 These are based on the ten census tracts in the western portion of the neighborhood. In 1980 the census asked about "Spanish" origin, and "Hispanic" on all other versions, but these were both under the category of race. The Polish counts come from the census question on ancestry.

34 See Abu-Lughod (1994).
35 In this study, seventeen of the fifty respondents were considered Old Timers. Two were (im)migrants; thirteen grew up in Williamsburg; two more moved to the neighborhood as adults. Nine residents lived on the Northside and eight on the Southside. The study also includes twelve Bohemians, eleven Condo Dwellers, and ten Former Residents. A table with the full sample and their ethnic identifications can be found in the methodological appendix.
36 See Gooch (1992). Published in *New York* magazine, it was one of the first major mainstream media pieces about Williamsburg's art scene.

CHAPTER 2. CLAIMING SPACE

1 See Short (2011a).
2 The alliance includes a "Community Committee" as an advisory board, but use of funds is ultimately decided by the board members.
3 See Wilson (1996); Byrne (2003); and Hyra (2015) for these arguments on the waxing and waning of political engagement.
4 See Putnam (2000).
5 See Deener (2007).
6 See Wherry's (2011) account of the role of special events and arts branding in the gentrification of North Philadelphia.
7 Levy and Cybriwsky (2010).
8 See Bourdieu (1984).
9 See Ocejo (2021).
10 See Addie and Fraser (2019).
11 See Small (2004).
12 See Marwell (2007); and Stabrowski (2015) for more details on the Southside's political machine.
13 See Susser (1982); and Bahrampour (2003) for the history of the People's Firehouse.
14 See Susser (1982: 186).
15 In her 1985 documentary *Metropolitan Avenue*, Christine Nochese tracks the creation of a coalition of local associations in Williamsburg, including Polish, Irish, Italian, Puerto Rican, Dominican, and Black residents. Throughout the film the individual associations and the coalition advocate together for more police protection, and protest the reduction of public services and the cancellation of a local bus route.
16 See Wiltse (2007) for more history about the racial tensions at McCarren Park pool.
17 From the Southside Los Sures website, www.southsideunitedhdfc.org.
18 From the El Puente website, www.elpuente.us.
19 The act brought together existing community action and job creation programs under one funding umbrella, giving block grants to states that distributed funds. It was a victory for Congress under president Richard Nixon, but CETA was later

dissolved by Ronald Reagan in response to a conservative argument that the private market would better benefit the city and that this sort of funding in inner cities was a waste of non-urban taxpayer dollars. See Mollenkopf (1983).
20 For more information on CETA, see "President Signs Manpower Bill" (1973).
21 Rumors spread among residents and in local media outlets questioning whether the fire was an accident or arson by Brodsky himself.
22 Foderaro (2012) details new racial tensions at the pool, thirty years after the initial problems. In reality, the three people who were arrested for fighting were from within the neighborhood.
23 See Hoffman (2012) for more context of the issues in Cooper Park.
24 Aaron Short (2012) also wrote about tensions in the park that spring.
25 See Carr et al. (1992).
26 Parts of this section were published in Timothy Shortell and Judith N. DeSena's edited volume *The World in Brooklyn* as well as in the *Open Urban Studies Journal*. See Martucci (2012; 2013) for more details.
27 Quotes in this section are from Colvin, Feingold, and Sweet (2008).
28 This quote and others in this section have come from an unpublished Williamsburg Walks summary report provided by an organizer through personal correspondence.
29 See Bélanger (2012) for more details on why the built environment matters during gentrification.
30 See Greenberg (2008: 11).
31 Eventually Williamsburg Walks merged with the Northside Music Festival. The ticketed concert event initially took place in local parks but added Bedford Avenue as a venue in 2017, absorbing Williamsburg Walks as its "Block Party." The music festival was organized by Northside Media, a company that promotes Williamsburg via the local *L Magazine*, as well as other events geared around food, music, and film. By 2019 the Northside Music Festival was defunct amid allegations that the founder was withholding tens of thousands of dollars from staff salaries. See Offenhartz (2019).
32 This quote comes from the website Nervepool, a digital archive of sorts, of Williamsburg's bohemian scene designed by Ebon Fisher. See Rose (1991).

CHAPTER 3. DANGEROUS ENOUGH
1 See McDonald (1986).
2 See Taylor and Covington (1988); and Covington and Taylor (1989).
3 See Kreager, Lyons, and Hays (2011).
4 See C. Smith (2014).
5 See Papachristos et al. (2011) for an overview.
6 See Barton (2016).
7 See O'Sullivan (2005); and Ellen, Horn, and Reed (2019).
8 See Dozier (2019) for a discussion of the harassment faced by homeless residents of Los Angeles's Skid Row during state-led revitalization efforts. See Huq and

Harwood (2019) for an ethnographic account of tenant harassment in Albany Park, Chicago.
9 See Pattillo (2007).
10 See Laniyonu (2018); and Beck (2020).
11 These numbers come from NYC Open Data, part of the New York City government website that provides open access to hundreds of datasets on education, crime, sanitation, and even a census of city trees, https://opendata.cityofnewyork.us.
12 See Stolper (2019).
13 See Kelling and Wilson (1982).
14 See Fagan, Zimring, and Kim (1998); Karmen (2000); and Harcourt (2009) for these arguments.
15 See Haldipur (2018) for a critique of broken windows policing.
16 Additional critiques of the relationship between visible "disorder" and crime can be found in Sampson and Raudenbush (1999); Fagan and Davies (2000); Herbert (2001); and Welsh, Braga, and Bruinsma (2015).
17 See Tissot (2015: 231), who references a 1979 survey of new residents in Boston's South End.
18 See Hipp (2010); and Sullivan and Bachmeier (2012).
19 See Sampson, Raudenbush, and Earls (1997).
20 See Pattillo (1998); and Browning (2002). Gibson et al. (2002) provide a quantitative study of collective efficacy and fear.
21 The crime rate data in this section come from the New York Police Department, which has precinct-level crime rates for the entire city. These figures were collected in late 2017. See the methodological appendix for more details.
22 Several news outlets have suggested that the proliferation of smartphones and personal laptops has caused some of this increase. Apple products alone accounted for more than 18 percent of reported larcenies in 2013.
23 See M. Sullivan (1989); and Skaperdas (2001).
24 See Brady (1983); and Hemenway, Wolf, and Lang (1986) for more information on arsons in New York during this time.
25 See Kasinitz and Hillyard (1995).
26 See Kreager, Lyons, and Hays (2011).
27 See Low (2001); and Atkinson and Flint (2004) for more details on the psychology of living in "gated communities."
28 See Anasi (2012).
29 See N. Smith (1996).
30 *Gut Renovation* is a 2012 documentary that tracks the development of the real estate grab in the 2000s and the effect it had on the artist and retail communities in Williamsburg.
31 For more on the pioneer narrative, see Zukin (1982); and Lloyd (2005).
32 See Mele (2000); and Sullivan and Shaw (2011) on the role of artists as "pioneers" in gentrification.

CHAPTER 4. SELLING WILLIAMSBURG

1 Between North Third and North Fourth Streets.
2 See Mejía (2019).
3 See Jones (2022).
4 Some descriptions and data in this chapter also appear in Martucci (2019).
5 See Young (2013); O'Connor' (2015); Williams (2015); and Rivera (2017).
6 See Gómez (1998); and Evans (2003).
7 BIDs are usually managed by a board of directors including local business owners and take on issues like garbage collection, hiring private security, and promoting local shops. In New York, $167 million flows through BIDs annually and some, like Manhattan's Lower East Side BID, are very active. Just across the bridge from Williamsburg, the Lower East Side has seen a concerted effort at neighborhood (re)branding. The former BID (now the Lower East Side Partnership) produced shopping and art gallery maps of the neighborhood, coordinated business owners for street festivals, and organized "gallery nights" with the aim of attracting visitors. Formerly a working-class manufacturing neighborhood similar to Williamsburg, the Lower East Side does attract tourists to a few museums in the area, but the BID was focused on cementing a local culture of upscale consumption.
8 There is a business improvement district in the eastern portion of the neighborhood, the Grand Street BID, but this is in an area that has experienced much less gentrification than the Northside.
9 See Lloyd (2005: 100).
10 Some archives of the now defunct ArtNetWeb can be found at www.artnetweb.com.
11 See Walljasper and Kraker (1997).
12 See Zukin (2010: 37).
13 See Jayne (2006); and Duyvendak (2011).
14 See Kinsella (2004).
15 See Moynihan (2014).
16 This quote comes from Supercore's now-defunct website, supercore.tv, which remained active for several years after the restaurant closed in 2014.
17 See Hubbard (2016); and Martucci (2019).
18 See Zukin, Kasinitz, and Chen's (2016) discussion of the "global toolkit of revitalization," where local actors including business owners, investors, and the state work in tandem to create a "local character" that ends up looking very similar to the local character of countless other neighborhoods around the world.
19 See the methodological appendix for more details on the Cole's reverse directories.
20 See Schlichtman and Patch (2008) for another example of the use of business directories to triangulate ethnographic and interview data.
21 See Patch (2004).
22 For a full overview of Brooklyn's fleeting DIY venues, see Leckert (2015).

23 See D. Sullivan's (2014) study of a healthy/organic grocery store in the gentrifying Alberta neighborhood of Portland, Oregon. The store opened in a location that was a former food desert, and while he found that 90 percent of local residents used the store at least once a year, white residents and those with at least a college degree visited the store more frequently. While he did not ask participants about their feelings toward the store, Sullivan speculated that racial and socioeconomic "symbolic boundaries" in terms of signage, aesthetics, and products affected use of the store.
24 See Lowe, Stroud, and Nguyen (2017) for a further discussion on how retail changes can shift who belongs in public spaces, and the surveillance and suspicion that can arise.

CHAPTER 5. VIEWS OF CHANGE

1 This finding is echoed in many gentrification studies that find that long-term residents view new businesses, improvements to infrastructure, and cultural projects as "not for them." See Freeman (2006); Watt (2013); García and Rúa (2018); Rigolon et al. (2020); and Tuttle (2020).
2 Impacts of gentrification without displacement include loss of ownership over space and cultural displacement (Shaw and Hagemans, 2015; Hyra, 2016); negative health outcomes (Gibbons and Barton, 2016); stressors on social and emotional well-being (Domínguez-Parraga, 2020); and increased police harassment (Laniyonu, 2018).
3 See N. Smith (1996: xv).
4 See Logan and Molotch (1987) for a discussion of growth agenda politics, and Angotti and Morse (2017) for an analysis of how this played out in Williamsburg.
5 See Horne (2015).
6 See Brown (2011).
7 See Mollica, Gray, and Treviño (2003) for more on this idea that gentrifiers socialize with, befriend, and perhaps even notice other gentrifiers more than non-gentrifiers.
8 See Halperin (2014).
9 See Furfaro (2013).
10 See Hogan (2017).
11 The summer before construction started, artist Karen Walker held an imposing art installation inside the refinery. The exhibit considered relationships of exploitation and power, including the connection between the sugar trade and slavery. You can see more about the show at www.creativetime.org.
12 For a more in-depth history of the sugar refinery, see Diamond (2017).
13 See Benzine (2022).
14 Artist and writer Steven Pritchard has written and lectured extensively on artwashing. See Pritchard (2019; 2020). See also Mould (2017).
15 See R. Sutton (2018).

CHAPTER 6. THE MYTHS OF GENTRIFICATION

1 See Lees (2008) for an overview of these arguments from the 1970s to the 2000s.
2 See Byrne (2003).
3 See "In Praise of Gentrification" (2018).
4 The concept of a "complete neighborhood" is most frequently referred to in city and town strategic plans. See also Talen (2018).
5 Retail plays a unique role in gentrification apart from amenities in general. Therefore, there is a separate section dedicated to retail below. In the present section, amenities refer to municipal services, medical care, public parks, and other non-retail institutions like libraries, community centers, or childcare providers.
6 The Federal Reserve Bank of San Francisco, the National Community Reinvestment Coalition, and Housing Matters in DC all recently published reports that refer to cultural displacement as a cost of gentrification. See "Gentrification and Displacement" (n.d.); Richardson, Mitchell, and Franco (2019); and Torres Rodríguez (2020). Cultural displacement has even become a concern in more rural versions of gentrification tourism. See Zhao (2019); and Lorenzen (2021).
7 See the sections on cultural displacement and symbolic ownership in the introduction and chapter 2 for more details and references to other work on this topic.
8 See Vo (2018).
9 Programs like the Downtown Revitalization Initiative, funded by the New York governor's office, obliquely reference "job creation." See "Governor Hochul Announces" (2023).
10 See Byrne (2003: 420).
11 See Curran (2004) on gentrification's impact on deindustrialization, and Meltzer and Ghorbani (2017) on the relationship between gentrification and employment more broadly.
12 See García and Rúa (2018) on the impacts of retail change for Puerto Rican older adults in Chicago.
13 See Lees (2008); Freeman (2009); Jonathon Jackson (2015); Embrick (2016); and S. Sutton (2020).
14 See Johnson (2018).
15 See Hwang (2015) for insight into how gentrification instead perpetuates racial inequality.
16 See Haag (2022).
17 See Mader et al. (2018).
18 See Brown-Saracino (2004; 2009).
19 See Bradley (2023) for a discussion of the rise and dissolution of the neighborhood's music scene through waves of gentrification. Reports by Create NYC and the Center for an Urban Future also document the loss of Williamsburg's artist population.

20 See Rucks-Ahidiana (2021) for a discussion of the racialized trajectories of gentrification.

CONCLUSION

1 See Giambrone (2018).
2 See Giambrone (2017).
3 See Banister (2017).
4 See Howe (2023).
5 See Schwartzman (2021).
6 See Sigler and Wachsmuth (2016) for an overview of how Casco Viejo has been gentrified through globalization, specifically by cosmopolitan elites who have worked together with local developers to exploit an international rent gap. They have profited by purchasing properties, evicting existing residents, and converting buildings into tourist apartments, hotels, and luxury residences.
7 See "Casco Viejo" (2014).
8 See Zukin, Kasinitz, and Chen (2016) for examples of these revitalization strategies.
9 It was accomplished in this project (granted, with a small N) by snowball sampling, or asking current-resident interviewees whether they knew anyone who had left the neighborhood and might be interested in speaking with me. While snowball sampling has its own issues in terms of generalization, this was an effective way of finding and contacting former residents. See the methodological appendix for more details.
10 See the methodological appendix for more details on deed transfer data.
11 These examples refer to Laniyonu (2018); and Gibbons, Barton, and Reling (2020), both informative quantitative pieces on gentrification but nevertheless relying on preexisting data.
12 The work of Daniel Munroe Sullivan stands out as an important outlier here. His quantitative surveys correlated demographic data like race, education, and tenure with measures of neighborhood belonging that included likelihood to shop at certain stores, participation in local arts events, evaluations of neighborhood disorder, feelings of trust, relationships with neighbors, and vulnerability around displacement. See his work on Portland in Sullivan and Shaw (2011); Sullivan (2014); and especially Sullivan (2006). See also Soytemel's (2015) research in Istanbul for a mixed-method approach, including Likert-survey questions on measures of belonging.
13 Community land trusts have recently seen success in cities from Oakland to Rochester. A report from the Urban Institute details some of the benefits and challenges of this model. See Velasco (2020).
14 In 2019 Brooklyn City Council member Steve Levin introduced a bill to reenact commercial rent control in 2019, but it lost steam when the pandemic began. He proposed the idea again in September 2021 to wide support from the City Coun-

cil, but there has been no further movement since then and Levin completed his final four-year term in December 2021.
15. In New York there are currently more than one hundred retail units owned by the New York City Housing Authority, which rent at market rate but only allows for a 3 percent rent increase per year.
16. See Angotti and Morse (2017) for more details on the community's 197-a plan and the city's rezoning.
17. In 2022 the real estate industry donated $150,000 to a committee associated with Elizabeth Crowley's campaign for Senate. She lost the race. Had she won, she would have represented Williamsburg, Greenpoint, and the gentrifying Queens waterfront. The real estate industry is typically one of the biggest contributors in New York's mayoral and gubernatorial races. See Joseph (2022).

EPILOGUE

1. See Marsh (2018).
2. See "City Finances Nearly 30,000 Affordable Homes" (2021).
3. See Brenzel and Larsen (2021).

METHODOLOGICAL APPENDIX

1. See Marwell (2007); and Deutsch and Casper (2021) for sociopolitical and historical accounts of the Williamsburg Hasidic community.
2. Jerome Krase and Timothy Shortell have written extensively on visual sociology as a method of urban research. See Krase (2017); and Krase and Shortell (2011), as well as Manzo (2013). See Harper's (1988) as well as Becker's (1995) seminal pieces on the topic.
3. In 2008 Jerome Krase shared his archive of Williamsburg photographs from 2000 to 2003, before the neighborhood's condofication. Throughout the 2010s, I repeated the photographs as streetscapes and local shops changed.
4. See Schlichtman and Patch (2008) for more details on their specific methodology.
5. This work was published in Zukin, Kasinitz, and Chen (2016).
6. See Brown-Saracino and Rumpf's (2011) quantitative analysis of articles containing the word "gentrification" from 1986 to 2006 as well as Lavy, Dascher, and Hagelman's (2016) content analysis of media in a gentrifying neighborhood in Austin, Texas.
7. Social Explorer provides demographic, voting, health, and crime-related information about the United States from 1790 to the present at www.socialexplorer.com.
8. The deed transfer information can be found on the New York City Department of Finance website under "Data and Lot Information." The DOF also hosts a "Digital Tax Map" that provides essential information for looking up deed transfer records.

BIBLIOGRAPHY

Abu-Lughod, Janet. 1994. "Diversity, Democracy, and Self-Determination in an Urban Neighborhood: The East Village of Manhattan." *Social Research* 61(1): 181–203.
Addie, Jean-Paul D., and James C. Fraser. 2019. "After Gentrification: Social Mix, Settler Colonialism, and Cruel Optimism in the Transformation of Neighborhood Space." *Antipode* 51(5): 1369–94.
Ahrens, Mareike. 2015. "'Gentrify? No! Gentefy? Sí!': Urban Redevelopment and Ethnic Gentrification in Boyle Heights, Los Angeles." *aspeers* 8: 9–26.
Altman, Irwin, and Setha M. Low, eds. 1992. *Place Attachment*. New York: Plenum.
Amsden, David. 2009. "The Billyburg Bust." *New York*, July 10, 2009.
Anasi, Robert. 2012. *The Last Bohemia: Scenes from the Life of Williamsburg, Brooklyn*. New York: Farrar, Straus and Giroux.
Angotti, Tom, and Sylvia Morse, eds. 2017. *Zoned Out! Race, Displacement, and City Planning in New York City*. New York: Terreform.
ArtNetWeb. 1996. "Resources." Accessed January 2017. http://artnetweb.com.
Atkinson, Rowland, and John Flint. 2004. "Fortress UK? Gated Communities, the Spatial Revolt of the Elites and Time-Space Trajectories of Segregation." *Housing Studies* 19(6): 875–92.
Bahrampour, Tara. 2003. "Neighborhood Report: Williamsburg. 'The People's Firehouse' Faces Another Fierce Battle of Wills." *New York Times*, April 27, 2003.
Baker, Joe, and Hadrien Coumans. 2020. "Home in Lenapehoking." *Urban Omnibus*, February 6, 2020. www.urbanomnibus.net.
Banister, Jon. 2017. "How Union Market Has Become the Front Line of DC's Activist-Developer War." *Bisnow*, September 21, 2017. www.bisnow.com.
Barton, Michael S. 2016. "Gentrification and Violent Crime in New York City." *Crime & Delinquency* 62(9): 1180–1202.
Barton, Michael S, and Colin P. Gruner. 2016. "A Theoretical Explanation of the Influence of Gentrification on Neighborhood Crime." *Deviant Behavior* 37(1): 30–46.
Beck, Brenden. 2020. "Policing Gentrification: Stops and Low-Level Arrests during Demographic Change and Real Estate Reinvestment." *City & Community* 19(1): 245–72.
Becker, Howard S. 1995. "Visual Sociology, Documentary Photography, and Photojournalism: It's (Almost) All a Matter of Context." *Visual Sociology* 10(1–2): 5–14.
Bélanger, Hélène. 2012. "The Meaning of the Built Environment during Gentrification in Canada." *Journal of Housing and the Built Environment* 27(1): 31–47.

"Benefits for Property Construction." n.d. New York City Department of Finance. Accessed December 2022. www.nyc.gov.

Benzine, Vittoria. 2022. "Two Trees Taps Photoville to Explore the History of the Domino Refinery." *Brooklyn Magazine*, October 17, 2022. www.bkmag.com.

Blasius, Jörg, Jürgen Friedrichs, and Heiko Rühl. 2016. "Pioneers and Gentrifiers in the Process of Gentrification." *International Journal of Housing Policy* 16(1): 50–69.

Bourdieu, Pierre. 1984. *Distinction: A Social Critique of the Judgment of Taste*. Translated by R. Nice. Cambridge, MA: Harvard University Press.

Bradley, Cisco. 2023. *The Williamsburg Avant-Garde: Experimental Music and Sound on the Brooklyn Waterfront*. Durham: Duke University Press.

Brady, James. 1983. "Arson, Urban Economy, and Organized Crime: The Case of Boston." *Social Problems* 31(1): 1–27.

Brenzel, Kathryn, and Keith Larsen. 2021. "Eric Adams' Cup Runneth Over with Real Estate Cash." *Real Deal*, October 7, 2021. www.therealdeal.com.

Brown, Tamara Mose. 2011. *Raising Brooklyn: Nannies, Childcare, and Caribbeans Creating Community*. New York: New York University Press.

Browning, Christopher R. 2002. "The Span of Collective Efficacy: Extending Social Disorganization Theory to Partner Violence." *Journal of Marriage and Family* 64(4): 833–50.

Brown-Saracino, Japonica. 2004. "Social Preservationists and the Quest for Authentic Community." *City & Community* 3(2): 135–56.

———. 2009. *A Neighborhood That Never Changes*. Chicago: University of Chicago Press.

———, ed. 2010. *The Gentrification Debates*. New York: Routledge.

Brown-Saracino, Japonica, and Cesraea Rumpf. 2011. "Diverse Imageries of Gentrification: Evidence from Newspaper Coverage in Seven US Cities, 1986–2006." *Journal of Urban Affairs* 33(3): 289–315.

Byrne, J. Peter. 2003. "Two Cheers for Gentrification." *Howard Law Journal* 46: 405–32.

Campo, Daniel. 2013. *The Accidental Playground: Brooklyn Waterfront Narratives of the Undesigned and Unplanned*. New York: Empire State Editions.

Carr, Stephen, Mark Francis, Leanne G. Rivlin, and Andrew M. Stone. 1992. *Public Space*. New York: Cambridge University Press.

"Casco Viejo: Heart and Soul of Panama City." 2014. *Alex in Wonderland*, March 12, 2014. www.alexinwonderland.com.

"City Finances Nearly 30,000 Affordable Homes in 2020." 2021. Office of the Mayor, City of New York, February 9, 2021. www.nyc.gov.

Colvin, Connie, Dana Feingold, and Alex Sweet. 2008. "Williamsburg Walks End Report." Accessed June 2009. www.billburg.com.

"Community Board 1: Williamsburg Waterfront 197-a Plan." 2002. Department of City Planning, City of New York. Accessed November 2016. www.nyc.gov.

Covington, Jeanette, and Ralph B. Taylor. 1989. "Gentrification and Crime: Robbery and Larceny Changes in Appreciating Baltimore Neighborhoods during the 1970s." *Urban Affairs Quarterly* 25(1): 142–72.

Cox, Kevin R. 1982. "Housing Tenure and Neighborhood Activism." *Urban Affairs Quarterly* 18(1): 107–29.
"Create NYC: A Plan for All New Yorkers." 2017. Department of Cultural Affairs, City of New York. Accessed July 2017. www.createnyc.org.
"Cuomo Announces Settlement with ExxonMobil to Provide for Comprehensive Cleanup of Greenpoint Oil Spill." 2010. Office of the New York State Attorney General, November 17, 2010. www.ag.ny.gov.
Curran, Winifred. 2004. "Gentrification and the Changing Nature of Work: Exploring the Links in Williamsburg, Brooklyn." *Environment and Planning A* 36(7): 1243–60.
Davidson, Mark. 2008. "Spoiled Mixture: Where Does State-Led 'Positive' Gentrification End?" *Urban Studies* 45(12): 2385–2405.
———. 2009. "Displacement, Space and Dwelling: Placing Gentrification Debate." *Ethics, Place & Environment* 12(2): 219–34.
Deener, Andrew. 2007. "Commerce as the Structure and Symbol of Neighborhood Life: Reshaping the Meaning of Community in Venice, California." *City & Community* 6(4): 291–312.
———. 2012. *Venice: A Contested Bohemia in Los Angeles*. Chicago: University of Chicago Press.
DeSena, Judith N. 1999. *People Power: Grass Roots Politics and Race Relations*. Lanham, MD: University Press of America.
———. 2006. "'What's a Mother to Do?': Gentrification, School Selection, and the Consequences for Community Cohesion." *American Behavioral Scientist* 50(2): 241–57.
———. 2009. *Gentrification and Inequality in Brooklyn: The New Kids on the Block*. Lanham, MD: Lexington Books.
Deutsch, Nathaniel, and Michael Casper. 2021. *A Fortress in Brooklyn: Race, Real Estate, and the Making of Hasidic Williamsburg*. New Haven: Yale University Press.
Diamond, Anna. 2017. "These Photos of the Abandoned Domino Sugar Refinery Document Its Sticky History." *Smithsonian Magazine*, December 19, 2017. www.smithsonianmagazine.com.
Domínguez-Parraga, Lidia. 2020. "The Effects of Gentrification on the Elderly: A Case Study in the City of Cáceres." *Social Sciences* 9(9): 154.
Donohue, Pete. 2006. "Oh, L, Not Enuf Trains! TA Says There's Too Few Cars for Surge in Riders." *New York Daily News*, July 7, 2006.
Dozier, Deshonay. 2019. "Contested Development: Homeless Property, Police Reform, and Resistance in Skid Row, LA." *International Journal of Urban and Regional Research* 43(1): 179–94.
Duyvendak, Jan Willem. 2011. *The Politics of Home: Belonging and Nostalgia in Western Europe and the United States*. New York: Palgrave Macmillan.
Easton, Sue, Loretta Lees, Phil Hubbard, and Nicholas Tate. 2020. "Measuring and Mapping Displacement: The Problem of Quantification in the Battle against Gentrification." *Urban Studies* 57(2): 286–306.
Ellen, Ingrid Gould, Keren Mertens Horn, and Davin Reed. 2019. "Has Falling Crime Invited Gentrification?" *Journal of Housing Economics* 46.

Elliott-Cooper, Adam, Phil Hubbard, and Loretta Lees. 2020. "Moving beyond Marcuse: Gentrification, Displacement and the Violence of Un-homing." *Progress in Human Geography* 44(3): 492–509.

El Puente: Leaders for Social Justice. 2017. "History." Accessed March 2017. http://elpuente.us.

Embrick, David G. 2016. "Thinking Diversity, Rethinking Diversity." *Humanity & Society* 40(3): 223–28.

Evans, Graeme. 2003. "Hard-Branding the Cultural City: From Prado to Prada." *International Journal of Urban and Regional Research* 27(2): 417–40.

Fagan, Jeffrey, and Garth Davies. 2000. "Street Stops and Broken Windows: *Terry*, Race, and Disorder in New York City." *Fordham Urban Law Journal* 28: 457–504.

Fagan, Jeffrey, Franklin E. Zimring, and June Kim. 1998. "Declining Homicide in New York City: A Tale of Two Trends." *Journal of Criminal Law and Criminology* 88: 1277–1324.

"Federal Superfund Cleanup Underway at Abandoned Hazardous Waste Site in Brooklyn, Williamsburg." 1998. US Environmental Protection Agency, September 17, 1998. www.epa.gov.

Firey, Walter. 1945. "Sentiment and Symbolism as Ecological Variables." *American Sociological Review* 10(2): 140–48.

Foderaro, Lisa. 1987. "A Metamorphosis for Old Williamsburg." *New York Times*, July 19, 1987.

———. 2012. "A Revived Pool Draws Tensions to the Surface." *New York Times*, July 4, 2012.

Forman, Adam. 2015. "Creative New York." Center for an Urban Future. https://nycfuture.org.

Fowler, Glenn. 1976. "Starr's 'Shrinkage' Plan for City Slums Is Denounced." *New York Times*, February 11, 1976.

Freeman, Lance. 2006. *There Goes the 'Hood: Views of Gentrification from the Ground Up*. Philadelphia,: Temple University Press.

———. 2009. "Neighborhood Diversity, Metropolitan Segregation and Gentrification: What Are the Links in the US?" *Urban Studies* 46(10): 2079–2101.

Fried, Marc. 1966. "Grieving for a Lost Home: Psychological Costs of Relocation." In *Urban Renewal: The Record and the Controversy*, edited by J. Q. Wilson, 359–79. Cambridge, MA: MIT Press.

Friedrich, Su, and Cathy Quinlan. 2012. *Gut Renovation*. New York: Outcast Films.

Furfaro, Danielle. 2013. "A Flea Too Many." *Brooklyn Paper*, April 30, 2013. www.brooklynpaper.com.

Gans, Herbert J. 1962. *The Urban Villagers: Group and Class in the Life of Italian-Americans*. New York: Free Press.

García, Ivis, and Mérida M. Rúa. 2018. "'Our Interests Matter': Puerto Rican Older Adults in the Age of Gentrification." *Urban Studies* 55(14): 3168–84.

"Gentrification and Displacement." n.d. Federal Reserve Bank of San Francisco. Accessed March 2023. www.frbsf.org.

Giambrone, Andrew. 2017. "DC Moves to Subsidize Development and Limit Access to Shelters." *Washington City Paper*, November 16, 2017. www.washingtoncitypaper.com.

———. 2018. "Court Ruling Clears Way for Major Mixed-Use Project in NoMa near Union Market." *Curbed*, December 17, 2018. www.dc.curbed.com.

Gibbons, Joseph, and Michael S. Barton. 2016. "The Association of Minority Self-Rated Health with Black versus White Gentrification." *Journal of Urban Health* 93(6): 909–22.

Gibbons, Joseph, Michael S. Barton, and Timothy T. Reling. 2020. "Do Gentrifying Neighborhoods Have Less Community? Evidence from Philadelphia." *Urban Studies* 57(6): 1143–63.

Gibson, Chris L., Jihong Zhao, Nicholas P. Lovrich, and Michael J. Gaffney. 2002. "Social Integration, Individual Perceptions of Collective Efficacy, and Fear of Crime in Three Cities." *Justice Quarterly* 19(3): 537–64.

Glass, Ruth L. D. 1964. *London: Aspects of Change*. London: MacGibbon and Kee.

Golash-Boza, Tanya, Hyunsu Oh, and Robert Kane. "Gentrification, White Encroachment, and the Policing of Black Residents in Washington, DC." *Critical Criminology* 31: 181–202.

Gómez, María. 1998. "Reflective Images: The Case of Urban Regeneration in Glasgow and Bilbao." *International Journal of Urban and Regional Research* 22(1): 106–21.

Gooch, Brad. 1992. "The New Bohemia: Portrait of an Artist's Colony in Brooklyn." *New York*, June 22, 1992.

Gotham, Kevin Fox. 2002. "Marketing Mardi Gras: Commodification, Spectacle and the Political Economy of Tourism in New Orleans." *Urban Studies* 39(10): 1735–56.

"Governor Hochul Announces East Harlem as the $10 Million New York City Region Winner of Sixth-Round Downtown Revitalization Initiative." 2023. New York State Governor's Office, January 19, 2023. www.governor.ny.gov.

Greenberg, Miriam. 2008. *Branding New York: How a City in Crisis Was Sold to the World*. New York: Routledge.

Greif, Meredith J. 2009. "Neighborhood Attachment in the Multiethnic Metropolis." *City & Community* 8(1): 27–45.

Gricar, Barbara Gray, and L. Dave Brown. 1981. "Conflict, Power, and Organization in a Changing Community." *Human Relations* 34(10): 877–93.

Guest, Avery M., and Barrett A. Lee. 1983. "Sentiment and Evaluation as Ecological Variables." *Sociological Perspectives* 26(2): 159–84.

Haag, Matthew. 2022. "Why a Lucrative Tax Break for Developers Is Likely to Die in Albany." *New York Times*, May 26, 2022.

Hackworth, Jason, and Neil Smith. 2001. "The Changing State of Gentrification." *Tijdschrift voor Economische en Sociale Geografie* 92(4): 464–77.

Haldipur, Jan. 2018. *No Place on the Corner: The Costs of Aggressive Policing*. New York: New York University Press.

Halperin, Rory. 2014. "Williamsburg's Frolic to Close on Friday." *Mommy Nearest*, September 24, 2014. www.mommynearest.com.

Harcourt, Bernard E. 2009. *Illusion of Order: The False Promise of Broken Windows Policing*. Cambridge, MA: Harvard University Press.
Harper, Douglas. 1988. "Visual Sociology: Expanding Sociological Vision." *American Sociologist*, 19: 54–70.
Hemenway, David, Kate Wolf, and Janet Lang. 1986. "An Arson Epidemic." *Journal of Behavioral Economics* 15(3): 17–28.
Herbert, Steve. 2001. "Policing the Contemporary City: Fixing Broken Windows or Shoring Up Neo-Liberalism?" *Theoretical Criminology* 5(4): 445–66.
Hipp, John R. 2010. "Resident Perceptions of Crime and Disorder: How Much Is 'Bias' and How Much Is Social Environment Differences?" *Criminology* 48(2): 475–508.
Hoffman, Meredith. 2012. "Cooper Park Barbecue Grills Bring Neighbors to a Boil." *DNA Info*, May 4, 2012. www.dnainfo.com.
Hogan, Gwynne. 2017. "Brooklyn Flea Cancels Williamsburg Site amid Growing Community Discontent." *DNA Info*, May 3, 2017. www.dnainfo.com.
Holt, Sidney L., Ana María del Río-González, Jenné S. Massie, and Lisa Bowleg. 2021. "'I Live in This Neighborhood Too, Though': The Psychosocial Effects of Gentrification on Low-Income Black Men Living in Washington, DC." *Journal of Racial and Ethnic Health Disparities* 8: 1139–52.
Horne, Sarah. 2015. "Williamsburg Baby Resources." *Williamsburg Baby*. Accessed July 7, 2016. www.williamsburgbaby.com.
Howe, Aaron. 2023. "The City and the City: Tent Camps and Luxury Development in the NoMA Business Improvement District (BID) in Washington, DC." *International Journal of Historical Archaeology*, January 2023.
Hubbard, Phil. 2016. "Hipsters on Our High Streets: Consuming the Gentrification Frontier." *Sociological Research Online* 21(3): 106–11.
Hummon, David M. 1992. "Community Attachment: Local Sentiment and Sense of Place." In *Place Attachment*, edited by Irwin Altman and Setha M. Low, 253–78. New York: Plenum.
Hunter, Albert. 1978. "Persistence of Local Sentiments in Mass Society." In *Handbook of Contemporary Urban Life*, edited by David Street, 133–62. San Francisco: Jossey-Bass.
Huq, Efadul, and Stacy Anne Harwood. 2019. "Making Homes Unhomely: The Politics of Displacement in a Gentrifying Neighborhood in Chicago." *City & Community* 18(2): 710–31.
Hwang, Jackelyn. 2015. "Gentrification in Changing Cities: Immigration, New Diversity, and Racial Inequality in Neighborhood Renewal." *Annals of the American Academy of Political and Social Science* 660(1): 319–40.
Hwang, Jackelyn, and Lei Ding. 2020. "Unequal Displacement: Gentrification, Racial Stratification, and Residential Destinations in Philadelphia." *American Journal of Sociology* 126(2): 354–406.
Hyra, Derek S. 2015. "The Back-to-the-City Movement: Neighborhood Redevelopment and Processes of Political and Cultural Displacement." *Urban Studies* 52(10): 1753–73.

———. 2016. "Commentary: Causes and Consequences of Gentrification and the Future of Equitable Development Policy." *Cityscape* 18(3): 169–77.
"In Praise of Gentrification." 2018. *Economist*, June 21, 2018. www.economist.com.
Jackson, John L. 2003. *Harlemworld: Doing Race and Class in Contemporary Black America*. Chicago: University of Chicago Press.
Jackson, Jonathon. 2015. "The Consequences of Gentrification for Racial Change in Washington, DC." *Housing Policy Debate* 25(2): 353–73.
Jacobs, Jane. 1961. *The Death and Life of Great American Cities*. New York: Vintage.
———. 2005. "Letter to Mayor Bloomberg and the City Council." *Brooklyn Rail*, April 15, 2005. www.brooklynrail.org.
Jayne, Mark. 2006. *Cities and Consumption*. New York: Routledge.
Johnson, Olatunde C. A. 2018. "Unjust Cities: Gentrification, Integration, and the Fair Housing Act." *University of Richmond Law Review* 53: 835–69.
Jones, Sasha. 2022. "Alo Yoga Inks Lease on Fifth Avenue." *Real Deal*, January 20, 2022. www.therealdeal.com.
Joseph, George. 2022. "Real Estate Pours $150K into Pro-Crowley State Senate PAC." *City*, August 10, 2022. www.thecity.nyc.
Karmen, Andrew. 2000. *New York Murder Mystery: The True Story behind the Crime Crash of the 1990s*. New York: New York University Press.
Kasarda, John D., and Morris Janowitz. 1974. "Community Attachment in Mass Society." *American Sociological Review* 39(3): 328–39.
Kasinitz, Philip. 1988. "The Gentrification of Boerum Hill: Neighborhood Change and Conflicts over Definitions." *Qualitative Sociology* 11(3): 163–82.
Kasinitz, Philip, and David Hillyard. 1995. "The Old-Timers' Tale: The Politics of Nostalgia on the Waterfront." *Journal of Contemporary Ethnography* 24(2): 139–64.
Keil, Roger, and Murat Üçoğlu. 2021. "Beyond Sprawl? Regulating Growth in Southern Ontario: Spotlight on Brampton." *disP- The Planning Review* 57(3): 100–118.
Kelling, George L., and James Q. Wilson. 1982. "Broken Windows: The Police and Neighborhood Safety." *Atlantic*, March 1982.
Kensinger, Nathan. 2022. "EPA Delays Cleanup of Brooklyn's Toxic Newton Creek Superfund Site until 2032." *Gothamist*, December 5, 2022. www.gothamist.com.
Kinsella, Kevin. 2004. "Life Is Elsewhere." *Languor Management*, June 9, 2004. www.reddomino.typepad.com.
Kirk, David S., and John H. Laub. 2010. "Neighborhood Change and Crime in the Modern Metropolis." *Crime and Justice* 39(1): 441–502.
Kostrzewa, Aneta. 2020. "New Business in the Old Neighborhood: Young Polish Shopkeepers' Responses to Commercial Gentrification in Greenpoint, Brooklyn." In *Gentrification around the World*, vol. 2, edited by Jerome Krase and Judith DeSena, 37–62. Camden: Palgrave Macmillan.
Krase, Jerome. 1982. *Self and Community in the City*. Washington, DC: University Press of America.
———. 2017. *Seeing Cities Change: Local Culture and Class*. London: Routledge.

Krase, Jerome, and Judith N. DeSena. 2016. *Race, Class, and Gentrification in Brooklyn: A View from the Street*. Lanham, MD: Lexington Books.

Krase, Jerry, and Timothy Shortell. 2011. "On the Spatial Semiotics of Vernacular Landscapes in Global Cities." *Visual Communication* 10(3): 367–400.

Kreager, Derek A., Christopher J. Lyons, and Zachary R. Hays. 2011. "Urban Revitalization and Seattle Crime, 1982–2000." *Social Problems* 58(4): 615–39.

Kurutz, Steven. 2017. "Bleecker Street's Swerve from Luxe Shops to Vacant Stores." *New York Times*, May 31, 2017.

Ladewig, Howard, and Glenn C. McCann. 1980. "Community Satisfaction: Theory and Measurement." *Rural Sociology* 45(1): 110–31.

Laniyonu, Ayobami. 2018. "Coffee Shops and Street Stops: Policing Practices in Gentrifying Neighborhoods." *Urban Affairs Review* 54(5): 898–930.

Lavy, Brendan L., Erin D. Dascher, and Ronald R. Hagelman. 2016. "Media Portrayal of Gentrification and Redevelopment on Rainey Street in Austin, Texas (USA), 2000–2014." *City, Culture and Society* 7(4): 197–207.

Leckert, Oriana. 2015. *Brooklyn Spaces: 50 Hubs of Culture and Creativity*. New York: Monacelli.

Lederer, Victor. 2005. *Williamsburg*. Charleston, SC: Arcadia.

Lees, Loretta. 2003. "Super-Gentrification: The Case of Brooklyn Heights, New York City." *Urban Studies* 40(12): 2487–2509.

———. 2008. "Gentrification and Social Mixing: Towards an Inclusive Urban Renaissance?" *Urban Studies* 45(12): 2449–70.

Lees, Loretta, and Martin Phillips. 2018. *Handbook of Gentrification Studies*. Cheltenham: Edward Elgar.

Lees, Loretta, Tom Slater, and Elvin K. Wyly. 2008. *Gentrification*. Oxfordshire: Routledge.

Lehrer, Ute, and Thorben Wieditz. 2009. "Condominium Development and Gentrification: The Relationship between Policies, Building Activities and Socio-Economic Development in Toronto." *Canadian Journal of Urban Research* 18(1): 140–61.

Leland, John. 2011. "In Williamsburg, Rocked Hard." *New York Times*, May 28, 2011.

Levy, Paul, and Roman Cybriwsky. 2010. "The Hidden Dimensions of Culture and Class: Philadelphia." In *The Gentrification Debates*, edited by Japonica Brown-Saracino, 285–94. New York: Routledge.

Lewicka, Maria. 2011. "Place Attachment: How Far Have We Come in the Last 40 Years?" *Journal of Environmental Psychology* 31(3): 207–30.

Ley, David. 1996. *The New Middle Class and the Remaking of the Central City*. Oxford: Oxford University Press.

Lloyd, Richard. 2005. *Neo-Bohemia: Art and Commerce in the Post-Industrial City*. New York: Routledge.

Logan, John R., and Harvey L. Molotch. 1987. *Urban Fortunes: The Political Economy of Place*. Berkeley: University of California Press.

Lorenzen, Matthew. 2021. "Rural Gentrification, Touristification, and Displacement: Analysing Evidence from Mexico." *Journal of Rural Studies* 86: 62–75.

Low, Setha M. 2001. "The Edge and the Center: Gated Communities and the Discourse of Urban Fear." *American Anthropologist* 103(1): 45–58.

Lowe, Maria R., Angela Stroud, and Alice Nguyen. 2017. "Who Looks Suspicious? Racialized Surveillance in a Predominantly White Neighborhood." *Social Currents* 4(1): 34–50.

MacDonald, John S., and Leatrice D. MacDonald. 1964. "Chain Migration Ethnic Neighborhood Formation and Social Networks." *Milbank Memorial Fund Quarterly* 42(1): 82–97.

Mader, Nicole, Clara Hemphill, Qasim Abbas, Taina Guarda, Ana Carla Sant'anna Costa, and Melanie Quiroz. 2018. "The Paradox of School Choice: How School Choice Divides New York City Elementary Schools." Center for New York City Affairs.

Manzo, Lidia K. C. 2013. "Visual Approaches to Urban Ethnography." *Urbanities* 3(1): 99–102.

Marcuse, Peter. 1985. "Gentrification, Abandonment, and Displacement: Connections, Clauses, and Policy Responses in New York City." *Washington University Journal of Urban and Contemporary Law* 28: 195–240.

———. 1986. "Abandonment, Gentrification, and Displacement: The Linkages in New York City." In *Gentrification of the City*, edited by Neil Smith and Peter Williams, 121–52. Boston: Allen and Unwin.

Marsh, Julia. 2018. "Manhattan Residents Sue MTA over Planned L Train Shutdown." *New York Post*, October 1, 2018.

Martucci, Sara. 2012. "Williamsburg Walks: Public Space and Community Events in a Gentrified Neighborhood." In *The World in Brooklyn: Gentrification, Immigration, and Ethnic Politics in a Global City*, edited by Judith N. DeSena and Timothy Shortell, 89–111. Lanham, MD: Lexington Books.

———. 2013. "Rethink Your Public Space: Community Events in Gentrified Brooklyn." *Open Urban Studies Journal* 6: 40–49.

———. 2019. "Shopping Streets and Neighborhood Identity: Retail Theming as Symbolic Ownership in New York." *City & Community* 18(4): 1123–41.

Marwell, Nicole. 2007. *Bargaining for Brooklyn: Community Organizations in the Entrepreneurial City*. Chicago: University of Chicago Press.

Mazer, Katie M., and Katharine N. Rankin. 2011. "The Social Space of Gentrification: The Politics of Neighborhood Accessibility in Toronto's Downtown West." *Environment and Planning D: Society and Space* 29(5): 822–39.

McDonald, Scott C. 1986. "Does Gentrification Affect Crime Rates?" *Crime and Justice* 8: 163–201.

Mejía, Paula. 2019. "Whisk's Williamsburg Location to Close after Monthly Rent Surges to $26,500." *Gothamist*, April 22, 2019. www.gothamist.com.

Mele, Christopher. 2000. *Selling the Lower East Side: Culture, Real Estate, and Resistance in New York City*. Minneapolis: University of Minnesota Press.

Meltzer, Rachel, and Pooya Ghorbani. 2017. "Does Gentrification Increase Employment Opportunities in Low-Income Neighborhoods?" *Regional Science and Urban Economics* 66: 52–73.

Mesch, Gustavo S., and Orit Manor. 1998. "Social Ties, Environmental Perception, and Local Attachment." *Environment and Behavior* 30(4): 504–19.

Mollenkopf, John. 1981. "Neighborhood Political Development and the Politics of Urban Growth." *International Journal of Urban and Regional Research* 5(1): 5–39.

———. 1983. *The Contested City*. Princeton: Princeton University Press.

Mollenkopf, John, and Manuel Castells. 1991. *Dual City: Restructuring New York*. New York: Russell Sage Foundation.

Mollica, Kelly A., Barbara Gray, and Linda K. Treviño. 2003. "Racial Homophily and Its Persistence in Newcomers' Social Networks." *Organization Science* 14(2): 123–36.

Mooney, Jake. 2007. "An Oily Ooze Seeps In, Origins Unknown." *New York Times*, April 1, 2007.

Mould, Oli. 2017. "Why Culture Competitions and 'Artwashing' Drive Urban Inequality." *Open Democracy*, September 14, 2017. www.opendemocracy.net.

Moynihan, Colin. 2014. "Born in Brooklyn, Now Making a Motown Move." *New York Times*, December 7, 2014.

Mumm, Jesse, and Carolina Sternberg. 2022. "Mapping Racial Capital: Gentrification, Race and Value in Three Chicago Neighborhoods." *Urban Affairs Review* 59(3): 793–831.

Noschese, Christine. 1985. *Metropolitan Avenue*. New York: Newday Films.

Ocejo, Richard E. 2011. "The Early Gentrifier: Weaving a Nostalgia Narrative on the Lower East Side." *City & Community* 10(3): 285–310.

———. 2014. *Upscaling Downtown*. Princeton: Princeton University Press.

———. 2021. "The Virtue of Opportunity: Moral Framing, Community, and Conditional Gentrification." *Social Forces* 70(2): 416–34.

O'Connor, Maureen. 2015. "How Tulum Became the Mexico of Williamsburg." *Cut*, May 10, 2015. www.thecut.com.

Offenhartz, Jake. 2019. "Northside Fest and SummerScreen Go Dark as Alleged 'Scam Artist' Boss Goes Silent." *Gothamist*, May 15, 2019. www.gothamist.com.

Open Space Alliance. 2017. "About OSA." Accessed March 8, 2017. www.osanb.org.

Osman, Suleiman. 2012. *The Invention of Brownstone Brooklyn: Gentrification and the Search for Authenticity in Postwar New York*. New York: Oxford University Press.

O'Sullivan, Arthur. 2005. "Gentrification and Crime." *Journal of Urban Economics* 57(1): 73–85.

Papachristos, Andrew V., Chris M. Smith, Mary L. Scherer, and Melissa A. Fugiero. 2011. "More Coffee, Less Crime? The Relationship between Gentrification and Neighborhood Crime Rates in Chicago, 1991 to 2005." *City & Community* 10(3): 215–40.

Parker, Jeffrey Nathaniel. 2018. "Negotiating the Space between Avant-Garde and 'Hip Enough': Businesses and Commercial Gentrification in Wicker Park." *City & Community* 17(2): 438–60.

Patch, Jason. 2004. "The Embedded Landscape of Gentrification." *Visual Studies* 19(2): 169–87.

---. 2008. "Ladies and Gentrification: New Stores, Residents, and Relationships in Neighborhood Change." In *Gender in an Urban World*, vol. 9, edited by Judith N. DeSena, 103–26. Bromley, UK: Emerald Group.

Pattillo, Mary E. 1998. "Sweet Mothers and Gangbangers: Managing Crime in a Black Middle Class Neighborhood." *Social Forces* 76(3): 747–74.

---. 2007. *Black on the Block: The Politics of Race and Class in the City*. Chicago: University of Chicago Press.

Police Department of the City of New York. n.d. CompStat Precinct Reports. Accessed April 2017. www.nyc.gov.

Porter, Libby, and Austin Barber. 2006. "The Meaning of Place and State-Led Gentrification in Birmingham's Eastside." *City* 10(2): 215–34.

"President Signs Manpower Bill Giving Localities a Larger Role." 1973. *New York Times*, December 29, 1973.

Pritchard, Stephen. 2019. "More Today Than Yesterday (But Less Than There'll Be Tomorrow)." *Nuart Journal* 2(1): 10–20.

---. 2020. "The Artwashing of Gentrification and Social Cleansing." In *The Handbook of Displacement*, edited by Peter Adey, Janet C. Bowstead, Katherine Brickell, Vandana Desai, Mike Dolton, Alasdair Pinkerton, and Ayesha Siddiqi, 179–98. Cham, Switzerland: Palgrave Macmillan.

Purifoye, Gwendolyn Y. 2017. "Transporting Urban Inequality through Public Transit Designs and Systems." *City & Community* 16(4): 364–68.

Putnam, Robert D. 2000. *Bowling Alone*. New York: Simon and Schuster.

Richardson, Jason, Bruce Mitchell, and Juan Franco. 2019. "Shifting Neighborhoods: Gentrification and Cultural Displacement in American Cities." National Community Reinvestment Coalition. www.ncrc.org.

Rigolon, Alessandro, Samuel J. Keith, Brandon Harris, Lauren E. Mullenbach, Lincoln R. Larson, and Jaclyn Rushing. 2020. "More Than 'Just Green Enough': Helping Park Professionals Achieve Equitable Greening and Limit Environmental Gentrification." *Journal of Park & Recreation Administration* 38(3): 29–54.

Ringel, Norman B., and Jonathan C. Finkelstein. 1991. "Differentiating Neighborhood Satisfaction and Neighborhood Attachment among Urban Residents." *Basic and Applied Social Psychology* 12(2): 177–93.

Rivera, Cristina. 2017. "Vintage Shopping in Shimokitazawa, the Williamsburg of Tokyo." *Runway Riot*, January 20, 2017. www.runwayriot.com.

Rose, Mark. 1991. "Brooklyn Unbound." *Nervepool*. Accessed March 2016. www.nervepool.net.

Rountree, Pamela Wilcox, and Kenneth C. Land. 1996. "Perceived Risk versus Fear of Crime: Empirical Evidence of Conceptually Distinct Reactions in Survey Data." *Social Forces* 74(4): 1353–76.

Rucks-Ahidiana, Zawadi. 2021. "Racial Composition and Trajectories of Gentrification in the United States." *Urban Studies* 58(13): 2721–41.

---. 2022. "Theorizing Gentrification as a Process of Racial Capitalism." *City & Community* 21(3): 173–92.

Sampson, Robert J. 2012. *Great American City: Chicago and the Enduring Neighborhood Effect*. Chicago: University of Chicago Press.
Sampson, Robert, and Stephen W. Raudenbush. 1999. "Systemic Social Observation of Public Spaces: A New Look at Disorder in Urban Neighborhoods." *American Journal of Sociology* 105(3): 603–51.
Sampson, Robert, Stephen W. Raudenbush, and Felton Earls. 1997. "Neighborhoods and Violent Crime: A Multilevel Study of Collective Efficacy." *Science* 277(5328): 918–24.
Scannell, Leila, and Robert Gifford. 2010. "Defining Place Attachment: A Tripartite Organizing Framework." *Journal of Environmental Psychology* 30(1): 1–10.
Schlichtman, John Joe, and Jason Patch. 2008. "Contextualizing Impressions of Neighborhood Change: Linking Business Directories to Ethnography." *City & Community* 7(3): 273–93.
Schuerman, Matthew. 2019. *Newcomers: Gentrification and Its Discontents*. Chicago: University of Chicago Press.
Schwartzman, Paul. 2021. "In a Once-Gritty DC Market, These Wholesalers' World Is Slipping Away." *Washington Post*, June 18, 2021.
Shaw, Kate S., and Iris W. Hagemans. 2015. "'Gentrification without Displacement' and the Consequent Loss of Place: The Effects of Class Transition on Low-Income Residents of Secure Housing in Gentrifying Areas." *International Journal of Urban and Regional Research* 39(2): 323–41.
Short, Aaron. 2011a. "Post-Concert Open Air Drug Market in Williamsburg!" *Brooklyn Paper*, September 21, 2011. www.brooklynpaper.com.
———. 2011b. "Catholics Save Relics from Out of Business W'burg Church." *Brooklyn Paper*, December 6, 2011. www.brooklynpaper.com.
———. 2012. "Pit Stop: BBQ Holes at Cooper Park Divide W'burg." *Brooklyn Paper*, April 18, 2012. www.brooklynpaper.com.
Shumaker, Sally A., and Ralph B. Taylor. 1983. "Toward a Clarification of People-Place Relationships: A Model of Attachment to Place." In *Environmental Psychology: Directions and Perspectives*, edited by Nickolaus R. Feimar and E. Scott Geller, 219–51. New York: Praeger.
Sigler, Thomas, and David Wachsmuth. 2016. "Transnational Gentrification: Globalisation and Neighbourhood Change in Panama's Casco Antiguo." *Urban Studies* 53(4): 705–22.
Skaperdas, Stergios. 2001. "The Political Economy of Organized Crime: Providing Protection When the State Does Not." *Economics of Governance* 2(3): 173–202.
Skogan, Wesley. 1990. *Disorder and Decline: Crime and the Spiral of Decay in American Neighborhoods*. New York: Free Press.
Slater, Tom. 2009. "Missing Marcuse: On Gentrification and Displacement." *City* 13 (2–3): 292–311.
Small, Mario L. 2004. *Villa Victoria: The Transformation of Social Capital in a Boston Barrio*. Chicago: University of Chicago Press.
Smith, Chris M. 2014. "The Influence of Gentrification on Gang Homicides in Chicago Neighborhoods, 1994 to 2005." *Crime & Delinquency* 60(4): 569–91.

Smith, Neil. 1979. "Toward a Theory of Gentrification: A Back to the City Movement of Capital, Not People." *Journal of the American Planning Association* 45(4): 538–48.

———. 1996. *The New Urban Frontier: Gentrification and the Revanchist City*. New York: Routledge.

———. 2008. *Uneven Development: Nature, Capital, and the Production of Space*. London: Verso.

Southside United HDFC-Los Sures. 2015. "About Us." Accessed March 2017. www.southsideunitedhdfc.org.

Soytemel, Ebru. 2015. "'Belonging' in the Gentrified Golden Horn/Halic Neighbourhoods of Istanbul." *Urban Geography* 36(1): 64–89.

Stabrowski, Filip. 2014. "New-Build Gentrification and the Everyday Displacement of Polish Immigrant Tenants in Greenpoint, Brooklyn." *Antipode* 46(3): 794–815.

———. 2015. "Inclusionary Zoning and Exclusionary Development: The Politics of 'Affordable Housing' in North Brooklyn." *International Journal of Urban and Regional Research* 39(6): 1120–36.

St. Nick's Alliance. 2016. "History." Accessed October 2016. www.stnicksalliance.org.

Stokols, D., and S. A. Shumaker. 1981. "People in Places: A Transactional View of Settings." In *Cognition, Social Behavior, and the Environment*. edited by John H. Harvey, 441–88. Hillsdale, NJ: Lawrence Erlbaum.

Stolper, Harold. 2019. "New Neighbors and the Over-Policing of Communities of Color." Community Service Society, January 6, 2019. www.cssny.org.

Sullivan, Daniel M. 2006. "Assessing Residents' Opinions on Changes in a Gentrifying Neighborhood: A Case Study of the Alberta Neighborhood in Portland, Oregon." *Housing Policy Debate* 17(3): 595–624.

———. 2014. "From Food Desert to Food Mirage: Race, Social Class, and Food Shopping in a Gentrifying Neighborhood." *Advances in Applied Sociology* 4(1): 30–35.

Sullivan, Daniel M., and James Bachmeier. 2012. "Racial Differences in Perceived Disorder in Three Gentrifying Neighborhoods." *Advances in Applied Sociology* 2: 229–36.

Sullivan, Daniel M., and Samuel Shaw. 2011. "Retail Gentrification and Race: The Case of Alberta Street in Portland, Oregon." *Urban Affairs Review* 47(3): 413–32.

Sullivan, Mercer. 1989. *Getting Paid: Youth Crime and Work in the Inner City*. Ithaca: Cornell University Press.

Susser, Ida. 1982. *Norman Street: Poverty and Politics in an Urban Neighborhood*. New York: Oxford University Press.

Sutton, Ryan. 2018. "Brooklyn's Waterfront Needs More Than Danny Meyer's Tacocina." *Eater*, July 5, 2018. www.ny.eater.com.

Sutton, Stacey. 2020. "Gentrification and the Increasing Significance of Racial Transition in New York City, 1970–2010." *Urban Affairs Review* 56(1): 65–95.

Talen, Emily. 2018. *Neighborhood*. New York: Oxford University Press.

Taylor, Clive C., and Alan R. Townsend. 1976. "The Local 'Sense of Place' as Evidenced in North-East England." *Urban Studies* 13(2): 133–46.

Taylor, Monique M. 1992. "Can You Go Home Again? Black Gentrification and the Dilemma of Difference." *Berkeley Journal of Sociology* 37: 101–28.

———. 2002. *Harlem: Between Heaven and Hell*. Minneapolis: University of Minnesota Press.
Taylor, Ralph B., and Jeanette Covington. 1988. "Neighborhood Changes in Ecology and Violence." *Criminology* 26(4): 553–90.
Tissot, Sylvie. 2011. "Of Dogs and Men: The Making of Spatial Boundaries in a Gentrifying Neighborhood." *City & Community* 10(3): 265–84.
———. 2015. *Good Neighbors: Gentrifying Diversity in Boston's South End*. London: Verso.
Torres Rodríguez, Sonia. 2020. "How Can DCC Reverse and Prevent Cultural Displacement of Black Latines?" Housing Matters: An Urban Institute Initiative, November 11, 2020. https://housingmatters.urban.org.
Towes, Owen. 2018. *Stolen City: Racial Capitalism and the Making of Winnipeg*. Winnipeg: ARP Books.
Tuttle, Steven. 2020. "Producing Diverse and Segregated Spaces: Local Businesses and Commercial Gentrification in Two Chicago Neighborhoods." *City & Community* 19(4): 845–69.
———. 2022. "Place Attachment and Alienation from Place: Cultural Displacement in Gentrifying Ethnic Enclaves." *Critical Sociology* 48(3): 517–31.
Valli, Chiara. 2016. "A Sense of Displacement: Long-Time Residents' Feelings of Displacement in Gentrifying Bushwick, New York." *International Journal of Urban and Regional Research* 39(6): 1191–1208.
Van Riper, Frank. 1975. "Ford to City: Drop Dead." *New York Daily News*, October 30, 1975.
Velasco, Gabi. 2020. "How Community Land Trusts Can Advance Racial and Economic Justice." Housing Matters: An Urban Institute Initiative, February 26, 2020. https://housingmatters.urban.org.
Vo, Lam Thuy. 2018. "They Played Dominoes outside Their Apartment for Decades. Then the White People Moved In and Police Started Showing Up." *Buzzfeed News*, June 29, 2018. www.buzzfeed.com.
Von Wirth, Timo, Adrienne Grêt-Regamey, Corinne Moser, and Michael Stauffacher. 2016. "Exploring the Influence of Perceived Urban Change on Residents' Place Attachment." *Journal of Environmental Psychology* 46: 67–82.
Wallace, Rodrick, and Deborah Wallace. 2001. *A Plague on Your Houses: How New York Was Burned Down and National Public Health Crumbled*. London: Verso.
Walljasper, Jay, and Daniel Kraker. 1997. "The 15 Hippest Places to Live." *Utne Reader*, November 1, 1997. www.utne.com.
Watt, Paul. 2013. "'It's Not for Us': Regeneration, the 2012 Olympics and the Gentrification of East London." *City* 17(1): 99–118.
Weil, Joyce. 2019. "Relationship to Place for Older Adults in a New York City Neighborhood Undergoing Gentrification: A Discourse Analysis." *City & Community* 18(4): 1267–86.
Welsh, Brandon C., Anthony A. Braga, and Gerben J. N. Bruinsma. 2015. "Reimagining Broken Windows: From Theory to Policy." *Journal of Research in Crime and Delinquency* 52(4): 447–63.

Wherry, Frederick. 2011. *The Philadelphia Barrio: The Arts, Branding, and Neighborhood Transformation*. Chicago: University of Chicago Press.

Williams, Gisela. 2015. "Brooklyn in Berlin: Eating and Cooking in New York City's 'Sixth Borough.'" *Travel and Leisure*, June 10, 2015. www.travelandleisure.com.

Wilson, William J. 1996. *When Work Disappears: The World of the New Urban Poverty*. New York: Knopf.

Wiltse, Jeff. 2007. *Contested Waters: A Social History of Swimming Pools in America*. Chapel Hill: University of North Carolina Press.

Woldoff, R. A. 2002. "The Effects of Local Stressors on Neighborhood Attachment." *Social Forces* 81(1): 87–116.

Young, Paul A. 2013. "Melbourne Meets Williamsburg: 10 Minutes in Fitzroy." *City Lane*, February 6, 2013. www.thecitylane.com.

Zaveri, Mihir. 2020. "2 Warehouse Halloween Parties Attended by Nearly 1,000 Are Shut Down." *New York Times*, November 1, 2020.

Zhao, Yawei. 2019. "When Guesthouse Meets Home: The Time-Space of Rural Gentrification in Southwest China." *Geoforum* 100: 60–67.

Zukin, Sharon. 1982. *Loft Living: Culture and Capital in Urban Change*. Baltimore: Johns Hopkins University Press.

———. 1996. *The Cultures of Cities*. Oxford: Blackwell.

———. 2009. "Changing Landscapes of Power: Opulence and the Urge for Authenticity." *International Journal of Urban and Regional Research* 33(2): 543–53.

———. 2010. *Naked City: The Death and Life of Authentic Urban Places*. New York: Oxford University Press.

Zukin, Sharon, Philip Kasinitz, and Xiangming Chen. 2016. *Global Cities, Local Streets: Everyday Diversity from New York to Shanghai*. London: Routledge.

Zukin, Sharon, Valerie Trujillo, Peter Frase, Danielle Jackson, Tim Recuber, and Abraham Walker. 2009. "New Retail Capital and Neighborhood Change: Boutiques and Gentrification in New York City." *City & Community* 8(1): 47–64.

INDEX

affordable housing: critique of, 159, 162, 169; new developments, 156; rezoning and 197-a plan, 23, 33, 59

Airbnb, 27–28; Casco Viejo, 163; during pandemic, 177; role in gentrification, 173

alienation, 10, 152

amenities: in condos/high-rises 3, 27, 45; luxury 60, 102–3, 106, 124; neighborhood, 20, 43, 134, 138, 141, 149, 154

artists, 14, 2, 32, 40, 121; art businesses and institutions, 9, 95, 98, 153; artists and gentrification, 4, 6, 16, 37, 59, 71–73, 90, 122, 137, 163, 166; causing cultural displacement, 11, 71–73; experiencing cultural displacement, 11, 46, 50, 115; scene, 15, 32, 41, 95, 114. *See also* Bohemians

artwashing, 141

authenticity, 11, 143; Bohemians, 104, 127, 148; corporate attempts at, 115, 127, 141, 164; danger and, 41, 89–91, 164; industrial, 141

avant-gardes, 6, 32, 41; culture and scene, 14, 43, 60, 71, 95, 113, 137; disappearance of, 35, 115, 158; perceptions of crime, 90

Bedford Avenue, 25; retail, 98–113, 162, 178; retail landlords, 166; Williamsburg Walks, 64–68

belonging, 2, 10; and cultural displacement, 8, 98, 150; lack of, 150–55; 173; public space, 62; retail and, 98, 116, 170; signals and, 52, 150

Bohemians, 6, 10, 40–42; and avant-garde scene, 32, 137, 166; claiming space, 71–73; and community organizing, 58–60; co-optation of scene, 50, 91, 111–14, 121; cultural displacement, 9, 106, 117; perceptions of social disorder and crime, 85–88; retail and institutions, 94–101, 104–6, 154–55; as urban pioneers, 89–91. *See also* identity attachment

brand, 8, 64; retail and, 92–97, 115; Williamsburg's reach, 161

Brooklyn, 3, 97; Brownstone Brooklyn, 43, 106; demographics, 36–38, 131–33; depictions of gentrification, 5

Business Improvement District, 94; Lower East Side BID, 205n7; Northside Merchants Association (NMA), 94

Casco Viejo, Panama City, 163–64

census: demographics and population, 8, 36–38, 131–35, 172; Social Explorer, 195

children: and gentrification, 129–36

City Council: and parks, 61; retail rent regulation, 170; and rezoning, 7, 33, 159, 162, 180

class, 11–12, 16, 57, 114, 155–60; middle-class, 32, 90, 152; upper-class, 149; wealthy, 3, 7, 9, 43, 94; working-class, 5, 34, 36, 94

Cole's Reverse Telephone Directories, 99–102, 193–94

Community Board, 51, 63, 87, 153, 170; 197-a plan, 33, 59; and rezoning, 33, 140

227

community organizations: Bohemians, 58–60; Condo Dwellers, 60–63; and neighborhood ownership, 50–53, 151; Old Timers, 53–58

CompStat, 77, 195

Condo Dwellers, 7, 14–15, 35, 42–43, 47; community organizing, 60–63; convenience, 106, 124–25, 148; COVID-19, 177; claiming space, 62–63, 70, 151; families, 132–36; gentrification, 47, 123–26; local neighborhood, 137–39; perceptions of social disorder and crime, 88–89; retail, 103–7, 115–16. *See also* investment attachment

condofication, 7–8, 45–47, 97, 134, 162, 172; perceptions of Bohemians, 87, 122, 153; perceptions of Condo Dwellers, 87, 128; perceptions of Old Timers, 45–47; in Washington, DC, 162

conflict: attachment style and, 17; and ownership, 2, 8, 48; and public space, 62, 139

consumption, 68–70, 107, 121; cultural, 11, 41, 97; upscale and luxury, 36, 97, 99, 115; and Williamsburg Walks, 71–73

COVID-19, 177–78; pandemic 4, 102, 113

creatives, 6, 27, 137–38; community, 41–42, 47, 98, 123

crime: and authenticity, 89–91; Bohemians, 85–88, 89–91; Condo Dwellers, 88–89; decrease, 32; and gentrification, 75–79, 147–149; Old Timers, 79–85; perceptions, of 78–79; in Williamsburg, 79

cultural displacement, 8–12, 44, 52, 150, 168, 179; of Bohemians, 117, 122; neighborhood ownership and, 17, 159; and retail, 11, 103, 98, 170; Williamsburg Walks, 69–70

Deener, Andrew, 52
deindustrialization, 30, 53, 84
disinvestment: and gentrification, 173; in New York, 5; resistance to, 53–58; in Williamsburg, 26–27, 35, 119–20

diversity: and gentrification, 155; integration, 147, 155–57; social mixing, 145Dominican Republic, 5; businesses, 98, 104; Dominican residents, 30, 40, 80

Domino: Park, 135, 140–144; luxury development, 159; Sugar Refinery, 29

East River State Park, 21, 50
East Village, 32, 40, 58, 126–127; and gentrification, 122
El Puente, 57, 141
ethnography, 4, 21, 48, 64, 101, 118, 187–88

factories, 140; and Bohemians, 16, 32; and Condo Dwellers 89; history, 29; and Old Timers, 5, 30, 84; rebranding, 34, 158
family: friendly, 126, 129–31; and gentrification, 133–36, 149; Old Timers, 5, 30, 39–40, 82–83; oriented, 119, 129
Former Residents, 44, 104; and art, 165–66
Fried, Marc, 9

Gans, Herbert, 9
gentrifiers, 6; children of, 135; early, 9–11, 58; and ownership, 52–53; and retail, 153; and surveillance, 76–78
Glass, Ruth, 5–6
graffiti: and authenticity, 89, 104; and gentrification, 134, 160; and social disorder, 43, 77
Greenberg, Miriam, 30, 70
Greenpoint, 10, 26, 101, 146, 170, 190, 195; rezoning, 33, 59, 61
gritty: and authenticity, 87, 104, 148; negative perception, 18, 79, 88, 103

Hasidic Jewish, 21, 24, 30, 190
hipster, 3; co-optation of, 91; culture, 6, 50, 94; hip destination, 3, 46, 95, 101, 113
Hunter, Albert, 13
Hyra, Derek, 51

identity attachment, 14–16, 40–42, 50. *See also* Bohemians

(im)migrants, 29, 38, 40, 188; businesses, 98, 104, 154; communities, 8, 30, 106; families, 5; language, 99; networks, 14–15, 146

industrial, 14, 29–30, 99, 107, 143, 172; aesthetic, 34, 140–141, 158, 162; and Bohemians, 32, 85, 137; and rezoning, 33

investment: corporate, 8, 49, 72, 107; and gentrification, 6, 23, 35, 115, 156; reinvestment, 5, 18, 150, 171

investment attachment, 14–15, 17, 42–43, 47, 49–50, 138, 149, 154–55. *See also* Condo Dwellers

Italy, 5; businesses, 98, 101, 104; Italian residents, 26, 30, 40

Jacobs, Jane, 5, 7

landlords, 166–67, 195; evictions, 57; harassment, 10; negligence, 31, 54, 84
L Café, 98, 105, 110
Lloyd, Richard, 11, 95
local: actors, 10, 39, 52, 99; neighborhood, 136–139; shops, 19, 95, 110, 167, 193
Los Sures: community organization, 57–58, 60; mural, 141–44; neighborhood, 141Lower East Side, 29–30; gentrification of, 11, 90
L train, 32, 175–76

Marcuse, Peter, 9
mayor, 170; Adams, Eric, 20, 179–81; Bloomberg, Michael, 6–7, 33, 129, 178; de Blasio, Bill, 140, 175, 178
McCarren Park, 26, 34–35
McCarren Park Pool, 49, 55; closing of, 26; parties at, 50–51; reopening, 62; tensions, 26, 55–56,
migration: chain migration, 30; from Manhattan, 3, 31–32, 41
Moses, Robert, 26

music: corporate, 9, 49; DIY spaces, 50, 121; scene, 32, 41, 95, 114, 207n19
myths, 20, 147–158

NAG, 59–61, 65–66
necessities, 5, 31, 60, 99; businesses of, 5, 31, 92, 107–11, 154, 170; lack of, 103, 116; and ownership, 98, 116, 155
necessity attachment, 14–17, 39–40, 47, 53–58, 83, 101, 119, 146. *See also* Old Timers
neighborhood: change, 3, 10, 46; ethnographic description of Williamsburg, 21–29; history of Williamsburg, 29–35; identity, 6, 11, 41, 91, 95 97, 135; popularity of, 3, 94, 163
neighborhood attachment style, 12–18; community attachment, 12; place attachment, 12. *See also* identity attachment; investment attachment; necessity attachment
New York Times, 62, 105, 127, 138; and gentrification, 95–96, 134, 179, 194
norms, 8; and claiming ownership, 11, 49, 53, 151; community events and, 70; surveillance and 76–77, 147–149, 153
Northside, 35–36; community activism, 54–56, 58–62; condofication, 45–47; crime, 83–85; description of, 21–26
nothing: authenticity, 121; Bohemians, 58, 103–4, 153; Condo Dwellers, 124; and gentrification, 18, 164, 173; narrative of void 126–29; Old Timers, 68, 70

Ocejo, Richard, 11, 52
Old Timers, 5, 8–9, 14–17, 39–40; claiming space, 31–32, 63; community organizing, 53–58; cultural displacement, 45–46, 64, 154; erasure, 116, 136, 142–45; exclusion, 68, 70, 142–45; families, 129–32; gentrification, 45–47, 63, 119–21, 145–47; local neighborhood, 136–37;

Old Timers (*cont.*)
perceptions of social disorder and crime, 79–85; retail, 103–4. *See also* necessity attachment
Open Space Alliance, 48–50
ownership: conflicts about, 2, 48, 56; and cultural displacement, 11, 147, 150–51; retail and, 98; symbolic ownership, 52–53, 69–71, 72, 167, 170–71

Patch, Jason, 107
physical displacement, 8, 10, 119, 125, 145, 155; avoiding, 4, 169
planned shrinkage, 31–32; resistance to, 51, 54–58
Poland, 5; businesses, 1, 101, 104, 108–9; Polish residents, 30, 38, 40, 98
police, 28, 42, 81; broken windows, 77–78; and gentrification, 76, 78, 87, 125, 148, 153
policing, 11, 53; at Williamsburg Walks, 67–68
pollution 34
public housing, 3, 27–28, 35, 169, 180; and gentrification, 75; New York City Housing Authority, 30; Williamsburg Houses, 28–30
public space: control of, 49, 50, 53, 56, 62; cultural displacement, 10, 70–71, 99; ideals of, 64; surveillance of, 76–77, 88; symbolic ownership, 8, 11, 52, 58, 64, 70, 71–72; temporary, 64–69
Public Works Administration, 30
Puerto Rico, 5; businesses, 98, 108, 153; Puerto Rican residents, 30, 38, 39–40

race: and gentrification, 10–11; of participants, 189; racial tensions, 26, 55, 62; segregation, 8, 32
real estate: and city government, 7, 33, 47, 169; co-optation of bohemian culture, 11, 122; investment 42–43, 47, 63, 91, 124, 138; tax incentives 33; Two Trees Management, 140–44
redlining, 27, 31, 160
religious: celebrations, 65, 69, 137, 142, 149; communities, 40; Hasidic, 190; institutions, 39, 148
reputations, 8; Bohemians and, 6, 41, 58–59, 89–91, 115; Condo Dwellers and, 63, 111; family neighborhood, 129, 134; gentrification and, 11, 113, 149; media and, 95; retail and, 99
retail: branding, 99; convenience, 124–25; cultural displacement, 9, 11, 103; data collection, 102, 193–94; exclusion, 97–101; family friendly, 133–34; gentrification, 35, 44, 91, 99, 106, 115; globalized, 99; identity, 97–101, 116, 167; landlords and, 166; myths of retail and gentrification, 151–55; perceptions of change, 103; signaling ownership, 10, 46, 52, 98, 116; upscaling necessity, 107–11
rezoning, 4, 7, 23; Bloomberg, Michael 33, 129; community plan, 33; displacement of artist culture 111, 166; Gowanus 180; resistance to 58–60

Sampson, Robert J., 78
Saracino-Brown, Japonica, 5, 157
Smith, Neil, 32, 90, 129
Smorgasburg, 21, 70, 138–39social disorder: attachment style and, 89; perceptions of, 19, 43, 78; policing of, 77
social mixing, 145
Southside, 36; community activism, 57–58; condofication, 140–44; crime, 80–83; description of, 27–29; families, 131–32
state-led gentrification, 4, 6, 8, 158, 160, 165; and crime, 75; justification for, 147, 164

stigma, 5, 149; destigmatize, 148
students: early gentrifiers, 6, 10, 14, 32, 37, 90,
suburbanization, 5, 30–31
Sullivan, Daniel, 98
surveillance, 9, 147–149, 155, 159–60, 173; 311 calls, 76–78, 148, 153
Swinging Sixties Senior Center, 56, 83, 103, 120

tax abatements, 7, 32, 156; Inclusionary Housing Program (421-a), 33, 156
Taylor, Monique, 10
tenure, residential, 12, 146–47, 156
tourism, 97, 138–39, 163

Union Market, DC, 161–64
urban pioneers, 6, 11; and danger, 89–91, 104; parenting, 130; and void, 127
urban renewal, 5, 9, 32, 160

void, perceptions of, 18, 105, 126–29, 153

Where is Williamsburg? (app), 3, 46, 161, 173
white flight, 5, 40, 90, 145
Williamsburg Walks, 19, 63–71; and cultural displacement, 70–71; and exclusion, 68; policing at, 67–68; symbolic ownership, 72
Works Progress Administration, 26

Zukin, Sharon, 32, 97

ABOUT THE AUTHOR

SARA MARTUCCI is a Lecturer in the Sociology Department at the John Jay College of Criminal Justice, City University of New York. Her research interrogates how inequality impacts experiences of daily life.

www.ingramcontent.com/pod-product-compliance
Lightning Source LLC
Chambersburg PA
CBHW020028040426
42333CB00039B/548